FIGHTING THE NIGHT

FIGHTING THE NIGHT

IWO JIMA, WORLD WAR II, AND A FLYER'S LIFE

Paul Hendum

Paul Hendrickson

 ALFRED A. KNOPF | NEW YORK | 2024

THIS IS A BORZOI BOOK
PUBLISHED BY ALFRED A. KNOPF

Copyright © 2024 by Paul Hendrickson

All rights reserved. Published in the United States by Alfred A. Knopf,
a division of Penguin Random House LLC, New York, and distributed
in Canada by Penguin Random House Canada Limited, Toronto.

www.aaknopf.com

Knopf, Borzoi Books, and the colophon
are registered trademarks of Penguin Random House LLC.

Portions of this work appeared in different form
in *Life, The Washington Post,* and *Literary Hub*.

Grateful acknowledgment is made to Wesleyan University Press
for permission to reprint an excerpt from "Stages on a Journey Westward"
from *Collected Poems* by James Wright, copyright © 2007 by James Wright.
Published by Wesleyan University Press. Used with permission.

Excerpts from letters of Larry Garland reprinted by permission of Marsha Phillips.

Library of Congress Cataloging-in-Publication Data
Names: Hendrickson, Paul, 1944– author.
Title: Fighting the night : Iwo Jima, World War II, and a flyer's life / Paul Hendrickson.
Description: First edition. | New York : Alfred A. Knopf, 2024. | "This is a Borzoi Book
published by Alfred A. Knopf." | Includes bibliographical references and index.
Identifiers: LCCN 2023017439 (print) | LCCN 2023017440 (ebook) |
ISBN 9780593321133 (hardcover) | ISBN 9780593321140 (ebook)
Subjects: LCSH: Hendrickson, Joseph P. (Joseph Paul), 1918–2003. | United States. Army
Air Forces. Night Fighter Squadron, 549th—Biography. | United States. Army Air Forces.—
Officers—Biography. | World War, 1939–1945—Aerial operations, American. |
World War, 1939–1945—Campaigns—Japan. | World War, 1939–1945—
Regimental histories—United States. | Fighter pilots—United States—Biography. |
Black Widow (Night fighter plane) | Hendrickson, Paul, 1944–
Classification: LCC D790.262 549th .H46 2024 (print) |
LCC D790.262 549th (ebook) | DDC 940.54/2528092 [B]—dc23/eng/20231019
LC record available at https://lccn.loc.gov/2023017439
LC ebook record available at https://lccn.loc.gov/2023017440

Jacket photograph: Hendrickson family collection
Jacket design by Chip Kidd

Manufactured in the United States of America

First Edition

For my grandsons, Jackson and Teddy

Long ago, in Kentucky, I, a boy, stood
By a dirt road, in first dark, and heard
The great geese hoot northward.
I could not see them, there being no moon
And the stars sparse. I heard them.
I did not know what was happening in my heart. . . .
Tell me a story.
In this century, and moment, of mania,
Tell me a story.
Make it a story of great distances, and starlight.

—ROBERT PENN WARREN, "Tell Me a Story"

Contents

FIGHTING THE NIGHT

Prologue

AMARILLO GOODBYE

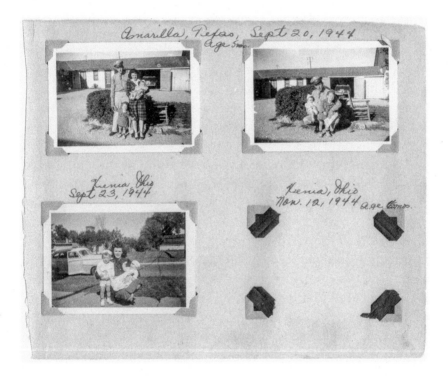

I AM LOOKING at a faded page from my broken-backed baby book.

On September 20, 1944, at about nine o'clock in the morning, two farm kids from Ohio and Kentucky told each other goodbye out front of a sad-sack-looking motor court in Amarillo, Texas. Perhaps the only thing extraordinary about the moment was how ordinary it was to its time and place. They were my parents, and they are dead now. No matter what else I might ambivalently say about what turned out to be their largely sorrowful sixty-one-year marriage, this part of their story seems to me absolutely good, even heroic.

My first lieutenant dad, twenty-five, pilot of a P-61 Black Widow, was leaving for the war. He was headed ultimately with his night fighter squadron to the Western Pacific. The 549th Night Fighter Squadron, which would soon get attached to the VII Fighter Command of the Seventh Air Force, didn't have its announced orders yet, but the rumor in the ranks among the squadron's nearly 300-man force—about fifty officers and the remainder enlisted men—was that they were going deep into the Pacific. The specific destination, which they wouldn't get to for a few more months (there would first be an outfitting and training stay in Hawaii, and then some less scary mission duty on Saipan), turned out to be Iwo Jima, that iconic scrap of sulfurous sand 760 miles from Tokyo, which my father, for the rest of his life, whenever he spoke of the war and his time in it, simply referred to as "Iwo."

He arrived on Iwo in a convoy of Widows in the third week of March 1945, a little less than a month after the Marines had immortally raised the flag on the summit of Mount Suribachi in the Battle of Iwo Jima, one of the bloodiest and dirtiest and costliest sieges of World War II.

For the next five and a half months, in his cockpit of backlit knobs and dials, my father flew approximately seventy-five missions, roughly 175 hours of logged time, most of it at night, off of what was named South Field on Iwo. His type of aircraft was a sleek and lethal thing, poisonous as the spider from which she'd taken her name, a combination fighter-bomber, a pursuit ship, from the Northrop Aircraft Corporation, with a twin-boom tail design and with a crew of three: pilot, radar operator, gunner. She was the first operational warplane of World War II to have been built specifically as a night fighter, powered by her Double Wasp 18-cylinder engines and armed with her .50-caliber machine guns and 20-millimeter cannons and, not least, rigged with state-of-the-art radar detection equipment sealed in her nose. Her M2 Browning machine guns, mounted in a rotating 360-degree turret atop the fuselage, could fire 800 rounds per minute: 560 rounds of ammo per gun, and all four guns able to fire simultaneously. She could carry 500-pound bombs—and even more than that on occasion. Altogether, she was like a small, tight orchestra of violence.

Like my dad, the Black Widow was coming very late into the war, at least into the shooting war, but she carried an undeniable mystique. I think it had to do with the idea of dark, of stealth, of working under cloud cover or in the glow of moonlight. "Fighting the night," I've heard my father call it, with the poetry of which he was often unconsciously capable. I have his old flight records as well as a two-inch stack of other documents that were in his military file at the National Personnel Records Center in St. Louis. (There was a large fire there in 1973, but somehow my dad's entire military service record was saved.) I've also acquired some of his old mission reports from Iwo. They were in a different government repository, in Montgomery, Alabama. For so many reasons, I am terribly saddened that my dad is gone, and not least because I can't ask him all I long to know, as a son, as a writer, about sultry days on Iwo and freezing nights at 10,000 feet and so many other aspects of the war that no amount of documentary record, regardless of how rich, could ever impart. I got him to talk about some of it in the years before he died, but never for long enough.

Once, I got to accompany him to a night fighter's reunion in Orlando, where I met some of his old squadron mates, including the CO—the commanding officer. That was in the nineteen-eighties. If a lot of it was paunchy old men drinking a little too much and telling their mythologized war stories, that's not all it was. "You can't imagine how happy I was to hear your old man was going to be here," somebody said, collaring me close, whispering it in my ear. I could hear the choke in his voice. It was the last night, at the big banquet. The speeches were going on way too long. The A/C wasn't working very well. When my dad and I were slipping out early, the same collaring voice issued a command: "Help your dad with that coat!"

I have my yellowing notes from that reunion, but they're still just notes. What I really long to hear is my father's voice. I've got his voice on one old scratchy cassette tape, and it's further true that my kid brother, Mark, himself a skilled pilot, found on the internet a recording of an hour-long oral history about the war that our dad did less than a year before he died, of which he said nothing to any of us. It feels like lost treasure of the Incas. But I guess I am talking about another voice altogether. He'd be about to turn 104 if he were alive, as I am writing this sentence.

"Really, I didn't do all that much in the war, Paul," he once said.

"But you were there, Dad."

"Yes, I suppose that's so."

The leaving, the going. With the same craving, almost a carnal craving, to know more, I find myself staring at a couple of old snapshots that my archival-minded mom so lovingly and carefully glued into my baby book more than three-quarters of a century ago. Here we are, our neophyte family of four, about to be separated as a nuclear unit, and who knows if forever, with two of the parties in the frame having no idea as to what is really going on.

My mom is only twenty-one and has already brought two babies into the world. I am the not-quite-five-month-old protected in her left arm and with part of her right. That's my squirmy older brother, Marty, between my parents. He's twenty-one months old. Like my parents he's also gone. It was such a hard life, enough of it of his own making, to my mother's constant sorrow and to my father's, often enough, violent anger. When Marty was dying a few years ago in the hospice unit of a Veterans Administration Hospital at Bay Pines, Florida, we listened to a lot of Tom Petty ("I Won't Back Down") and spent some time in between talking about how angry my father seemed in the late nineteen-forties and through the fifties, when the two of us were growing up, trying to outrun his wrath. There wasn't recrimination in our talk so much as love, an increasing depth of understanding. I'm able to see much more clearly now that my father came home from the war with PTSD and didn't know how to escape it except to take it out savagely on his sons' backs with his belt, which he'd peel right off his pants. Sometimes he went after us with boards he retrieved from the basement. In our childhood, Marty and I used to take nighttime baths together, sitting in the tub comparing our welts. Is it any wonder we both fled as teenagers into the same Catholic preparatory seminary? He went first, I followed. But that's another story, or at least not the story for right here.

My mom's name is Rita. Her middle name's Bernardine. Not too long removed from this Amarillo moment, in a far Pacific place, the words "The Rita B" are going to get artfully scrolled in curvy white on a glassy black side panel below the Plexiglas cockpit on the right side of my father's P-61. I asked my dad once who did the paint job on *The Rita B.*

"Damned if I remember, Paul. You just grabbed somebody in maintenance and said, 'Listen, I want you to put my wife's name on my airplane and make it beautiful.' And the guy would have snapped to and said, 'Yessir, Lieutenant.'"

I have another treasured picture. It's of my father grinning in front of the spanking artwork. He's in his one-piece coverall flying suit and inflatable Mae West life preserver and unbuckled oxygen mask and skintight leather aviator's cap. The big black machine is hovering above him, casting its shadows in dark slashing angles on the blinding white tarmac. It almost looks like a modernist painting, maybe something Edward Hopper would have tried at his easel if he took a sudden whim to monochrome. On the back of the picture are these barely legible words: "How do you like my

plane's name?" I'd bet anything he wrote the message and immediately posted the picture to the States.

When Marty and I were kids, we were so proud that our dad
was an aviator—a commercial airline pilot. No one else we knew
had a job like his. I have written in another place of how we used
to brag to our classmates on the grammar school playground that
he could fly the crates the planes came in. I think that's a line from
a Cagney movie.

Rita B. has gotten up this morning and put on her smart Scotch-
plaid suit and slingback pumps, has combed out her thick Irish
coils of raven hair. She's ready for the day, or at least is pretend-
ing so. I wonder what this motor lodge set them back last night—
three bucks? And did they get any sleep? And were we all in one
bed? And was there some attempt at silent lovemaking once Marty
and I were finally down for the night? How could there not have
been?

I said they were two farm kids out of Ohio and Kentucky. My
mom's farm town was and is a little place called Xenia, which is in
southwestern Ohio, not far from Dayton. (It's pronounced Zeen-
ya.) The land there is rich and black and rolling and loamy. Both
my parents are buried in Xenia, and Marty, too, and an infant sibling brother named David, and a nearly lifelong emotionally ill
brother named Ric (emotionally ill, but who nonetheless almost
made it to seventy-one, and then the coronavirus swept through
his Illinois nursing home, and Ric had no chance), and about two
dozen other extended family members on my mom's side. Xenia
is where Rita B. is headed today, perhaps pulling out in the next
thirty minutes. She and another Army Air Forces wife named Edy
Kessler (her husband, Charles, a pal of my dad, fellow 549er, is also
going to Iwo in his Black Widow) will shortly get into my parents'
car, with Marty and me in tow, and drive across the rest of the Texas
Panhandle, and into Oklahoma, and up into Missouri, and through
Illinois, and then across Indiana, and finally into Ohio, something
like 1,100 miles in a little less than four days. Two wartime women,
barely out of their teens, on those bumpy two-lane wartime roads,
already heartsick from missing their men, and overtired, too, with
Marty and me squalling in the car, with my mom and Edy heating

up the Gerber's strained peas on hot plates at night in the motel rooms, both of them reading the road maps and checking the oil and refueling at the gas stations, obeying the wartime restrictions on speed limits, changing the poop-filled cloth diapers and searching on the floor of the car for the talc and safety pins—all of this and more. For all that I have thought about what my father faced in the war, I know I am guilty of not considering enough, not nearly, of what my *mother* did in the war, what so many mothers had to do in their own shouldering ways and circumstances. Oh, yes, I should add: Edy Kessler was several months pregnant. So I wonder if she wasn't fighting motion sickness and morning sickness all the way across. Her family lived in Teaneck, New Jersey. That's where she intended to wait out the war through her fear and prayers. My mom was going to wait it out in the same way in Xenia, at 8 Mechanic Street, in the home of her mother and father, whom I knew all throughout my childhood as "Pop" and "Nonna." Pop was my substitute father while my father was overseas. Pop was a corn and wheat and soybean farmer, who'd been too old for the war.

The story of how my parents arrived at their going-away moment in the scuffed-dirt motel courtyard at the back end of the war starts with Xenia. I know some of this must begin to sound like the script of a Hollywood B-movie produced especially for the war effort, but, however cliché and Frank Capra–seeming, our family legend is that my parents had bumped into each other, almost literally, at a Xenia roller rink on a Friday night three and a half years before, as my mom twirled in her chaste tights and lace-up skates past the good-looking soldier boy.

This would have been in the early part of 1941, ten or eleven months before Pearl Harbor. Everything was so speeded up then. America wasn't in the war yet, but who didn't know it was coming? Rita B. was still in high school, seventeen or eighteen then. (Her birthday was in early February.) She was angling for the lead in that spring's senior-high production at St. Brigid High School, of a comedy farce called *Peggy Parks*. (She'd get it, too, and the

Xenia *Evening Gazette* would report that she "gave a splendid performance and made a nice stage appearance.") Rita B. had a size 16 waist. Rita B., even (or especially) then, knew how to work her wiles, her will.

And the lank soldier boy, who was four years older? He was over with a buddy from Patterson Field in nearby Fairfield, Ohio. Almost certainly he was in uniform, the better to snag the glances of the local girls. He had a hot-looking convertible and a sergeant's stripes on the sleeve of his Army Air Corps blouse. He was off a sharecropper's farm in Morganfield, Kentucky, third-born in a Depression family of nine kids. He introduced himself to people as Joe Paul Hendrickson, and the way it came out of his mouth was the way it had always come out back on the farm in western Kentucky, as if it were really one name, one word: *Joepaul.* (After the war, when he hired on with Eastern Air Lines, flying out of Midway Airport in Chicago, he would gradually drop his second first name; it was as if he had begun to Yankee-fy himself, at least in superficial ways.)

The soldier boy, with his blunt farmer's hands, with his cocky grin, had a small vertical divot that rode down the middle of his chin and was destined to get more pronounced in the years up ahead. The soldier boy, who had been able to go only to high school before his enlistment in the Army Air Corps in 1937, tended to use double negatives and could slide into metaphor without truly understanding what a metaphor was. ("We'd better get out of here before a fire starts licking at our boots," he'd be apt to say if he were sitting in the balcony of a movie theater and suddenly smelled smoke curling from below.) If he weighed one hundred and thirty-five then it must have been partly due to a couple of wrenches in his back pocket. At this stage he was still working under the hood of the big, throbbing machines instead of being able to strap on a parachute and climb inside their cockpits and take them up into the air. It wouldn't always be like this, he'd promised himself—and possibly the high school girl at the skating rink that night, too. One way or another, he was going to get into flight school. He was going to become an officer, an aviation cadet. When they met, he wasn't really a lowly grease monkey any longer. He'd been a mechanic crew chief for a couple of years, supervising the other grease monkeys. Still, the gleam in his flying eye had yet to be realized.

The Capraesque newsreel, the forties cliché in sepia: The sergeant from the local airbase and the newly graduated schoolgirl were spooning at a double feature in a Xenia movie house on a Sunday afternoon in early December of that same year, 1941, when the lights went up suddenly and the panic-stricken manager ran down the aisle to cry that the Japanese had just attacked America. I heard this story a lot in my childhood and take the essence of it to be true. My parents' generation could remember precisely where they were when they first heard about Pearl Harbor in the way my generation can remember exactly where they were on November 22, 1963.

They got married two months later. It was a high Mass on a Tuesday morning at St. Brigid's. The newlyweds left for a two-night honeymoon in nearby Richmond, Indiana. (*Gazette:* "The bride's going away costume was an aqua crepe ensemble, with which she wore navy accessories, and a corsage of gardenias and violets.") The next month, March, my dad burned through three or four noncommissioned ranks and then took the oath of office for a wartime officer's commission. For the next thirty months they lived in fourteen towns and cities, one field or base or depot after another. "We left Xenia on March 23, 1942," my mother once told me. "Every two months the government was transferring us somewhere else." She ticked them all off for me, and I scribbled them down in my journal, and damn if she didn't have them in the precise sequence, by almost the exact dates, as I've lately discovered from poring over my dad's military records and some family documents.

It was out to San Bernardino (San Berdoo, as I remember them speaking of it in my childhood, as if they had an insider's knowledge of the cool way to say it), and, no sooner having arrived in California, it was back East, to Hartford, Connecticut, for some TDY (temporary duty) schooling at a Pratt & Whitney aircraft engine factory. They crisscrossed the country by Pullman car and Greyhound and, sometimes, in their own car.

When it was by automobile, they rolled into the next place with their two sticks of furniture and their wedding gifts (at least the useful ones, like pots and pans) and rousted up some cheap housing. Santa Ana, Bakersfield, Scottsdale (it's next door to Phoenix, where Marty was born at the end of 1942), Yuma (where my dad got his wings), La Junta, Orlando, Kissimmee, Ocala, El Centro, Fresno—I haven't said them all, and not in the right order, and I will fill in more later, but you get the idea: their own blurring gazetteer of America. Two rural kids from the Midwest and the border South seeing the continent, one coast to another, the great, flat feel of the land right there at their steering-wheel elbows. What was it like to spy the California High Sierra for the first time? What was it like to glimpse from five miles off those bone-white grain elevators standing up so spookily and beautifully on the Nebraska plain? I wish I knew. I never asked.

Once, in California, on a Sunday afternoon, they got to go to a studio-audience broadcast of Jack Benny's coast-to-coast radio program. Once, in Times Square, at the Paramount, they got to see the Ink Spots in a live performance. The Paramount was a 3,664-seat palace at 43rd and Broadway. I remember my dad once telling me, sort of whistling it through his country-boy teeth, that he had never realized somebody could build a "picture show" that large. Decades after the war, when he was captaining big jets for his airline into and out of LaGuardia, he'd say: "New York? Shooee, Paul, that's the jumping off place of the world." He meant the grime. He meant the congestion. He meant the seeming ridiculous cost of everything. He meant what he regarded as the shocking incivility. Never mind that he himself had grown up in a deeply uncivil society of another kind, which is to say a segregated society, and that he held some of his ingrained racial bigotries nearly till his last breath, even as I witnessed him struggling against them. But, again, that is not the story I am telling here, at least not right now.

In Hartford, and with my mom two months pregnant, they found a two-dollar-a-week room in a boardinghouse with the toilet down the hall. "Your dad would be at work all day and I'd ride a bus downtown and look in the shop windows," my mom once told me. "I had terrible morning sickness. We didn't have any money. But I wanted to see what was in those windows."

They knew, of course, what lay behind and under all of their adventuring: my father's departure for the war. At nearly all of these assignments, he was training on different aircraft, building his hours and skills. It was the B-25 Mitchell bomber in La Junta, Colorado. It was the Douglas A-20 Havoc in Orlando. Toward the end, it was the P-61 at Hammer Field in Fresno, where the 549th NFS was formed and where I came along, on April 29, 1944. In the entire course of the war, only 706 Widows got built (as opposed to 9,816 B-25s), so getting into a P-61 squadron was like gaining membership in an elite aviator club. (For one thing, you had to have superior nighttime vision; at his death my dad's distance vision was still nearly 20-20 in both eyes without glasses.) He was so highly trained by the time he went over. I believe all of that training helped save his life in more ways than one—it kept him stateside longer than a lot of other flyers.

Bakersfield (where they'd been posted at least once before) was the last stop before the motor-court goodbye. The late summer of 1944 must have been wrenching: They knew the leaving was near. In Amarillo that morning, they got up and got Marty and me dressed and got dressed themselves and ate breakfast and went outside and stood for some pictures. Later that morning, my dad and Charlie Kessler went out to the local Army airfield and hitched a ride on a government transport back to Bakersfield, to rejoin their unit. (Their squadron commander had given both lieutenants a small leave to accompany their wives as far as Texas.)

So the men flew westward that day. And the women drove eastward.

That same afternoon, in California, my dad logged an hour and twenty-five minutes of training in a P-61. It wasn't *his* P-61, his *Rita B.* Black Widow serial number 42-39516 hadn't yet been assigned to First Lieutenant J. P. Hendrickson. (She was still on the assembly line at Northrop in Hawthorne, California.) The reason I know that my dad logged some flying time at Bakersfield Army Air Field on the same day that he and my mom told each other goodbye in Texas is because the record of it is in his military file. As I say, that file, which got saved from the 1973 fire, is gold. But it's not the same as having my dad in front of me to ask what he might have felt that afternoon, above Bakersfield, in his goggles and jumpsuit, practicing turns and rolls and dives and then shooting an approach, having departed his family a few hours before, not knowing if he'd ever see them again. By then my mom and Edy and their unaware charges were probably somewhere up into Oklahoma, starting to think about that night's stopover.

I'd give a lot to know what my parents said to each other at the Amarillo last. And I never got around to asking. Not in any specific way.

But I *can* report one small, fine, specific thing about the four-day Amarillo-to-Xenia run, which ended on September 23, 1944. Go back to my baby book and take a closer look at the third image on the page. Do you see anything surprising? I had to look at it an awfully long time before an obvious question struck: How is it that she looks so spiffy? Her hair is combed out, her collar snugged up tight. Marty and I are clean as a new penny. See the flung-open car door? I think these two war wives and the two cleaned-up babies have hit Xenia just seconds ago. They've hopped out—heck with the door. And Edy or maybe Nonna or Pop decides to document the arrival for the scrapbook, for my baby book, on the sidewalk outside of 8 Mechanic Street. Is it late afternoon? I think so. Nonna must have supper on. Surely, we'll all sleep fine tonight.

My mom died in Florida in 2015, at ninety-two. My dad had died at almost eighty-five twelve years before. About a year before she died, I was sitting with her in her nursing home and talking about various things. I had my baby book. We studied the third picture on the page.

"But you look so spruced up, Mom."

She didn't quite snicker in my face. "What, Paul, do you think I was going to go in on my parents looking like something the cat dragged in? Of course I was spruced up. I stopped at a gas station outside of town and took you and Marty and my suitcase into the women's restroom. First, I got you two all scrubbed and dressed. And then I wriggled out of what I was wearing and put on nylons and a new dress I'd especially saved. I put on my makeup. Wouldn't anybody have done that?"

I'm not so sure, Mom, if you're somehow reading this.

In any case, I keep staring, trying to dream myself in. That's what the rest of this is about. It's meant to be a reported memoir rather than a memoir per se. It's a kind of journalistic search for my father, although really for both my parents, and for some others, too, who flowed in and out of their lives, directly or indirectly, in a period of American history just beyond the reach of my conscious memory. But as is already evident, time won't always stay back there, but will thrust forward for glimpses of the nearer past and continuing present. Time, like memory, seldom draws itself in a straight line. Like jazz, it can have its own inner logic. I've made this point before in the books I've written, and the idea of time as a trombone seems only truer to me now. Some of these thrusting-forward glimpses—again, already apparent from what you've read—have to do with family sorrow and costs that got paid. But these are notes meant mostly for a minor key. The major key is the prewar and wartime forties, when so much about my parents' lives seems to me to have been something close to heroic, wholly good. Millions of other American couples, in the same age range as my parents, also had no choice but to throw themselves against one of the largest events in human history. And even as I say this, I recognize the historical fallacy of trying to over-romanticize the so-called Greatest Generation. They were that, even if they were also so many other human and flawed things. If this book is mostly about my father and mother in the best years of their lives, I nonetheless have a strong hope that if I set it down as conscientiously as I can, you who are reading it will also be able to hear some connecting chords to your own family's history.

Regardless, it's the storytelling path an octogenarian son and old shoe-leather reporter is choosing to take, with only feints and shadows cast toward all the rest.

PART ONE

BEGINNINGS

Sundays too my father got up early
and put his clothes on in the blueblack cold,
then with cracked hands that ached
from labor in the weekday weather made
banked fires blaze. No one ever thanked him.

—ROBERT HAYDEN, "Those Winter Sundays"

IT'S ONE OF THE THINGS *that moves me most about his life—the leap my father seemed to make through time and space from a Depression farm boy sitting on wagon tongues in baking Kentucky hayfields, dreaming of airplanes, to someone who, not even two decades later, was piloting airliners out of what was commonly called, when we were kids growing up ourselves, "The World's Busiest Airport."*

The title of world's busiest belonged first to Midway on the southwest side of Chicago, when, as I've already noted, my dad had started out, after the war, in mid-1946, for $225 a month as a copilot for Eastern Air Lines in those old workhorse and tail-dragging DC-3s. And then, in the late fifties and early sixties, when the high-whined turboprops and first generation of jets came in, the title got passed to O'Hare International on the northwest side of the city. We'd moved up closer to the city by then. He'd made captain by then. I think my father flew something like ten different aircraft for Eastern, from the prop age to the jet age, from Martin 404s to DC-7s to Lockheed Electras to Super Connies to the 727 Whisperjet, before his thirty-year commercial aviation career was over. Before he couldn't pass the company physicals anymore because of his weakening heart. And for almost all of that time, he worked out of either Midway or O'Hare as his home base.

Which, somehow, he always referred to as "the field." They were all fields to him, whether a weedy single strip of macadam or some vast complex of crosshatched runways. That was his Kentucky past calling. The taking-off place and the landing place was the field. I remember him saying that when we were small, my older brother, Marty, and my younger brother Ric and I, lining up to tell him goodbye as he was leaving on a "trip" (all he ever called it) with a two- or three-night layover—maybe down to Miami, with plenty of stops along the way, and then working back through some of those same stops, maybe Atlanta, Charlotte,

Raleigh-Durham, Charley West (what he always called Charleston, West Virginia), Louisville, Indianapolis, home.

As I wrote elsewhere: "Sometimes he had to leave in the middle of the night, and then I would hear him moving at the front of the house, talking to my mother, his voice waving through my sleep as though through water. Other times he left after supper, or on Sunday after church, or before Marty and I got home from school."

Say the leaving was in the daytime, after school, late afternoon, just when other fifties fathers might have been arriving home from work. Out in the driveway, with our family's green Oldsmobile 88 idling beside him, he'd be in his captain's hat, with the beautiful medallion of a red falcon on the brim, and the scrambled egg on the visor, and in his starched dress shirt with the epaulets on the shoulders, and in his dark blue woolen uniform with the gold buttons on the jacket and the raised gold stripes on the sleeve. He smelled of talc and Old Spice. He'd be holding his thick and beat-up old black leather satchel case stuffed with manuals—his "brain bag," he called it. He'd set it in the trunk, along with his metallic silver suitcase. The emperor of the air was going off. Which often enough was an incredible relief. It was as if the house—our lives—could slump again. The fact that he was going away for the next two or three days created in me a queer feeling of both loneliness and euphoria. This was the two-edged sword we lived by: terrified something bad might happen to him on a winter night up there in the high and the mighty, and the simultaneous joy of being free for the moment of his often explosive and arbitrary-seeming temper. Two-edged because of course we loved him, craved his approvals. Two-edged because of course there were plenty of times when he seemed the best dad in the world.

"Well, honey, I'd better head for the field," he'd say. He and my mom would kiss goodbye. Marty and Ric and I would shake his strong hand. I don't remember ever once trying to kiss him. It was impossible to do that. Sometimes there might be a semi-hug.

That other kind of field: I remember him telling me not too long before he died, when I was more overtly trying to get him to speak about flying and the past, and specifically about Kentucky, of how he was once sitting on the tongue of a wagon in a sweltering Union County hayfield when overhead came this terrible roar, and then this huge shadow darkening the earth all around him. His voice grew soft, as if recounting a gauzy dream.

"It was a Ford Trimotor, Paul. It was silver. It flew right over top of me. I was out there all alone. I would have gotten the strap for sitting on that tongue instead of working. I heard it coming before I could see it. It came over the rise. It seemed about a hundred feet over my head, as if it was going to land and pick me up, or maybe drop a ladder down. I could make out the pilot in the little window on the side of the fuselage under the wing. Must have been about '32. I was fourteen or fifteen. It went right on past me, the noise just huge. I was trembling. It landed in a big pasture on the other side of Morganfield. The next day the people who owned it, and who were barnstorming it through the countryside, along with a biplane that was doing acrobatics, started taking people up for a dollar a ride. I got a ride. I have no idea where I got that dollar. A dollar? Who had a dollar? After, when I told my folks I was someday going to fly airplanes, my mother said, 'Joe Paul, if you want to commit suicide, why don't you just go out there and jump off the barn?'"

My dad wasn't Wiley Post or Lindbergh, but it was his own kind of leap, and he made it. None of it would have happened without World War II. But it's also true that the leap could not have been made without my father's force of will, his certainty in self. None of his other siblings ever possessed this quality of character to the extent he did. Why the third-born in a sharecropping family of nine kids in far rural and unelectrified western Kentucky should have had such vision and vaulting ambition is something I won't try to answer here. It was just in him. I doubt he ever quite understood it himself. To reference the beautiful Robert Penn Warren poem at the start of this book: Something was happening in a boy's heart. He didn't know what it was. Those great geese in the moonless thirties night were honking him northward, away from Union County, even if there is a whole other sense, or so I believe, in which my father never left Morganfield and Union County at all.

Long Ago in Kentucky

Morganfield, mid-1930s

SUCH A SERIOUS GAZE, almost unnerving. I can't say it's untypical. In his baggy and high-waisted dungarees turned up at the cuff. In his coarse-looking work shirt, which must have been rubbed so many times across the washboard by my grandmother that the coarseness of the cloth, with its glints of bluing in it, may actually have felt soft as lanolin against his skin. With his fist held tight on that bridle, right at the edge of the bit, showing the horse who's boss. With the slightest stoop to his shoulders that I remember so well the entire time I knew him. My father told me once that he felt self-conscious when he went into the service because he seemed taller than everyone else around him. But at his tallest, he was only six-foot-one, and he doesn't look quite grown out to that here. "I'd've been handsome if I ever stood up straight," he used to say.

Yes, serious-looking, and with that pencil of cig that's probably a roll-your-own and that he's holding so naturally between index and middle finger. I remember him holding his smokes like that, down low, against his trouser leg, with his slightly raised thumb poised to flick off the ash reflexively. My dad smoked them one after the other when we grew up—unfiltered Camels and Chesterfields and Luckies. Then he went to menthols with filters. Long into my adolescence, he was still a four-pack-a-day man. And then, speaking of force of will: One day, right in the middle of a Kool or Salem or whatever it was (at least this is our family legend), he threw the cigarette down out in the yard and crushed it and cursed it and walked away and never touched one again. And, of course, once he'd quit, he became a zealot against them, eager to show his contempt for weak people addicted to nicotine.

How old would he be in this photo? I'd guess about seventeen or eighteen, in which case it's about 1935 or 1936, and he's either a junior or a senior at Morganfield High School. They're living out on the Will Tom Wathen farm, cropping on the share again, because the bankers have foreclosed on the family again. "I remember when they foreclosed on Daddy," my father once told me. "Back then, when you lost the farm, they took everything—we had our clothes and a team of horses. They even took the furniture."

Such an odd and on the other hand entirely understandable way to say it: "losing" the farm, as if you've inadvertently dropped something out of your back pocket. When what you're really trying to acknowledge in the least humiliating way possible is your shame. It wasn't as if you didn't try. You just couldn't make the payments. You and your wife had too many mouths to feed. It wasn't your fault. Maybe you couldn't even make the $148.33 of yearly taxes due on your land to satisfy the state, the county, the school board, and the road commission. Never mind payments to the bank or other title holder for the property itself. And then one day there was your name on page seven in the weekly *Union County Advocate* under the one-column headline: "SHERIFF'S SALE FOR TAXES." At the courthouse door next Monday, between the hours of 11 and 3, the sheriff or his deputy intend to sell you out, auction off all you have, or at least preside over the selling off, and this is the official published notice of it to all your neighbors (some of whose names are also on the list). Because you don't have $148.33.

This kind of indignity is interwoven into the history of my extended family's farming roots in Kentucky. Those roots go back in Union County into the nineteenth century, and in other parts of the state they predate the American Revolution. The roots are about family and hard work.

What I have just described literally happened to my great-grandfather in 1932 and 1933—he couldn't make the bundled state/county/school/road taxes on his 205 acres, about four miles out of town, off the Crawley Road. His name was Philip Kincheloe Hendrickson, and he seems often to have gone by "P.K." or "Kinch." (The name has variant spellings; it's pronounced KINCH-low.) In his pictures, he looks like somebody out of the James Gang, or maybe one of Cole Younger's boys. I never knew him, but I knew his son, George Hendrickson, my dad's dad, my grandpa, and, in fact, I knew him very well. I was almost nineteen when he died. I was in the seminary, and the priests let me come to Kentucky in that frozen February of 1963 for Grandpa Hendrickson's funeral. Something shocking happened at the reading of the will in the parlor after the burial, with everyone assembled: My dad and all the others who had moved off the farm to make their way in the world got disinherited. My dad left town in a rage. He swore he was going to contest the will in court. He never entirely got over it. It wasn't the money.

About six generations of Hendricksons have broken Union County soil, are still breaking it. That includes two of my first cousins, Jimbo and Keith, and their own sons, men now in their thirties and forties. They don't do it with two mules and a plow and a mouthful of dirt. They ride in air-conditioned cabs with leather seats and built-in stereos atop monster pieces of machinery that can plant twenty-four rows of corn seed in a single swath and for which they are paying on time—the multi-hundred-thousand-dollar machines, that is. Along with payments on the land.

Yes, Hendricksons have broken the soil, and often enough the soil has broken them. It's much truer for some of those earlier generations than the latter, although in another way it's still the old story: You do the work, and the bankers hold all the money cards, or seem to. It was the evil New York Life Insurance Company that dispossessed Kincheloe Hendrickson in 1932. He had been a farmer for half a century in Union County, and they took it all away from him when he was nearly seventy-three. He moved to Louisville. After he died, in 1946, the family brought him back for burial in Union County, and his small stone is there now, one side of it popping up out of the earth, as if in protest of what was done by faceless people in suits in faraway cities.

You don't have to go back three or four or five Hendrickson generations in Union County to sense how hard it was. The family my father grew up in got foreclosed at least once in the mid- to late twenties, and then again, a few years later, before they went back to farming on the share. My dad's family sharecropped through most of the thirties, until he left home for the service. Actually, it's a sadder story than that: Kincheloe had put up his own farm as collateral in September 1931 to try to help save my grandfather's farm—and both father and son, Kincheloe and George, ended up losing what they had. There was a great bitterness and a family falling-out.

Eventually, it healed.

The place of my father's birth sits on the western edge of what some Union Countians still refer to as the Great Western Coal Field. It's tucked into a semi-hidden and hard-to-get-to crook of the state, west of Owensboro, southwest of Evansville, Indiana, across the river from Shawneetown, Illinois, not really close to anything you'd describe as urban. Even now, with America having long since shrunk itself down in driving and flying times with superhighways and big metropolitan airports, you'd still have to *want* to get to tiny Morganfield and sparsely populated Union County.

In the War Between the States, which is what some locals still call the Civil War, Union County, in the torn state of Kentucky, went largely Confederate. In the 1850 slave schedules, there were

484 slave owners in the county—and somewhere in the neighbor-hood of 3,200 slaves, both Blacks and mulattoes. In the next cen-sus, 1860, out of a total population of almost 13,000, there were a reported 3,105 slaves—a ratio of just more than three whites to one slave. Best I can discover, decades before the Civil War, Hen-dricksons, at least my line of Hendricksons, hardly ever owned any slaves: They were too poor. I'm not remotely suggesting this gets my collective family history off the hook of America's greatest shame and sorrow. My father comes from a region of racial bigotry. That was the legacy he grew up in. Did he throw around the "n" word when I was a child, growing up on the edge of Chicago? I'm afraid he did, now and then. Did he get more sensitive to the word as he aged? Unequivocally yes, and I don't think all of it was due to the way he recognized the world had changed on him.

The Ohio River, looking as wide and brown as the Mississippi at this far point in its 981-mile meander, curls left along Union County's entire western edge, forming a natural border. Another famous river—Indiana's Wabash—empties into the Ohio, on the opposite shore, at about the halfway point in this natural-forming border. The Green River is not far from here, either. This little hidden neck of Kentucky has some storied American waters in its vicinity and near-vicinity.

The Ohio's alluvial riches create a deltalike effect that makes Union County's bottomlands and lowlands incredibly fertile. It's some of the most productive growing ground in all of Kentucky. The topsoil can go two feet deep. Something like half of Union County's 363 square miles is made up of broad bottomland. You can easily get a two-crop season in many of these fields. Through the decades, corn, wheat, oats, tobacco, soybeans, rye, barley, clo-ver, timothy, bluegrass, sorghum, hemp, flax—all of it and more has been produced here in astonishing abundance. It's a place of cattle and hogs, too, or was. (The hog business tended to dry up for my farming first cousins.) In middle summer, it's as if the entire county is field-sheeted in green.

I can remember as a child visiting down on the farm with my parents. Grandma and Grandpa and my dad would get in the car after supper and drive the back roads. They'd be inspecting my grandparents' own fields, the fields of their neighbors. I'd be in the back, overhearing both the envy and the pride.

"High corn, Mom," my dad would say, looking out the window at somebody's farm. Maybe it was the John Robinson farm. Or the Jerry Thompson farm. Or the Jack Young place. In Union County, the names of farms are like street addresses. Even if the original owners are no longer farming them. The names attach, and they stick. Through generations.

"High corn, Joe Paul," Grandma would agree. Then, to fortify themselves, they'd turn back for an approving look at Hendrickson fields, to assure themselves theirs was just as high.

And yet there's another wealth in Union County's God-given wealth: *Under* all this potential crop richness, if the rains have come and the pestilence hasn't, lay the black gold. Union County's coal seams have been known to go thirty-one feet in thickness. To quote from an old statewide Kentucky biennial agricultural report (its date is 1895): "Thus it will be seen, that under every acre of land in this county there lies hid an acre of coal over thirty feet thick." A couple of feet of black alluvial topsoil, and under it all the black rock, waiting to be picked and shoveled. Some of my relatives have worked in the mines of Union County, where there can be far faster paydays—and also much higher costs that perhaps weren't necessarily reckoned when they signed up to ride deep down under the field sheets of green on somebody's coal train.

"Gary Mike, he went into the mines" is how they say it. He's a first cousin a little younger than I am. Another first cousin was a face boss at Peabody Coal. Another first cousin lost an arm to the mines. In some places in the county, you can see the terrible coal scars on the hillsides.

Morganfield, still just a little bitty place, had about 2,500 people when my dad was growing up there, or outside of it, on a succession of poor farms. At best, the population is maybe only a thousand or so more than that now, and the whole county itself is no more than about 14,000. But like almost any county seat, Morganfield has always assumed a far greater importance than its actual numbers. It was ever a farm town, but it had its gentry. It had paved sidewalks. It had a passenger railroad and bus lines. It had its own chapter of the United Daughters of the Confederacy. It even had a future governor of the state, Earle C. Clements, who, later on, in the United States Senate, became the Democratic whip to Senate Majority Leader Lyndon Johnson. When I was a child and getting to spend maybe two weeks of every summer down on the farm, Morganfield had a drive-in movie and a motel called the Forty Winks. The town's African Americans, segregated in every way, lived on the west end of Morganfield. They still live there.

Looking again at this old black-and-white of my father in his dungarees and too-serious gaze: If it is 1935 or 1936, then he's got about another year and a half at home. My older brother told me that our dad once told him, when they both had had a little too much to drink, that his mother came to him a few months after his high school graduation and said, "Joe Paul, you're going to have to leave. There are too many of us at home." Maybe Grandma, such a tough old country woman, saw that, with Joe Paul's force of will, he had a better chance of making it out there on his own than some of the others. Better, perhaps, than the next brother up, my Uncle Phil, the second-born of the nine. He was such a decent man. I knew him my whole life until his death in 1991. Uncle Phil also left the farm and ended up, after the war, molding steering wheels for a lifetime of work for a division of General Motors in Dayton.

It goosebumps me to realize that five of my grandparents' eight sons on that dirt-poor sharecropping farm of the thirties went to World War II—and that all five survived. In terms of distance, and in other ways, too, my father easily went the farthest out. But the others—Phil, Tommy, H.C., Gerald: Each enlisted in a branch of the service, willing to risk his life, and each got back safe. I've long heard the story of how my on-their-knees grandparents kept a folded flag with five stars in a front window of their lamplit farmhouse.

I think what I love most about this photograph, one of the very few of him on the farm I possess, is how weathered and outdoorsy and just plain unwashed my dad looks. He's a boy of the fields. He's a boy of hard work. The day's grime is on him, the week's grime, around his wrist cuffs, in the rim of his neck, beneath his nails.

"Did you ever have to work on Sundays?" I asked my dad once. I think I was trying, without even really knowing, to get at the grime—how you wore it, almost like your clothes.

"Nope. Just the chores. No in-field work. Nope, a free day. Church day. Mass day."

He paused. "I remember, even on Sundays, after church, we'd come home in the wagon and put the horse in the pasture, and then Daddy would walk out into the corn rows. All he wanted to do was see things grow. If he couldn't see things grow, he didn't want to live."

It's odd to me that such a deeply rural mid-South family was so fervently Catholic. The Catholic roots, as best I can search it out, go about four generations back. It hasn't wavered much. Some of my first cousins pray the daily Rosary on their knees in the living room.

If this is a Saturday, and I have no real idea of that, end of the latest layer of grime, my dad will probably get his weekly bath this evening. He and his siblings used to take them, he told me once, in galvanized metal washtubs outside under the trees, at least in the warmer months, which in western Kentucky can go to seven months of the year. They'd haul out the water from buckets heated on the big wood-burning stove inside. My dad said they'd practically have the water wore out by the time everybody in the family had a bath, because you can't afford to draw a fresh bath for each kid. You got your time in the tub according to your rung on the ladder.

If this is spring or summer of 1936, then my dad, a few months before, has suffered a ruptured appendix. They took him to a hospital in Evansville for the surgery—and what did that cost my grandparents, who couldn't have had any kind of health insurance? He had a tonsillectomy when he was eight. And when he was two, in 1920, he came down with both whooping cough and measles. When he was born, at the end of October 1918, the world was about seven months into the Great Influenza Epidemic, which would last two years and kill somewhere between

20 and 50 million people worldwide. Union County didn't escape the scourge.

This classified notice appeared in the *Advocate* on February 13, 1936, about three weeks after my dad's surgery in Evansville: "FOR SALE—Pure timothy hay, also Red Top and Lespedeza mixed, some soy bean hay and one pair smooth mouth mules— G.E. Hendrickson, Morganfield, Ky. Tel 175-J." In its own way, the ad astonishes me: The family had a telephone. Could the two events, the rushing of the third-born to Indiana, the need to raise some cash, have been related? I bet so.

"I remember coal-oil lanterns hanging from finger-hooks in darkened rooms," my dad said once, the poetry rolling right up. Another time, he said: "We had four fireplaces in the Wathen house. It was our sole source of winter heat. Daddy would buy a wagonload of fine crushed coal to bank the fire at night. Starving it of oxygen, is what you're basically doing." Another time, he said: "Daddy put shoes on our feet, we didn't go barefoot, Paul, I know that." Another time, he said: "We picked it by hand, you know." He was talking about the corn. "Two wagons loaded by dinner, one and a half after dinner." There was no such thing as sweet corn—the family would eat field corn, just like their stock. By "dinner," my dad meant the noontime meal.

All of these things he seemed to say so lovingly, as if all the poverty and hardship had gone right out of his memory.

We were standing once at one of the Smithsonian history museums on the National Mall in Washington. We were looking through a glass case at a cutaway of an early American schoolroom, with its primitive chalkboard and crude desks bolted to runners.

"I went to first grade in a room like that, Paul," he said. "It was a one-room schoolhouse. It was called Seven Gums. I guess because it was out on Seven Gums Road. This must have been about '24. One big room and there'd be three or four in every class, and the teacher would work with, say, the sixth or seventh graders, while the other ones were supposed to be tending to themselves. Can you imagine how much studying went on when the other side of the room is full of noise?"

"How'd you get to Seven Gums School?"

"Rode a horse. No. I guess I was too young at that point. That was later. We walked, or Daddy took us in inclement weather in the buckboard. Let's see, I guess it was about three or four miles, yes, from the Buckman place, where we were living then, to Seven Gums."

Again, the pride, strange to my ears in terms of the words themselves: "Daddy would never say it twice. He couldn't afford to. He had too many kids. There were too many of us. He told you to do something, and you were already moving. If you weren't, he'd get a chair or the first thing he could pick up and start coming for you." This is so at odds with the kindly old figure I remember from my fifties childhood. That man had pearl-colored hearing aids and a knobbed hickory cane and a hitch in his gait that almost seemed rhythmic. He held up his khaki pants with suspenders. His big straw hat was rimmed with sweat. There was a big flag of red kerchief in his hind pocket. Far from violent, this man seemed only gentle. I think I can even remember him calling me "honey." Grandpa Hendrickson was in his late sixties then and was still working on the farm six days a week with several of his sons.

The last child in this former sharecropping family was a girl. Eight boys and a baby girl.

Her name's Margena. As I write this, she's the last alive, deep in her eighties. She always had it so easy, my Aunt Margena insists. She got to bathe inside, at least after the family acquired indoor plumbing, which wasn't until sometime in the forties, well after my dad had left home. She never had a hand laid on her, she insists. She even went to college—in far-off Louisville. She married a well-to-do boy who lived in town. There's almost a seventeen-year gap between my dad and his baby sister. She was only two and a half when he left for the service in the late fall of 1937. By the time Margena was growing up, or at least by the time she had gotten into college, in the fifties, my grandparents had become almost prosperous. They weren't cropping on the share anymore. They owned their own land and were adding to it. They'd made it all the way back from penury and foreclosure. In the early sixties, my grandparents even managed a Chevy with air-conditioning.

"Daddy would buy a Chevy, you know, if it was built on a donkey," my father once said.

I can remember my grandmother saying, "If the rig's a-going, I'm a-going." Meaning, if someone pulled the Chevy out of the shed, intending to take it to town for errands, she sure well enough was going along, too.

It was Grandma Hendrickson who seemed to run the show when Marty and I would visit the farm every summer. Grandma had us grandkids from up North scared about half to death. Her name was Martina. She was broad in the beam and stumpy in the legs. She could talk louder and cackle louder than anybody in the room. She wore paisley dresses with her stockings rolled below the knees. She loved to slap down gin rummy cards on a foldout card table. I remember her fanning herself with her skirt when the weather got beastly. If I was hanging around the house for too long in the morning, Martina would bark, "Now, you go on and get out there in the yard before Grandma gets after your rags."

Not long ago, as I am writing this, my Aunt Margena, always so good to me (we are only nine years apart), sent me a picture, probably taken around 1930. It nearly flattened me. "All the boys except Leon," she said in a phone call. "He isn't born yet. Neither am I.

That's your dad on the far left in the second row. He hasn't begun to shoot up yet. Aren't they something?"

What nearly flattened me are those citified duds. Where in the world did they get them?

Margena said she had no idea. So, on a recent visit to Morgan-field, I brought out the picture and showed it to my Uncle Leon, whom we always knew as Lonnie. He is the eighth-born son, and in his own way, like Margena, someone who got spared so much of the hardship (not to say the strap or the picked-up chair). I always loved my Uncle Lonnie, almost thirteen years younger than my dad. Like Uncle Phil, near the top of the ladder of kids, there was a softness, even a sweetness, in Lonnie, who was down at the bottom. I think he was always my grandmother's favorite. He lived the longest of any of the sons: soon to turn ninety (in the summer of 2021) when I visited him and his wife, Eva Clare, who'd been his high school sweetheart, and whom he had married almost seven decades before. She's always been my favorite aunt, or, really, aunt-in-law.

When I knew Uncle Lonnie on the farm, he was a thickset man. He had a stutter, or at least a stammer. Now he was a thin old man in a darkened and hot living room on North Morgan Street with the afternoon TV playing at deafening levels. He kept fiddling with his COVID mask; it was half dangling from one ear. He was putting it on sideways. Eva Clare came over to fix it. No one knew, of course, but he had about eight months to live.

I showed him the picture. Was this when you were living out at the Wathen farm? I asked.

"No, that wouldn't have been our place, I don't believe," he said, after a minute. "That doesn't look like ours. I'm pretty sure this is a studio picture." He ran his index finger down the center of the picture. "I wonder if the studio furnished the clothes. I kind of think they did."

Of course!

Uncle Lonnie moved his finger over to my dad. "I don't know, Paul, your dad, he just had some kind of . . ."

"Drive?" I ventured.

"Yes, that's the word I'm trying to say. I guess the rest of us never understood that drive. I still don't know how he did what he did. It's a mystery. It's almost a miracle."

Uncle Lonnie moved his finger three over from my dad to the pomaded figure on the far right in the second row: my Uncle Lindle. "Well, he was a rebel, wasn't he?" he said.

Lindle, as the oldest son, didn't have to go to World War II. He stayed home to farm. He ended up having three wives and several families and an itinerant life. Of his first family of seven kids, by his first wife, there's one left—my first cousin Becky, who still lives in the vicinity. Becky and I are the same age, and we used to be sort of kissing cousins. Until recently, as I am writing this, Becky had an unwell older brother, Jerry, who still lived locally. Becky and Jerry, who refused to go to their father's funeral in 1988, told me shocking stories of their father's violence when they grew up— "shocking," except in another sense no. Jerry was in his eighties, with ALS, and failing, when I stopped in to see him. What would either have had to gain at that point by not speaking the truth, as they could recall it, to a first cousin who'd been long out of touch? Even if you discounted 50 percent of it (and I don't), what about the remaining 50? Stories about beating a mule half to death with a wrench because the mule couldn't make the hill with a wagon of picked corn. Stories about beating a child out behind a shed, and afterward the beaten kid crawling around the corner on all bloody fours. There is a story that when Uncle Lindle was still in high school, in early 1933, he got his girlfriend Sarah Graves pregnant, and my grandfather George was so shamed that, after the shotgun wedding (across the river in Illinois), he made his eldest take his pants down to his ankles and had him bend over a stump, and then beat him with a tree limb while his new wife stood watching.

What passeth down. Yes, I am convinced my father came home from the war with bad PTSD, and took it out on his sons, or at least on Marty and me, who were the two oldest. But there is another sense in which I now believe he was only doing in return what was done to him—that his anger and violence and eruptive tendencies were the result of the war and all of his past, and all of it working together. And, by the way, maybe Grandpa Hendrickson was only doing to his sons what in turn had been done to *him*. And on back, as far as you want to march it. By that measure, you could almost understand, if not forgive, a man for beating a mule, never mind a child, half to death because the mule wouldn't make the hill with a loaded wagon. Who knows what the child had ever done? Except I want to say something else: I never saw any of my Uncle Lindle's violence. I just heard about it. What passeth down. What hides underground.

Uncle Lonnie and I didn't talk of any of this. We shifted the subject back to my dad—and flying. Suddenly an old man seemed about three decades younger.

"Do you remember that time Joe Paul brought you and Rita and Marty and Eric down in that new airplane he'd bought?"

I nodded. It was a cream-colored V-tailed Beechcraft Bonanza, with a snappy red trim. My dad had been a pilot for Eastern for seven or eight years. He and another Eastern pilot had gone in together on the purchase of their own private plane, something to fool around with when they weren't flying the line. So, naturally, the third-born, who had already gone so far past his raisings, wanted to fly his new plane down to the farm to show it off, show himself off. The little Bonanza could seat five—two in the front, and we three kids squeezed into the back. I remember how we buzzed the farm. Grandma came running out of the house waving a dish towel as my father kept making low passes over the barn and the chicken coop and the outhouse and the main house. We then flew on down to a little town called Sturgis, a few miles away, which had a landing strip, and where one of the brothers picked us up. The next day, my father began taking his family up, one at a time. None of them had ever been up before. Grandma refused to go. Grandpa went, though. For years after, my father loved telling the story.

"I said, 'Now, Daddy, everything's going to be just fine. But I'm going to ask you not to touch anything.' And Daddy said, 'Joe Paul, don't you worry, I'm not going to touch a goddamn thing.' And I said, 'Good, Daddy.' And he said back, 'Uh, Joe Paul, do you think you could try to keep it low and under the wires?'"

Uncle Jimmy went up. Then it was Leon's turn. He was reliving it all now on the eve of turning ninety. "Oh, Lordy," he said, nearly coming out of his chair. "I was in that little airplane with your dad and I was praying out loud. I didn't care what he thought. I said, 'Joe Paul, I'll do anything if you just make it quick and get me back down on the good ground of Morganfield.'"

Although Morganfield and Union County are the Hendrickson ground which I have loved for more than seven decades, it turns out that the Hendricksons of my line didn't originate there. They originated, at least in Kentucky, about nine counties and 200 miles southeastward—in a place called Adair County, and, specifically, in a verdant little cove tucked between ridges that's known as Cane Valley. I don't propose to tell a genealogy story here, except in its barest bone, even if I do believe that the tale lines up in rough ways with some great American mythology. Whenever I asked my father where we came from, he used to say: "Hell, I don't know, Paul. I always heard we were descended from horse thieves. We were too busy working the farm to try to find out where we came from." There may have been horse thieves in the bargain, but there was some heroism, too, not least Civil War heroism.

I am convinced that my father lived and died with no clue that his great-grandfather (which is to say Kincheloe's father) had fought on the side of the Union as a private in Company C of the Thirteenth Kentucky Volunteer Infantry. That he was at Shiloh and the Siege of Corinth and was in the Knoxville Campaign and the Atlanta Campaign and the Battle of Kennesaw Mountain. That he served for three years and four months, entering as a private and coming out as a private. His name was George Hendrickson, same name as my father's own father, my grandfather. I have stood at *that* George Hendrickson's stone in Cane Valley Cemetery in Cane Valley, Kentucky: my great-great-grandfather, my Civil War grandfather, George Hendrickson, who saw duty and undoubtedly some stark terror in some of the most famous place-names of the war. His stone is under a sassafras tree. It's on one of the highest points of land in the valley—you almost get a 360-degree view. (In the country, the old folks always said that you built the cemetery on the highest ground, to get it closer to heaven.)

Written on my great-great-grandfather's stone are these words, still perfectly readable from when somebody chinked them in back in 1898: "No pains, no griefs, no anxious fears can reach our loved one sleeping here."

The gist of the genealogy: The Hendricksons of my line seem to have come out of the British Isles somewhere in the mid- to late eighteenth century and landed in the Virginias or maybe the Carolinas. From there they eventually made the trek westward. They would have come westward in one of two ways: on foot through the Cumberland Gap, which is that iconic notch where Kentucky and Virginia and Tennessee all join together, or down the Ohio, on a flatboat, possibly from as high up as Pittsburgh, landing at what today is known as Maysville, Kentucky. One way or another, they got through the Gap or off the docked flatboats to Adair County, which is in the southern part of the state, about an hour east in driving time of what is now the medium-sized city of Bowling Green.

Let all the rest of the specifics of it go. Because it is my Civil War ancestor, George Hendrickson, fighting on the side of the Yankees, who interests me most in this long line, and for a specific reason: I've discovered an uncanny parallel between him and my father. George Hendrickson of Company C (to repeat the lineage: He is my grandfather's grandfather; he is Kincheloe's father; he is my dad's great-grandfather; he is my great-great-grandfather) mustered in at age twenty-six, on the last day of December 1861. When he told his wife (her name was Martha Winfrey) goodbye at Cane Valley that December, he had two little children, the younger of whom was just past two: namely, my great-grandfather-to-be, Kincheloe. He even had a third child on the way.

Eight decades later, when *my* father kissed *my* mother and *his two* little children goodbye in that scabby motor lodge courtyard in Amarillo on September 20, 1944, not knowing if he'd ever see them again, he was five weeks from turning twenty-six.

Two Hendrickson sons in a direct bloodline going off to war at the same age, with two babies and a wife in their prayerful wake.

But there's more. George Hendrickson fought at the Battle of Shiloh on April 7, 1862. It was his first test under fire. According to after-action battlefield reports, the Thirteenth Kentucky, which was attached to the Army of the Ohio, heroically held its ground. The night before, the boys, which, of course, is what they were, had tried to get sleep out on the open ground in a sheeting rain. According to the reports, written three days after the battle, the rebels had "opened a heavy fire with shot and shell, which ranged over the battery." In return, the Thirteenth "poured in a heavy fire on the enemy's lines, thinning their ranks and driving them from the field." Apparently, no one of the Thirteenth turned and ran. There were eight killed, and thirty-seven wounded, and twenty missing. My ancestor wasn't among them.

And eighty-three years later, not quite to the day, on April 11, 1945, George Hendrickson's great-grandson, my dad, stationed on Iwo Jima, flew his first intruder mission on a nearby island, at a place called Chichi Jima (Chichijima today), and faced what I have now come to believe was his most terrifying night of the war. I can't tell that story yet—I need to save it for its rightful place—but I'll relay this much: My dad had been on Iwo for only about three weeks. He had already flown a string of nighttime missions, mostly patrol around the island, but this was his first real test in *The Rita B*. Eighty-three years between these separate moments of terror, plus or minus four days: Private George Hendrickson on the ground at Shiloh in Tennessee, with the bullets singing over his head, and First Lieutenant Joe Paul Hendrickson at about 10,000 feet, strapped into his capsule in the far Pacific, caught in the enemy's searchlights.

In chapter three of MacKinlay Kantor's 1955 Pulitzer Prize–winning novel, *Andersonville,* an unnamed soldier of the Thirteenth Kentucky gets a cameo. "In the lines near Knoxville," the author wrote, "a boy from the Thirteenth Kentucky slid his rifle across a rock, elevated the sight slightly, and fired at a dark shape which had been drifting in front of him through the thickening mountain dusk." The dark shape was a Johnny Reb. The fictional boy from the Thirteenth, whom I like to dream was my great-great-grandfather, got him. Popped him. He could hear the yelp.

———

And so, the end of this part of the story, which is really only the beginning, or even the start before the start, which is to say the moment when my father left Union County behind, when he got off the land for good, when he rose up out of all his roots and rode a bus up into Illinois and entered the Army Air Corps, even if, as I have tried to say, he never really left Union County behind and in larger ways never even got off the land itself.

Did Grandma really tell him he had to go? I don't know. Certain things are fact: There had been an epic flood in February 1937—the Ohio rose so high that it put some of the houses in Uniontown four or five feet under water. (Uniontown is six miles north of Morganfield, directly on the river.) That flood beat out the epic 1913 flood. That flood, even if it didn't seem directly to affect the higher-ground tenant lands my grandfather farmed, had to have set nerves further on edge. My dad's high school graduation was in late May. Morganfield High School couldn't afford a yearbook, but the graduates, the young men in their coats and ties, the young women in handsome dresses, got their portraits taken for a display in the *Advocate*. (Astonishingly, Bill Bauer, a Morganfield historian, found the program from the Baccalaureate Night, on May 23, 1937: an eight-by-ten sheet, folded in half, thin as parchment, the paper gone the color of weak weak tea. There's my dad's name, "Joe Paul Hendrickson," in column one of the Class Roll.)

That summer he worked on the farm. A few years hence, when he is up for promotion, and his superior officers have asked him to write a brief autobiography, he will describe himself as "an assistant supervisor and helper on father's farm" in the time before he left home.

That summer, Amelia Earhart and her plane went down in the Pacific without a trace.

That September, in Nuremberg, the Nazis held the largest rally in Germany's history. Adolf Hitler screamed and waved from the high-up podium.

Joe Paul turned nineteen on October 28. Three weeks later, on Tuesday, November 16, 1937, the week before Thanksgiving, he departed. Ten-pound bags of cornmeal were going for 19 cents at Waggener's Grocery. The upcoming big high school football game between Morganfield and Sturgis was getting a lot of ink and talk. I bet my dad never even got to attend a high school football game.

He left on a Greyhound. Surely, Grandma and Grandpa brought him in. The northbound schedule ran morning buses to Evansville at 7 and 11:15, one in the early afternoon, and a final bus at 8:05 p.m. I'm thinking he took the one at seven o'clock. He was headed, with a transfer at Evansville, up Route 41, and via other roads, to Chanute Field, at Rantoul, Illinois. He had boot camp ahead of him, but the Air Corps Technical School had already promised him a place in its airplane mechanics class, starting shortly after the turn of the year.

I've done a lot of thinking about that journey, something like 230 miles. This rawboned farm boy, who didn't know anybody in Rantoul, or, really, the wider world (if not literally true, then spiritually so), sitting toward the front of a Greyhound with his cowlick and pasteboard suitcase, peering out the window, wondering what the rest of his life might be like.

TIME-BEND. I squint and see my father ready to go on a routine patrol mission on Iwo. He's fully garbed and climbing into The Rita B's *cockpit on a drop-down ladder behind the nose wheel well on the underbelly of the fuselage. Such a tender and slender-looking little plexi box with all those switches and levers and knobs and gauges and dials in front of him. He's got on his oxygen mask, and his Polaroid goggles, and his shoulder-strap .45 Luger pistol, and his leather aviator's cap, and his parachute, and his uninflated Mae West with a pocket in the front to hold his shades and a pen flashlight and possibly a notebook. He's in his one-piece flight suit, cinched at the waist. Over top of that he's got on his leather flying jacket with the yellow sheepskin fur on the collar and on the cuffs of the sleeves. Cold up there tonight, even with these extra layers.*

Belted in, he's adjusting his headphones and doing a dozen other pre-liminary tasks. One of the early tasks is to secure the bulletproof canopy. It sits on a hinge on the left side of the cockpit. Once he reaches up and swings it over and locks the canopy in place, he'll really be sealed inside his "greenhouse." More than once when I was growing up, I remember him calling the cockpit of a Black Widow that: the greenhouse. There was room for only one person in that narrow-glassed slot: himself. There was never any pilot backup on a Widow—that was both her glory and her tragedy as a hybrid warship with a crew of three. She'd been designed that way for maximum effectiveness—sort of the art of elimination, no matter, or maybe because of, all of her advanced technology. But the point is, your fate rested with the guy in the cockpit, the one who had his cool hand, turned blue by the power of beauty, on the control stick. That's an image in a haunting and morally layered poem about the Black Widow by the poet James Dickey—more later about Dickey and on how his strange story intersects with my dad's and even my own.

My dad's gunner, Leo Vough, is sitting immediately above him, in another tight plexi box. My dad's radar operator, the R/O, is in the rear, belted into his own bulletproof bubble with his own scopes and gauges and gizmos. That man, Jack Kerr, out of Woodbridge, New Jersey, is my godfather. Back in Fresno, Flight Officer Kerr stood up for me at my baptism.

Soon enough my dad will be begin reciting—out loud, to himself—the checkoff list prior to taxiing and takeoff. I may be somewhat off on some of the sequence here, but I know I'm close enough, because I watched my father do much paler out-loud versions of the same ritual many times, long after the war, long after he was retired from his airline career at Eastern, but still a man possessed of the almost narcotic dream of flying, sailing around the country at 12,000 feet and 161 knots in his nifty little single-engine Beechcraft Debonair, which he used to keep parked in a rented hangar at a general aviation airport in the western suburbs of Chicago. The "Deb," as he always called her, was a different model and faster version of that cream-colored V-tailed Bonanza that he had bought, or cobought, a couple decades before, when he was new at Eastern, the one in which he'd buzzed the farm, the one in which he couldn't help showing off.

I used to fly with him in the Deb in those "retired" years every chance I could get, which wasn't often enough. I was in the East, leading a different life.

He flew as a private pilot until he was deep into his seventies, and he probably would have done it till he was past eighty, had not the hated "Feds," as he always called them, stopped licensing him because of his creeping health problems. And yet I will say that even when he could no longer fly as a private pilot, he was one of the most fit and agile people of his age group I've ever known. He never let his stomach go slack in the way of some old aviators and athletes. In the final few years of his life, I saw him still able to take the front steps of our house two at a time when he would come over to visit us in the East, hell with his failing heart, which had been failing him in serious ways for more than a decade.

But the ritual of getting set to go, even or especially in the little Beech Debonair: There was something beautiful, incantatory, about it. I'm talking now about the checkoff list, with the machine shaking below you, with the sound of the prop coming through the glass like a smooth table saw. Thinking back on it helps me to imagine a little of what it must have been like, so many years before, in the dark, in his Widow, on Iwo, alone in his greenhouse.

If I was going up with him in those long after-years of his professional career, feeling such pride and confidence and awe about what he could still do, just the two of us going for a little spin around the pea patch, as he liked to call it, he'd pass over to me a laminated card, and I knew then that I'd better have my part of the ritual down pat, or else face his frowning disapproval. That disapproval was something I feared for almost as long as I knew him, up to the moment when he died, in a hospice room outside Tampa in 2003, with its absurd wallpaper, with the irradicable whiff of urine seeming to float right out of the woodwork.

It was call-and-response, as if we were in some strange church.

"Mixture," I'd say, reading from the card.

"RICH," he'd shout.

"Prop," I'd say.

"HIGH RPM," he'd shout again.

"Throttle," I'd say.

"HALF OPEN," he'd shout back.

After we had worked down the list, he'd take back the laminated card and stick it in a side pocket of the door hatch and give me one of those Attaboy, Paul *grins and brush his knobby farm-boy hand affectionately against my knee. Sometimes he'd rest it there for a second or two. Invariably, he'd say something like:*

"Well, son, I suppose we better be off like a herd of turtles before we lose our nerve."

Or: "What do you say, Paul, we try to cheat old lady death one more time?"

And up we'd go.

I've never been able to fly a lick, never had the wit or patience or nerve to take a flying lesson, but in his own way my father was co-opting me, and we both knew it, into momentary participation in the thing he loved almost more than anything else in life. It makes me sad to say, but I think he loved it more than his own family. I do believe he was happiest up there in his wild blue yonder. He said to me once, talking of some of the great heartaches in our family: "You know, Paul, all of my troubles begin once I get back down on the ground." Of his five children, four sons and a daughter, only one of us, my kid brother Mark, a superb pilot, fourteen years my junior, in his mid-sixties now, with whom I think I would be willing to go to Antarctica in a single-engine plane, chose to follow him into his profession.

"It's something I've never really been able to explain," I remember my dad once saying. "The feeling I've always gotten from flying." I've heard Mark say much the same thing.

Sometimes, in those long after-years, when we'd be up together, just the two of us, side by side, as if loosed from all else in the world, not least from our long struggle of just trying to know how to talk to each other, he'd casually pass the wheel to me without any warning and then I'd try to hold the nose of the Deb semi-steady for a few minutes against the horizon.

Attaboy, Paul. *The ultimate quiver of approval.*

The Road to South Field on Iwo Jima (1)

Old Chanute Field brochure

WHEN I WAS GROWING UP, it was just another good Nonna story, among so many Nonna stories: the time my maternal grandmother wrote to Eleanor Roosevelt, trying to keep my dad from being sent overseas to the war. She wanted the president's wife to intervene in some way so that my father would be ordered to stay stateside and take care of his newly pregnant wife. "Wanted" would be putting it mildly. This was June 1942. My father had been in the service for four and a half years then. My dad had been Nonna's son-in-law for four months then. If it was a good story later, it wasn't so funny at the time. I'm not exactly clear on when my father found out, but when he did, I don't think he spoke to her for a while. He felt Nonna's interference was going to hold back his career. Apparently it didn't hold back a thing. Indeed, I'm wondering if Nonna's famous letter, famous in our family, didn't do my dad sly good with some military superiors who had unstoppable mothers-in-law of their own.

I picture Nonna writing her letter to the first lady—in blue fountain-pen ink on two sheets of plain, white, eight-and-a-half-by-ten stationery, the kind you might buy at Woolworth's—late at night, in one take, at an oilcloth-covered table in her Ohio farm kitchen. Her husband, my Pop, unaware, has gone off to bed. Even if he'd been awake and aware, I doubt Pop might have tried to halt Nonna. Once she set her mind to something, the more so if it had anything to do with perceived harm to family, Nonna was her own force of nature.

Her first name was Isadora, shortened to Dora. She was first-generation Irish, deeply religious, descended from Conleys and Murphys. She was reed thin. She was a fifties health cultist, with all sorts of wild-seeming theories, which turned out to be not so kooky, after all, in the years after she was gone.

Nonna told me once, in reference to my brother Marty, who was often in trouble as an adult of one minor kind or another, that she would mortgage her house and anything else she possessed, if it came down to saving him from jail (which he was threatened with a time or two in his life). It wouldn't have mattered to her that she might be enabling his bad gambling habits or bailing him out of other kinds of debts, some of which weren't minor. "He's my flesh and blood, Paul," she said. That was that.

In her Eleanor letter, some of her sentences crowded the margins, and Nonna also employed a string of ampersands and other abbreviations: not a second to waste.

She put the date at the top: "June 20, '42."

Dear Mrs. Roosevelt:

　　Please pardon me for taking up your valuable time but I am coming to you for a very grave matter. You being very broad-minded, I know you will do something about this matter about which I am making an appeal.

My daughter (Rita Kyne Hendrickson), the wife of 2nd
<u>Lt. Joseph Paul Hendrickson</u> is three months pregnant & of
course is expecting a baby the last of November or the first
of December. They were married in February and she is 19
years old. I am making sacrifices and all of us are willing to
make sacrifices to win the war but as many of the soldiers
are being sent overseas we naturally feel like he may get
orders sometime to go. Don't you think he is greatly needed
in this country now and it is very important that he be with
her the next 6 months to come? She will be needing medical
care & attention from him & he will be worried & sick if he
isn't with her so I think it would be the death of the three
of them. . . . You as the mother of six children can see how
important it is that he be left in the States & I know can &
will do something about it.

Toward the end: "I am enclosing stamps for your sending of registered mail about this matter—to whom I do not know." Tagged
on: "I will appreciate this Mrs. Roosevelt & always remember you
as a friend & thank you. You see I can talk frankly to you on this
subject as 'woman to woman.'"
    In her P.S.: "Please give it your immediate attention."
    She signed it, "Mrs. Bernard Kyne, Xenia, Ohio, R.3. Cin. Pike."
The "Cin" stood for Cincinnati. Pop and Nonna's farm sat off the
Cincinnati Pike, a few miles south of Xenia. It's the farm where
my mom grew up.
    I wonder if FDR's wife even saw it. It seems clear somebody
on her staff saw it (and possibly pocketed the stamps). About two
weeks later, a high officer in the Adjutant General's Office in Washington wrote to Nonna in his best, straight-faced, governmental
voice. (I can see Nonna's letter getting passed around the office:
Hey, Guys, check this one.)
    "Dear Madam," began Major General J. A. Ulio.

Reference is made to your letter of June 20, 1942, addressed
to Mrs. Roosevelt, in the interest of your son-in-law, Second
Lieutenant Joseph P. Hendrickson, in which you requested
that he be assigned to some unit which will not leave the

United States. Your anxiety in this matter is appreciated, however, this office regrets very much that no assurance can be given at this time of Lieutenant Hendrickson's continued duties within the United States.

The adjutant's reply was dated July 3, 1942. That same day, my mom and dad, innocent of it all, were aboard the Super Chief, out of Chicago, headed back to San Bernardino, where they'd been posted several months before, and where my dad would now await orders in the fall for flight school. The day before, on the 2nd, they had left Xenia by rail, had changed in Dayton for Chicago, had arrived in the Windy City on the morning of the next day, had spent that day seeing a few sights, and at suppertime had boarded for the Coast.

A week earlier, my dad had graduated from eight weeks of temporary duty propeller school at Pratt & Whitney's headquarters in East Hartford. My mom had left Connecticut ahead of my dad and had taken the train to Ohio, via Penn Station in New York, and my dad had then followed her to spend five or six days at the farm with her and his in-laws. Probably he had helped out Pop with some of the chores. He and Pop always got along beautifully.

July 3, 1942, was a Friday. The next day, the national holiday, and the day and night following, this much-in-love couple, just kids, with my older brother, Marty, starting to grow inside my mom's stomach, were rolling through Dodge City and Albuquerque and Gallup and Winslow and Seligman and Needles and Barstow, and then right on into San Berdoo in the early hours of the third day out. Sounds pretty sweet: getting to spend the 4th of July, even or especially with a war on, on the crack train of the Santa Fe Railway, looking at their country from the other side of their Pullman glass.

Somehow, I had forgotten all about Nonna's letter. And then, several years ago, I opened my dad's thick (and saved) military file at the national archives in St. Louis, and there it was, first document in the folder, staring up at me, its original, hilarious self, not even yellowed or curled. Nonna died in 1978, but suddenly I had her back. I hooted, drawing looks from the other researchers in the reading room.

My dad's nearly eight-year road to the shooting war stretched and wound from late November 1937 to March 20, 1945, when he and his fellow flyers of the 549th Night Fighter Squadron touched down a little before noon with their Widows on a length of asphalt in the near-shadow of Mount Suribachi.

To say the obvious: My mom is much in the picture, too, once she enters the picture.

Go back to that callow Kentucky kid, an enlistee, raw recruit, a few weeks from having turned nineteen, nine days before Thanksgiving, on his Illinois-bound bus. I have to think he was aware that morning of not too much more than his own scared going. The Second Sino-Japanese War had recently begun. The summer before, the Spanish Civil War had broken out. A few months hence (on March 12, 1938), Hitler, preceded by forty tanks, would stand in an open touring car in his brown storm trooper uniform returning the hysterical salutes of his worshippers as he rolled into Vienna in the Anschluss, the forced annexation of Austria into Nazi Germany. All these distant conflicts, and more besides, were grim prologue to the coming event of history my parents were going to get caught up inside of without any say of their own. I saw a statistic recently that stunned me: There were something like 300,000 American airplanes in World War II. And the person sitting inside the cockpit of *The Rita B* would be one of the sixteen and a half million American men and women who served in the war in one capacity or another.

It seems to me that in at least several ways the recruit was unwittingly lucky. If the place where my dad was headed was larger by a quantum than anything he'd yet known, in another way it was only on the edge of becoming something truly large, even gargantuan. In that sense, Chanute Field was a synecdoche for what was about to start happening in the American armed forces in general. The base, begun in World War I, was named for aviation pioneer Octave Chanute, friend of and adviser to the Wright brothers. Within a few years, Chanute had become the headquarters of all the mechanics courses and other technical training for the entire air department of the U.S. Army. Said another way (and this from an official government history): "From 1922 to 1938 Chanute Field provided the only technical training for the small peacetime air arm of the U.S. Army." *Sleepy* peacetime air arm of the U.S. Army, even if, in some sense, Hitler was already on the doorstep. My point is that my dad didn't have to travel to California or Mississippi or Texas (where the Enlisted Mechanics Training Department had first been organized in 1917). That might have swamped him. His new home at the Air Corps Technical School (the official name when he joined up) was half a day's bus ride up from Morganfield. All the training to become an "A&E" guy was at tiny and flat Rantoul, about 130 miles south of Chicago, just north of the twin towns of Champaign-Urbana, home of the University of Illinois. A&E stood for airframe and engine. I used to hear my dad say it with pride when he talked about how he became a flyer, an officer, from the very bottom of the enlistment ranks. "I worked my way up through A&E, Paul," he would say. "Damn tootin', I did." He knew airplanes, machines, from the inside out. His whole life, he worked with his hands. He overhauled cars and rebuilt washing machines and took apart the backs of watches for neighbors. When he flew airliners worth six million dollars, he was still making a living with his hands. White-collar hands.

So Chanute was this very large thing sitting astride this very small and still rural thing. Rantoul was an even smaller farm town than Morganfield. It had one main street. It still has one main street—I walked it recently and stared at the abandoned marquee of the Home Theatre, wondering if the name alone had drawn in a homesick boy on his first Saturday night pass.

He would have gone through a white gate and reported to the Receiving Barracks. They would have given him a cot inches from the next cot with a board sticking out of the wall about four feet above the cot. In the board were a dozen holes—with hangers in them: his closet.

Within weeks of his arrival, the number of enlisted men at Chanute was up to 1,280, the most in its history. And yet this number—and the amount of sudden new construction—would quintuple after 1938, as my father was finishing up the first phase of his

military life. Congress was on the verge of appropriating millions
for what came to be known as Chanute's "Great Renaissance"—
hospital, theaters, administration buildings, warehouses, hangars
into which you could taxi a Boeing 747 (if such a plane had existed
then).

Chanute Air Force Base (as it came to be named) closed in 1993.
More than two million students had gone through. The old buildings hang empty. You can drive out onto the cracked tarmac and
nobody will stop you, or no one stopped me. I drove right up to the
open door of one of the hangars, trying to see him in there, pulling
on wrenches. Gearhead.

First came Basic. He got done before Christmas. They let him
take a bus back to Morganfield on a three-day leave. (The event
made the *Union County Advocate*.) In February, with boot camp
over, his coursework began: in ignition, propellers, engine over-
haul, toolmaking, metalwork. The hangars served as classrooms—
freezing in that winter, sweltering in that summer. I've scoured
the old photo files in the 1938 Chanute archives. Is that him in the
back of the first row? Probably not. (I used a magnifying glass.) I
couldn't find any of his grades in the archives, but I have to think
he had a leg up on most of his classmates because of all he knew

about tools and machinery on the farm. There must have been a
few other farm boys.

Here he is, second from left, second row: graduation day,
August 5, 1938. So boyish, although in three months, he'll be
twenty. Notice the fine erect posture. Temporary correction. He's
gotten some of his classmates to autograph the picture and put
their forwarding address on the back. They're all headed in different directions.

Next assignment (after home leave) is San Antonio, at Kelly
Field. He's starting to see a bit of the world. I know next to nothing about his thirteen-month stay in Texas at two Army airfields
other than that they made him, on arrival, a crew chief on two
interwar trainers called the P-12 and BC-1—so I can only think
he'd graded high in his six months of instruction at Chanute. What
I do know is that he fell hard for the state itself. For the rest of his
life, "Texas," the word alone, represented for my father a kind of
atavistic cowboy dream. (In midlife he took to wearing boots and

cowboy hats.) He loved the food, the music, the sun pasted in the wide-open sky—and doubtless he loved the women, too, which he would have called girls. One of his expressions when I grew up, to describe almost anything in life that seemed grand, was: "Rich as a farm in Texas, Paul." He and my mom used to speak of retiring from Chicago to "San Antone" once his airline career was done. Years after I left home, they tried it, briefly, disastrously, not in San Antonio, but in the Rio Grande Valley, down on the Gulf Coast. But their lives together had been too long damaged for any kind of realistic new start. This was in the late eighties. I called my parents a few times in the months that they were living in McAllen. Practically the next thing my siblings and I heard was that my mom had driven off on Christmas morning from the "townhome" on which they had too quickly put down their money. (They had bought it fully furnished, down to napkins and silverware. The taste of the seller was so garishly at odds with their own. It's one of the few rash financial decisions I ever knew my father to make.) Not that they broke up, though. They never broke up, not on paper. They were too Catholic, for one thing among many things. The long agonies and occasional truces and part-time-living-together arrangements would go on and on and on, until the end. I'm not saying there wasn't sudden and deep tenderness in there sometimes, too, and their own kind of loyalty. There was. There was.

On December 1, 1939, my dad got new orders to Patterson Field in Fairfield, Ohio. He was back in the approximate region of his birth, maybe seven hours distant from Morganfield by car—with his own wheels. Three months before, he had gotten his official Air Mechanic rating. He was assigned to a bombardment squadron. Early the next year, he got his Corporal Second Class Air Mechanic rating. Seven months and thirteen days later, on September 15, 1940, he was promoted to Sergeant First Class Air Mechanic. He'd been in the service not quite three years. By then he'd transferred out of bombardment and gone to a transport squadron—I can only think he did so because he sensed new opportunity, faster rise. He was crew-chiefing on a Douglas bi-motor transport. Within three months, another jump, although still stationed at Patterson. Three months later (on April 1, 1941): a promotion to Staff Sergeant. The "noncom" (noncommissioned officer) is starting to earn decent pay. Another car comes somewhere in here, this time a convertible, not some clunker off the secondhand lot. I have a picture of him in Kentucky with his foot up on the bumper of his new rod with the white ragtop. He's brought it home on furlough to show the folks. The good-looking soldier's in civies: black suit, black tie, slicked hair.

Also coming in here: the Friday night Xenia roller rink meetup with the younger daughter of Dora and Bernie Kyne, who live out on the Cincinnati Pike. I like to imagine it happening—that initial encounter, my mom's chaste twirling in her white lace-ups past the Air Corps boy—on the first Friday of February in 1941, the 7th, in which case Rita B. is still seventeen, but only for four more days. Oh, who knows if it was even on a Friday? But it's our family story.

And I'll bet "Slam" was on hand that night, too. I can't say the number of times I heard this name when I grew up, always with something sorrowful and contained beneath it, especially if my father was the one saying it. Slam was Bernard Xavier Slamkowski. He was from East Chicago, Indiana, up on Lake Michigan. He and my dad had made fast friends at Patterson. They were the same age. He was a champion swimmer. He was a good-time Charlie— you can see it in the photographs. He's nearly always grinning, a muscled kid who's likely up to no good, especially with the ladies. After high school, Slam had worked in factories and had attended Michigan State University, before enlisting in the Air Corps in August 1940.

I've wondered, in fact, if Slam wasn't the one who first winked at and waved to Rita B. to pull over to the rail for a snatch of flirty talk that night at the Xenia rink.

In any case, Slamkowski was going to serve as my dad's best man a year later. Slamkowski was going to get married eight months to the day (in Florida, assigned to a new base) from when my parents got married. And Slamkowski was going to die—shot down by the Japanese, with three crew members, when my dad was still in training stateside and my mom was six months pregnant with me—about two years after that night, on January 18, 1944, while commanding a C-46 transport over the Himalayas for the "ICW" of the "ATC." Any Allied pilot in World War II knew what those abbreviations stood for: the India-China Wing of the Air Transport Command.

"Japs got him flying over the Hump," I remember my father saying. My whole life, my talkative father tended to speak in laconic ways about tragic events, in or out of the air. It wasn't because he didn't feel the grief of it, I think it was the opposite. I think at its core the trait had to do with the profession he'd chosen: Ever, a built-in risk. Part of the bargain. Hence, a certain fatalism. When tragic events did occur, why waste the extra words? I remember once (it was 1975), when one of his fellow captains at Eastern crashed a big jet coming in for a landing at JFK in New York, killing more than a hundred, including the entire flight crew, and my father saying, "Wind shear got him, Paul." Period. This contained aspect in the face of no-going-back events was so at odds with the other man, the Kentuckian who could yarn your head off, if he felt like it.

Not long ago, as I write this, I looked up the details of Slam's death. The language of the official accident report has its own clipped tone. The pilot and his crew had taken off after midnight from Sookerating, Burma. The mission was to resupply the Allied forces in Yunnanyi, China. "Approximately 1325 pilot called in he was being attacked by enemy aircraft. . . . Pilot was at 16,000 feet diving for cloud cover at 14,000 feet. No further contact was made." The "diving for cloud cover" did it for me: terse, yes, but not without something else sliding in beneath: the terror that must have ensued. The transport was armed with a lone Tommy gun.

Fifteen months after he was shot down, in April 1945 (my dad was in his second month on Iwo), Lieutenant Barney Slamkowski's widow got presented with a folded flag and the Distinguished Flying Cross at American Legion Post Number 17 in Gary, Indiana. Slam and his crew wouldn't be officially declared dead until January 1946, five months after the war was over and my dad was back safe with his wife and two children on Mechanic Street in Xenia.

The roller rink meetup was in the early part of 1941, and a marriage proposal came on the back end. I think my mom may have gotten her ring a day or two before Christmas—which is to say two and a half weeks after Pearl Harbor on December 7 and a world now altered. But I believe the deal to have been sealed long before Christmastime 1941. I think they'd fairly swooned for each other in the previous spring before my mom had graduated from St. Brigid High School. Maybe the double-swooning happened right at the roller rink. My mom was offered a scholarship that spring to "The Mount" in Cincinnati, and she turned it down. The Mount was Mount St. Joseph College for women, run by the Catholic order of the Sisters of Charity. She had other plans. Her parents had to know what was up. I can't imagine Nonna not objecting: Her daughter was way too young. If she *had* gone to the Mount, it's unlikely I would exist.

What she did instead that summer and fall after graduating was to work as a secretary and office manager at Cox Insurance and Marshall Real Estate. In her nine-decade life, it was the only job she ever held outside the home. I believe that this fact, or the effect of it, boundaried her life in immeasurable ways. For a long time, she was a world-class homemaker who would iron a shirt at midnight in the basement. She was always more involved in our lives than my father. But my mom never had a chance to earn her own paycheck and reap the psychological benefits. Not that my father would have stood for a minute of her working outside the home.

After Pearl (more specifically, the week after Christmas), my dad gets posted to another TDY stint: three weeks of electric propeller study at the Curtiss-Wright Corporation in Caldwell, New Jersey. Caldwell is thirty miles from Manhattan; I bet he never went over. About January 20, he's back to Ohio and his girl and Patterson Field. Pop and Nonna announce the marriage. The wedding is set for February 17 at St. Brigid. My mother is a celebrity in the Xenia paper. They refer to her as the "bride-elect." On her birthday (the 11th), two columns in the *Evening Gazette:* "ATTENDANTS CHOSEN BY RITA KYNE FOR HER CHURCH WEDDING TUESDAY." Six days later (after another story in the meantime): "MISS RITA KYNE BECOMES BRIDE IN IMPRESSIVE CHURCH SERVICE HERE." Pop and Nonna have fifty guests out to the farm for the reception. Slam is making toasts. Grandma

Hendrickson and my Uncle H.C. and my Aunt Margena (just a little kid) have driven up the day before from Morganfield. (They're being put up out at the farm.) Even though it's February, Grandpa Hendrickson can't come because of needing to tend the stock and do the winter chores.

I stare at a photo of my parents on their wedding day. He is twenty-three, she barely nineteen. Years later, when I was in the seminary, my folks used to come for holiday visits. I remember how some of the priests at the school seemed nearly apoplectic at my mother's movie-star beauty.

Joe Paul has his slight stoop. Rita B. has that pursed willful look I'd know anywhere. This picture is my own version of Sharon Olds's poem, "I Go Back to May 1937," with those magnificent, sorrowful lines:

> I want to go up to them and say Stop,
> don't do it—she's the wrong woman,
> he's the wrong man, you are going to do things
> you cannot imagine you would ever do

I told earlier of my father's burning through the high noncom ranks over the next month.

Early in March, he took the oath of office to become an officer. To quote from an old document: "Honorably discharged March 22, 1942, convenience of the government, to accept commission as 2nd Lt. Army of the United States." The next day, the officer and his bride pulled out for the Coast, driving to the San Bernardino Air Depot. Their blurring gazetteer of America had begun. On page one of *The New York Times* that day, the first line of a three-deck headline, latest dispatch from London: "1,400 U.S. PLANES SMASH AT BERLIN."

I'm thinking that it was about four nights and five days across, an extension of their honeymoon, unless there was a *Hurry up, we need you out here* from my dad's superiors. I'm pretty sure Marty was conceived on this trip, in one of the squeaky beds of the roadside motor courts: He was born almost exactly nine months after, and he didn't arrive early.

There was so much newness, love, excitement, in their lives—it's all I can imagine. Scary things were swirling above their heads, over which they had small control. Okay. They'd live inside the fact. Millions of others were doing and feeling the same.

They got out to San Bernardino (it's about an hour east of Los Angeles), and, feeling flush from wedding-gift dough, took an apartment off the base that they soon realized they couldn't afford. "Number 1306 E Street," my dad remembered, six decades after. "Sixty dollars a month. Fully furnished, with a big Philco console radio in the living room. You paid by the week. We weren't there long. Shooee."

I already referenced Jack Benny's famous coast-to-coast radio show (sponsored by Jell-O), and of how my parents got to attend a Sunday live broadcast. They'd been in California for barely two weeks. Two days later, in Xenia, this headline: "SOLDIER AND BRIDE AT BENNY BROADCAST." Every time I look at the piece, which Nonna fed to the *Gazette,* I laugh out loud. "Second Lieut and Mrs. Joseph Hendrickson (Rita Kyne), San Bernardino, Calif., formerly of this city, were guests at Jack Benny's broadcast from Hollywood, Calif., Sunday, according to word received by Mrs. Hendrickson's mother, Mrs. Bernard Kyne, Cincinnati Pk." It reads as if Jack himself had arranged for passes to be left at the front door. Actually, Nonna goofed. The show wasn't in Hollywood. The comedian, about the hottest thing in radio, had brought his troupe to Camp Haan Army Base in Riverside, California, about twenty minutes from San Berdoo.

As I wrote earlier, "no sooner" had they arrived in California than they were yanked back East, to Hartford. My dad, remembering: "I don't think we were in Berdoo but about five weeks. I'm a new engineering officer. All I want is flight school. I don't know yet if that's coming, but I think it is. A high officer called me in at three in the afternoon and told me to be on a train at seven o'clock. I ran home and packed. I made it, too. Four other junior officers and myself. Several days to Chicago, change trains, on to New York and then Connecticut. Played cards all the way. Your mom followed about a week later."

Yes, she did, and I've heard her own account. She had an upper berth in a sleeping car, which meant she had to squirm into her pantsuit pajamas behind the pulled woolen curtains. There was a guy down below. Next day, he invited her to the club car. He suggested they sit and write some letters together. He had other things on his mind, though. She fended him off. Later, a letter to my mom from him, with "Please forward" on the envelope, would show up at the Kyne farm on Cincinnati Pike. I can picture how that went over.

She was probably about six weeks pregnant. It never occurred to me until lately that during the nine months she carried Marty—the pregnancy would have been confirmed in California, possibly by a base doctor—my mom traveled back East and lived in a Hartford rooming house. Which meant she had to find a second obstetrician there. And then, later in the summer, back in California, she would have had to reconnect with her first doctor—or maybe even another—who, in any case, wasn't going to deliver my brother come that December. That doctor would be in Arizona. Just the anxiety of all this change, in her first pregnancy.

My mom entrained to Ohio, stayed a few days with her parents. The three left for New York City. My dad met them on the platform at Penn Station. This was the weekend when they got to see the Ink Spots at the Paramount. Pop loved the Ink Spots. The quartet crooned the hit war tune "Don't Sit Under the Apple Tree (With Anyone Else but Me"). It was a full bill: not just the fabulous Spots, but Woody Herman's swing band, a couple comics, a noir crime feature starring Veronica Lake and newcomer Alan Ladd. Ten days or so before, reviewing *This Gun for Hire* in *The New York Times,* lead critic Bosley Crowther wrote: "Not since Jimmy Cagney massaged Mae Clarke's face with a grapefruit has a grim desperado gunned his way into cinema ranks with such violence as does Mr. Ladd." Nonna must have despised the movie, although I can see Pop going for it.

My own pop must have been going pretty intensely for his two months of crammed classwork at Pratt & Whitney. He finished up toward the end of June and caught a train for Ohio, arriving (according to the *Gazette*) on the 25th. Five days earlier, Dora Kyne had sat down late at night at her oilcloth-covered farm kitchen table (or so I imagine it) and wrote her secret plea, one mother to another, to the first lady of the United States.

IN THE OPENING *of a beautiful and brief and relatively little known essay, "My Father," the great British-Zimbabwean novelist Doris Lessing wrote: "We use our parents like recurring dreams, to be entered into when needed; they are always there, for love or for hate; but it occurs to me that I was not always there for my father." It occurs to me that maybe I, too, wasn't always there for my father; occurs to me that he might have actually welcomed opening up to me more about what he did and didn't do in the war, all that was routine and boring about it, all that suddenly wasn't. He's been dead for nearly two decades, as I write these words, and what I have come to believe is that he was basically scared out of his skull for the whole time he was overseas, at least in the shooting zones. I can see the entirety of this more clearly now, even if the individual pieces remain jagged.*

My brother Marty once said, "Paul, don't you remember how Dad was always wearing his squadron flight jacket around the house? He'd come home from an airline trip, and he'd put on his flight jacket."

I had forgotten. And it was true. This was before my kid brother, Mark, and kid sister, Jeannie, were born. The jacket was seamed and worn, its leather like the seat of an old Jaguar.

Only a handful of times after I was grown—on my own, making my way as a journalist, and aware there was storytelling gold for me in those wartime Black Widow hills—did I ever try to nudge my father on it: the fear he must have felt. I'm not sure why I didn't work at it harder. It's one of my many regrets now that I didn't ask him more directly about it. I am haunted by what I don't know about my father, and long to know. I'm haunted because I've lost my chance.

On the other hand, maybe that's just fantasy—and some self-indulgence. Maybe Doris Lessing's beautiful lines are only that: beautiful lines, at least in terms of my father's life and mine. Maybe we wouldn't have been able to talk about his fears any more than we ever did—which is to say not very much at all, and then mostly in a kind of code—had we had all the time in the world together. My father wasn't built for introspection, even though he could get his feelings hurt surprisingly easy. He didn't like to dwell on the meanings of things. His profession ruled against it. He liked to kid me that "meaning" was for writers. He used to say to people in my earshot, "I just don't see how someone can make a damn living from writing, although I hear that some people do." I also used to hear, secondhand, that, actually, he was extremely proud of the living I was trying to make, so alien to his own. And there are other moments when I think: Maybe they weren't so alien, our occupations, and that he sensed it. We were both trying to navigate our way to something. Except that mine didn't have the implicit threat of physical danger in it.

And yet sometimes it would come out without any code in it at all. Here is one of the four or five times when we spoke directly, unambiguously, of his fear. The talk didn't last long. It was on the telephone, and so we didn't have to be looking at each other. I was writing a freelance piece for Life magazine. (This was in 1990. My day job was as a reporter for The Washington Post.) I had sold the editors on the concept of trying to chronicle "the greatest Thanksgiving meal of the twentieth century," which is to say the one that occurred on November 22, 1945, when millions of American servicemen, all those fathers and husbands and uncles and cousins and elder brothers (and military women, too, let it be added, in my wakefulness), made it back from overseas, whole or partly whole, to the family table. My dad was one of the millions—I'll tell more specifics of that arrival toward the end of this book.

I had gone around the country finding eight or ten representative stories, representative vets. But I hadn't spoken to my father, not until the last minute, when the piece was practically due. It would have been obvious to speak to him, of course, to try to pull things out of him. I kept putting it off. I remember my wife, Ceil, asking me if I was going to call my dad. And then one day I dialed him at the family cabin in northern Wisconsin, up near Lake Superior.

"Bear country," he barked, in his customary greeting. Like Texas, living in the Great North Woods, as he loved to call it, was one of his lifelong dreams. He and my mother had been able to realize the dream in the *mid-fifties with the purchase of a two-room pine-board cottage sitting on a small blue lake amid white birches surrounded by national forest. It was just about as far up in Wisconsin as you could go. He kept improving it over the years, enlarging it. (My father could do anything with a hammer and a saw and a box of nails.) The place was in our family for almost half a century. Toward the end, which wasn't too long before my dad's death, my parents sold it off quickly, stuffing family memorabilia into trash bags and putting them out by the road for collection before my siblings and I could stop them. All it did for my father—the losing of Wisconsin—I am now convinced, was add to his sense that his time on the earth was about over. The sale was in the early 2000s.*

Somehow, he always seemed to catch the phone from up there on the first ring. He and my mom were living in their separate places—mostly.

"It's about the Thanksgiving of 1945, Dad," I told him. "Not the meal itself, of course, you understand."

"But what it represented," he said.

"Exactly."

After another couple of minutes, I said: "But what exactly would that holiday have meant to you?"

He went straight in. "I guess it was a little something like, 'My God, I just don't have that constant—'" There was a pause on the line. "'—threat of dying anymore.' It's not at you. It's gone, that thing you don't want to talk about but that's always there in the background. See, I'd been fighting people who wanted to die for the emperor, least that's what they told us. I had a beautiful wife and two little boys back home. Hell, I didn't want to die for anybody, Paul. I just wanted to get the hell out of there."

"I'm glad you didn't," I said. "Die."

The Road to South Field on Iwo Jima (2)

My mom wearing my dad's silver wings on the day he won them: June 22, 1943

THE EXACT BEGINNING of my father's airplane in American aviation history is anybody's argument, but it's safe to say that January 30, 1941, was a crucial crossing point. Which was right in the time range of the heart-swoon, the coup de foudre, at the Xenia roller rink, if that's what it was.

January 30, 1941, is when the undersecretary of war in Washington, D.C., approved a top secret contract for $1,367,000 for the time-urgent development of a pair of prototype models of a new kind of war machine. The challenge was to build a "night interceptor pursuit plane," carrying a device that would enable her to "see and distinguish other airplanes" in pitch blackness. Not a fighter plane, no. Not a bomber, not exactly. This hybrid craft would fairly glisten and bristle with firepower, including cannons and machine guns and bombs on racks beneath her wings. She'd have enough fuel for a 1,200-mile range. She'd carry a minimal crew. She'd be able to climb fast and get down fast. She'd be capable of tight turns and speeds above 350 miles per hour. She'd be able to fight the darkness in a way no airplane in history had yet fought it.

The nightly blitzing of London by Hitler's Luftwaffe in the fall of 1940 had driven the urgency among the generals in Washington. The fighter pilots of the Royal Air Force could protect their airspace by day. But at night, London was an exposed wound.

A West Coast entrepreneur and aeronautical engineer named Jack Northrop had gotten the contract. In a blitz of time, after a couple of secret meetings back East (a critical one had occurred at Wright Field in Dayton in October 1940), he and his chief of research had come up with the basic design specifications for an all-metal, twin-engine, twin-boom craft with a skinny fuselage. Northrop had a company in his own name that was only a year old. (He was well known in the industry and had worked at both Douglas and Lockheed.) Once the contract had been approved, he and 125 engineers worked nearly around the clock at their plant in Hawthorne, California, in metropolitan Los Angeles, not far from LAX. Eighteen months from the January 30, 1941, approval, XP-61, Number 1 ("XP" for "experimental"), took off in secret and landed in secret at Northrop Field. "Jack, you've got a damn fine airplane," the company's senior test pilot is supposed to have said, after he'd dead-sticked her right back in. The date was May 25, 1942, about four weeks before my unstoppable maternal grandmother executed a stealth thing of her own to Washington, D.C.

In truth, the making of the Black Widow was closer to a three-and-a-half-year all-out effort from the moment of the prototype contract approval in early '41, to the point when the actual warship entered combat service almost simultaneously in Europe and the Pacific. That was in April and May of 1944, just when I was getting born out in Fresno, just when my father's squadron—the 549th NFS—was getting activated at Hammer Field.

Over a period of about four years, the P-61 would go through something like thirteen different variations and models. (Early models came off the assembly line in the fall of 1943.) The most numerous production model was the P-61B. That's the model my father flew on Iwo Jima, with her wingspan of 66 feet, her length of nearly 50 feet, her full height of just over 14 feet, her takeoff weight of 30,000 pounds (armored and payloaded and sometimes carrying extra fuel tanks), with her Hispano M2 20-millimeter cannons and her Browning .50-caliber machine guns. But despite such bulk, my father's airplane was still capable of a 2,000-foot-per-minute rate-of-climb. Her service ceiling, as it was commonly called, was above 30,000 feet. (She could get to 25,000 feet in less than thirteen minutes.) Propelled by her twin 2,000-horsepower Pratt & Whitney 18-cylinder radial air-cooled engines, she could sail at a top speed of about 375 miles per hour, and in an emergency could be redlined into the 400s. Such numbers were practically unheard of for a craft of such dimensions. Except she wasn't really bulky at all, not in flight. That's the odd thing about her: Only the numbers seemed so.

But the most high-tech thing about the Black Widow was what got secured in her tubular nose. To quote Stephen Joiner, an aviation historian-journalist whom I admire and have come to know among some other aviation writers who've helped me greatly, what got hidden in the nose cone of *The Rita B,* no less than what got hidden in the nose cones of the approximately 700 other Black Widows built by Northrop, was something called the SCR-720: a "spinning, thirty-inch scanner-receiver dish antenna" that could "sweep the sky with a knife-like beam." This microwave radar dish had been manufactured in secret at Western Electric. Again, quoting Joiner: This star-war-like device would be able to direct "interceptors to within one hundred yards of intruders in total darkness."

No wonder she holds such a legend, even though (like my father) the P-61 entered the war so late, after so many gone lives. What adds to it is that she has now all but vanished. There are only four Widows known to be in existence. *The Rita B* isn't one of them. (I have a pretty good idea of what happened to her after the war.)

There are various versions of how the Widow got her name. Here's one: At the end of a shift, a worker at Northrop was walking through the plant. He looked up at a spanking-new P-61 with her glossy black finish, with her serial number lettered back by her tail in fingernail red and also with a thin and bright red band striped around her fuselage up near the propellers. (The band served as a warning signal to stay clear of the blades.) "I don't know. Looks like a damn black widow spider to me," the worker said aloud.

In one way or another, the name got fixed. Some Widow pilots during the war had a red hourglass painted on the belly of their poisonous machine.

The P-61 stayed largely a secret to the American public for a long time. On the night of January 8, 1944, a reported 100,000 spectators crowded into the Los Angeles Coliseum for an Army-Navy show. In the paper the next day, there were accounts of "something fast and dark flashing through the stabbing searchlights." A voice on the public-address system cried to the startled crowd: "Ladies and gentlemen: What you just saw, if you looked fast enough, was America's newest fighting plane, the Northrop P-61 Black Widow!"

In early summer 1942, after Nonna's letter, my married dad is still some thirty-three months from touching down with his unit on South Field on Iwo.

They got back to Berdoo. (Did the farm kids try out the dining car of the Super Chief with its starched linen tablecloths and monogrammed silverware? I hope so.) They reclaimed their Chevy convertible. Probably, they lived in base housing. In Hartford, my dad's superiors had told him he seemed a very good bet for flight school, if he could pass the physical, and that he and my mom should be ready, on short notice, for the next move. (On May 15, in Hartford, he'd completed a form for "Pilot Training in Officer Grade," and the next day had gone downtown to Superior Court to get it notarized. That must have goosebumped him: It was becoming real.)

Later that summer, he got formal word. He'd been in the service for not quite five years. They arrived at Santa Ana Army Air Base in the last week of September. My mom was in her last trimester. Santa Ana is in Orange County, below Los Angeles, a bit inland. My mom told me once: "We quickly found a place in Newport Beach. It was about twenty minutes away from the base. Not because we wanted to live on the ocean. We were Midwestern kids. It was near a church. I wanted to walk to Mass every morning, while your dad had taken the car to work."

In their nine weeks in Santa Ana, my prayerful mom had to locate yet another baby doctor.

First day, he would have reported to the Classification Center. It was a strange Air Corps base: no planes, hangars, or runways. Santa Ana was "Preflight." It was where aviation cadets—some of whom were hotshot college boys who'd gained admission to flight school almost upon completion of boot camp—took tests and got separated out into their eventual specialties: as bombardiers, radar operators, or the big prize, pilots. There were IQ tests, physical stamina tests, psychological tests. After a couple weeks, the superiors tacked up on a board the names and the specialties. My high school dad had made it. After that, and for the next seven or so weeks, the preflight training for pilots consisted of eight to ten hours a day of physics, mathematics, airplane identification, radio code—and a lot of phys ed. I wonder how he did at those games of organized softball. As a child, I was always struck by my father's somewhat awkward throw. He had natural hand-eye skills, he was a better-than-average golfer, and a fearsome pool player, but he apparently never had time, in his own growing up, to develop a throwing arm.

He finished on December 1. They gave him four days to get to the next school, in Arizona. This was "Primary." This was where he would solo—or wash out.

A few weeks before, Pop and Nonna had come out on the train from Ohio to help out after the arrival of my older brother. My dad once said: "I remember driving across the California desert. Your mom is in the middle, eight months pregnant, with her legs spread out, Nonna's over on the window, Pop's in the back barricaded by a couple of chairs and our wedding gifts."

He took his eight weeks of primary flight training mainly at Thunderbird Field II in Scottsdale. There were three flight training schools for the Air Corps in the Phoenix valley. Scottsdale wasn't anything like the country-club place people associate with the name today. A lot of it, especially up where the airfield was located, was desert and cactus in the shadow of the parched-looking McDowell Mountains. The field had opened for training in the previous June. All told, 5,500 U.S. Army Air Force pilots would go through.

The four arrived in Phoenix and stayed in a motel for a couple nights before finding a rental at 2217 North 23rd Place: a one-story pink rectangular house. It's still pink. I was walking up and down in front of it on the sidewalk not long ago, as I write this, arousing placid Sunday morning curiosity, baiting myself to go up and knock on the door. I did, but nobody was home.

Pop answered an ad in the paper for a part-time Santa Claus job at a Sears store. He rode the bus downtown every morning. It got him out of the house while the women waited.

My brother was born in a nearby Catholic hospital at 5:10 p.m. on December 28, 1942. Which is to say that Marty arrived not quite halfway through my dad's training, right around the time he would have been scheduled to solo. Did he go up by himself a day or two after the 28th, or maybe a day or two before? After he got down safe, did he feel like he was king of the world? A brand-new son, a nearly lifelong dream fulfilled. I can find no record.

What I do know, because he said it once, is that it happened in a PT-13 Stearman. That's the biplane, made by Boeing, in which thousands of World War II American airmen first learned to fly. Such a textured beauty, sitting back on her haunches, with her rear wheel looking almost as small as something you'd see on the wheelbarrow in your garage. Two open-air seats, the one in the front occupied by the instructor, the one in the back ("the rear pit") occupied by the terrified student. An exposed Lycoming radial air-cooled engine. Tilted glass windshields, with their little glass side panels. Delicate guide wires between the thirty-two-foot rag wings.

Up front, flying at, say, 106 miles per hour, the silk-scarved instructor is shouting his one-way commands through a Gosport voice tube. The student can't talk back. That's the point.

He wouldn't have been sitting in the rear pit on the day when he went up alone.

At Thunderbird II, he learned how to hold enough rudder in his climb, learned to do banks and glides and stalls and spins and loops and slow rolls. It was stick-and-rudder work on a rudimentary flying machine. He was getting all the "stick time" they could throw at him, which came out to about two hours per day. The rest of the day belonged to ground school.

He would have had his first check ride at twenty hours, his next at forty hours, his final at sixty. At each check, or in between, some of his classmates would have washed out.

In the winter Arizona light, someone snaps a picture.

He's the one kneeling, in his Snoopy hat and pushed-up goggles. The way his arms are slung over his bony knees: so casual, cocky. The other flyboys look pretty easy, too.

He graduated on February 4, 1943. They gave him a week to pack up and get back to California, this time to an airfield in Bakersfield.

He'd passed Primary; next was Basic. His start date is February 12. Pop and Nonna have now departed on the train home to Ohio.

At Bakersfield (it's north of Los Angeles), middle of February to early April, in basic flight training, he takes courses in navigation, meteorology, radio communication. It's a more sophisticated kind of flying, in single-engine monoplanes. Again, the tension-filled twenty-hour check ride, and then at forty, and then at sixty. In pilot lingo, he learns about "needle, ball, and air speed." He gets introduced to instrument flying.

They're living on base, in units stacked in a row. My mom has turned twenty. She's gotten back her eighteen-inch waist. Probably she had it back within weeks of Marty's birth.

Another graduation: April 12. This time they give my dad almost two weeks to get to the next stop, for "Advanced," where he'll earn his wings—or won't. His advanced flight training occurs at Yuma, in far southwestern Arizona, which in 1943 seems about as remote and desolate as craters of the moon. And hot as Hades, besides.

Which is why they both decide that my mom and Marty will wait for him across the state line, in El Centro, California—plenty hot itself, but with a little more civilization.

He's in Class 43F. The first wave of cadets has arrived only that January, so his group is among the earliest to train at Yuma Army Air Field. This is twin-engine work: the AT-9 ("AT," as in Advanced Trainer), the AT-17, the AT-19. They're all used to make the gap between single-engine aircraft and multi-engine combat planes. He learns how to handle two throttles at once to make the thing taxi in a straight line. Here, ground school takes a rear seat. There's also much practice on the aerial gunnery range. Captain Barry M. Goldwater is director of ground training. He's just another high officer, not someone who'll make a different kind of American history.

It's 100 degrees in the shade in Yuma on June 22, 1943. My mom is there to see her husband get his silver wings pinned on. "Your dad put them on me a couple hours later," she once told me.

I love the pictures of him in his Yuma yearbook. But it's the old surviving yearbook itself, with its thick maroon cover and tattered binding, that's the more treasured thing to me. It may have been the only school yearbook of my dad's life. He gave it to me a few years before he died. It was as if he was saying, silently: *I know you're going to do it anyway. This may help.*

In the next fifteen months, my parents moved from Arizona to Colorado to Florida and back to California. And then it was the goodbye in Texas. But even then, my dad would have another six months before he saw Iwo.

A core question, for which I have no clear answer: Why did my father decide to sign up for night fighters? Typically, the system for training pilots for the war was to subdivide the instruction into the four stages which I have just been describing: Preflight, Primary, Basic, and Advanced. After that, you got "transitioned" by your superiors into one or more combat training aircraft in a tactical unit. You tended not to have a say; you went where they thought you should go. That happened to my parents after Yuma: They got immediate orders for Colorado, where my dad transitioned into B-25s (one of the most famous airplanes in all of World War II, seeing service in nearly every theater, a medium-range bomber with a crew of five, the formal name of which was the North American B-25 Mitchell Bomber).

In La Junta (it's in southeastern Colorado, on the plains), from July 1 to September 1 of 1943, my dad logged 150 hours in B-25s. It was low-level daytime flying with heavy emphasis on gunnery and navigation. Two things happened in these two months: I got conceived, and he threw in his hat to become a night fighter. Did he do it because of the challenge? You had to have exceptional vision. You had to be highly skilled in things like dead reckoning. You had to be willing to learn blind landings. You needed a natural feel for instrument flying. Some of these things he already possessed, and for the others he would soon prove to have a high capacity to absorb. And yet another thought has come to me, after some talk with my pilot brother, Mark: Perhaps he sensed that becoming a night fighter would keep him in the States for a longer time, since this was a new kind of flying art in the Army Air Forces.

His was a family of three when he volunteered, but a fourth member was coming. Did this weigh on him? I'd like to think so, even as I strongly suspect he wanted to see if he had the right, stylish stuff to fly the "night iron," as I once heard him call it. Was that kid in the hayfield who'd trembled when the Ford Trimotor flew right overhead daring himself to make another leap? Probably the decision, like so many decisions, was a hybrid one, not unlike the plane he would pilot on Iwo. But it must have scared them both, that he was challenging himself to see if he was good enough to fight the night in a new high-tech warship.

La Junta was done. They packed up again, bound for Florida, to the Fighter Command School, Night Fighter Division, at the

AAF School of Applied Tactics. It was headquartered in Orlando. They went via Xenia (so the route was straight across the Midwest, and then a sharp hook due south). They stayed in Ohio for five days and delivered the happy news of a second child on the way. In central Florida, for the next four months, my father flew out of three fields—at Orlando, Kissimmee, and Dunnellon—and they lived briefly in each of these places and even in a fourth, Ocala. The training was principally in two craft: the A-20 Havoc medium bomber and the P-70, which was little more than a radar-equipped A-20 repurposed as an interim night fighter. To quote Stephen Joiner again: The training was "high-and-low-altitude flight in total darkness, radar-guided interception maneuvers, collaboration with ground controllers, and blind landings." It was as if the volunteers were learning to fly all over again.

My dad had to learn how to sleep all over again. He'd rise in the late afternoon. He and my mom, who was in her second trimester, got hooked on radio soap operas and quiz shows.

Marty didn't have a crib. "He had a pulled-out drawer," my mom told me once. "All those places we lived, we always put him in a pulled-out dresser drawer."

On December 20, 1943, in the middle of the night, in a P-70A, in which he'd already logged ninety hours, the second lieutenant husband and father sustained what you'd almost want to call a "fender-bender," except that it didn't involve another plane, and that it caused considerable damage to his own, and that it got a twelve-page report in his permanent record. I have to think the incident mortified him, not to say the word "carelessness" that got written in a large hand across one of the pages that asked for "Specific Causes."

It was a taxiing accident, at 12:15 a.m., at Dunnellon Army Air Field. From the report: "Other aircraft have been taxiing over this area for the past six months with no similar accident. . . . Constant use of the stabilized areas adjacent to the runways and taxi strip have resulted in rutted and rough ground. . . . The cause of this accident was due to improper taxiing." What happened is that his plane caught a rut on the taxi ramp in the darkness and the nose wheel collapsed. The props of both engines folded downward and inward. The fuselage buckled. He wasn't injured, but the two- or three-hour cross-country training mission had to be scrapped. By daylight, someone from headquarters came with a camera to document the damaged plane. He signed an official "Pilots Statement." He wrote his name above his typewritten name, "Joseph P. Hendrickson," and his signature was large and black and fluid, as if he was saying: *I won't hide from this.* My father always had strong, beautiful penmanship. I've long thought his handwriting was a clue to the other man—some secret, artistic impulse never realized.

It must have been an awful Christmas.

Jack Kerr was up with him that night. (He, too, had to sign a formal statement.) A bit ago I mentioned his name in passing. He was two and a half years younger and a couple inches shorter than my father. They'd recently teamed up as pilot and "radio observer" (a deliberately vague term, in these pre-Widow days, for the radar operator, or R/O). Through the rest of the war they'd be together as close friends and hugely dependent partners. Five months before the stubbing of the P-70's toe on the rutted runway, his hometown Jersey paper published this item beneath the headline, "STUDIES RADAR": "Word has been received here that Staff Sergeant Jack H. Kerr has been assigned to take specialized training. . . . Sgt. Kerr . . . is stationed in Florida, but the exact location is not divulged." My parents never saw him again after the war. But, as with Slam, I used to always hear his name. My disappeared godfather, who came home from the war, I am convinced, with deep emotional scars, which had their consequences.

In early 1944, my expectant parents got transferred again—back to California, this time to Fresno, in the San Joaquin Valley. The Air Force had decided to relocate almost all its night fighter training from Florida to several California sites. (It made sense to have the training posts closer to Northrop's plant.) Fresno's Hammer Field became the central headquarters for the 481st Night Fighter Operational Training Group. This was the umbrella organization beneath which (as one local journalist put it) the various training units practiced their "aerial combat skills in the black of total darkness." Almost overnight, Hammer Field turned into one of the busiest fields in the military. *Fresno Bee,* February 24, 1944 ("HF NIGHT FIGHTERS LEARN TO KILL IN DARK"): "It's the Night Fighters based at Hammer Field that cause the nightly uproar of airplane motors over Fresno and vicinity. Night after night, in moonlight and in darkness, they roar off the runways in P-70s, learning and practicing the intricacies of night-fighting tactics."

My folks would be in Fresno for six months. That must have felt luxurious.

As they'd done several months before, they had made the cross-country trip at a kind of ninety-degree angle, only in reverse: north-ward to Ohio to pick up Pop and Nonna in Xenia (who'd offered to help out again in the last stages of my mom's pregnancy), then straight across the prairies and the plains and the Rockies to the Coast. There were five people in the car—six, counting me. Marty was thirteen months old. They arrived safely and again scrambled for lodging. They found a bungalow with a brick porch on the edge of downtown, at 133 North Broadway. More importantly—I have to think—the rental was within ten or fifteen minutes of both St. Therese Catholic Church and Saint Agnes Hospital, the latter staffed by an order of nuns from France. I got born there at 8:30 a.m. on April 29. Two days later, on Monday, May 1, the 549th NFS also got born, which is to say it got officially activated as a tactical night fighter squadron bound eventually for the combat zones. The squadron was assigned to the Fourth Air Force. Twenty-one days later, on Sunday afternoon the 21st, I got baptized at St. Therese, with Father Delaney pouring the water on my head, and with Jack Kerr promising to look out for my spiritual welfare. My mom put it all down in my baby book, listing the various nightgowns and rattles and utility bags and booties that came as gifts from relatives and also from some of my dad's superiors and squadron mates and their spouses.

Within days, my dad was training in a P-61—and wearing high-intensity, infrared goggles in the cockpit. The Widows had arrived at Hammer. Overseas, in Normandy, the greatest seaborne invasion in history was about to commence.

Pop and Nonna went home on the train. On June 29, my father got promoted to first lieutenant. He was twenty-five. It had taken two years. In late July, the 549th, not yet at full strength, moved down to Bakersfield. The squadron's operations officer divided the "air echelon" into three "Flights" of four crews each. He appointed my dad team leader of Flight C. Several weeks later, something scary happened. While practicing routine gunnery in a P-70 near Muroc Dry Lake in the Mojave Desert, and then preparing to land at Muroc Army Air Field, my dad discovered his plane's hydraulic pressure had suddenly failed. He kept making passes, quick turns, banks. He got the main landing gear down, under the wings, but the nose gear wouldn't shake loose. He was beginning to run out of fuel. He asked his radar man over the radio if he wanted to bail out. "Well, what are you going to do?" Jack Kerr said. "I'm going to ride her in," my father said. "Then I'm sticking, too," Kerr answered. Rather than land at the base, my father told ground control and his superiors he wanted to attempt to get down on the softer surface of the dried lakebed. They said okay. He came in at full throttle, no flaps, tremendous speed, holding the nose slightly upward. The plane hit the earth so hard that, just as he hoped, the force of it knocked open the nose wheel door and the gear flopped out. He jammed down on the stick. The P-70, on its locked three wheels, bumped along for a quarter of a mile before coasting to an easy stop. No injuries or damage, not even a blown tire. In his monthly squadron report, the 549th's historical officer, whose job was to record the daily minutiae and nonminutiae of the unit, wrote, with beautiful understatement: "Lieutenant Joseph P. Hendrickson in P-70B-2 #43-10234, made a successful forced landing at Muroc Lake in California." Could the plane have nosedived on landing and turned into a fireball? *Maybe so, son,* I can hear my father answering.

This happened on August 8, 1944. Five weeks later, early on September 20, my parents told each other goodbye at a sad-sack Amarillo motor lodge. The squadron commander, Major Joe Payne, had given my father and his fellow flyer Lieutenant Charlie Kessler a week's furlough so that they could accompany their scared spouses (and my unaware brother and me) as far eastward as the Texas Panhandle. But you've heard this part.

Here would be the rest of it, in a fell swoop. More or less.

The 549th NFS kept readying itself for war. On September 4 (two weeks after the goodbye), my father had another potentially close call. From the monthly squadron report: "The left filter of P-61A aircraft flown by Lieutenant Joseph Hendrickson caught fire after landing." According to his flight record, he had been aloft for five hours that day and had made two landings. For the rest of September, he flew nearly every day. The following month, on the 4th, the 549th got its orders. The entire unit troop-trained north-ward from the Bakersfield depot to Fort Lawton on Puget Sound in Seattle. On October 12, they boarded a troopship. It was an eight-day sail to Hawaii (with some retching over the sides by air-men who didn't have their sea legs) before Oahu hove into sight. The unit disembarked and got trucked up to Kipapa Airfield not quite in the middle of the island, about seventeen miles north of Honolulu. They slung their gear into wooden lockers in tarpaper shacks with screened doors, six men to a shack, officers on one side, enlisted men on the other.

At the moment, they had two airplanes—and neither was a Widow.

Oahu is forty-four miles long and thirty miles across. In the fall of 1944, it was perhaps the busiest military airspace in the world. Orlando had been hectic, Hammer Field had been hectic, but the volcanic island that the Japanese had surprise-attacked three years before was insanely crowded with aircraft. If you counted the emer-gency landing strips, there were fifteen airfields on Oahu, serving the Navy, the Marines, the Air Corps—and each branch seeking to claim its priority airspace. Kipapa (in Hawaiian it means "pav-ing the way") was up on a plateau. The field had been cut out of sugarcane plantations. It had two crosshatched 5,000-foot runways, each ending in a steep gulch with zero tolerance for a poor land-ing. Hickam and Wheeler and Bellows: These were the far more famous fields on Oahu during World War II, and yet Kipapa Air-field was the place that paved the way for hundreds of units bound for the fighting zones. So many warplanes had come through—the

B-26 Marauder, the B-24 Liberator, the P-40 Warhawk, the B-17 Flying Fortress. But in the fall of 1944, Kipapa belonged largely to the P-61 squadrons. My dad's squadron got assigned to the VII Fighter Command of the Seventh Air Force. Through November and December, the unit's Widows began arriving on transports from the mainland. The big boats brought the planes to Hawaii in a disassembled state. At Hickam, crews of Seabees off-loaded them by crane and began reattaching the wings to the fuselages. Afterward, the waiting pilots climbed in and flew their designated ship up to Kipapa—where some fantastic and ribald and sentimental nose art would soon get painted on.

Except that this scenario didn't quite play out with my father. When his designated Widow came in, he was just getting discharged from the hospital at Schofield Barracks, a name that would be made famous after the war by James Jones in his great novel *From Here to Eternity.* Somebody else had to fly my father's reassembled plane for him up to Kipapa.

What I know, in and amid my longings to know so much else: *The Rita B*—or the Widow that was soon going to get christened *The Rita B,* serial number 42-39516—had come off the lines at Northrop in Hawthorne in late November. On December 6, she was shipped by train up to Oakland. On December 16, she left the mainland with other P-61s on a transport, arriving at Pearl on Christmas Eve—which, I repeat, is the day my father got out of the hospital, after a sixteen-day stay, weighing about 120 pounds. I once had a picture of him within a day or two of his release. He's got a white towel around his neck and he looks very wan. I can't find that photograph. But I have another of him outside his tarpaper barracks. He got discharged from General Hospital at Schofield perhaps the week before. He's regaining his weight.

Perhaps his illness was absolutely no more and no less than what is recorded in his military file, except that there's a part of me that wonders otherwise. Wonders if it was more than a serious hemorrhoid operation (internal and external) with unexpected blood loss. Why does something unproven and unknown lick at my doubts from what is in his official record? Because of something he once said to me, in code, yes, but said all the same. We were up flying. I

don't remember how it arose. But I remember how he said it, and
I wrote it down when we were back down on the ground: "You
know, Paul, I almost missed the damn war, out there in Hawaii,
after all those years getting ready for it. How do you like that?" He
paused: "Getting ready for it was almost worse than the going."
Was he hinting at an attack of nerves? I once asked Marty what he
thought about this. He thought I was flat wrong. But if I'm not,
then it makes me love and miss my father more than I already do.
He was afraid of going, and afraid of not going. He didn't want to
be left behind, and he wished he could get the hell out of there.

He didn't miss the war or get left behind to catch up to his unit
later. He got well. He got his plane. Through January and into
mid-February, he and his fellow flyers in the squadron, along with
their R/O's, ran their routes, did their patrols. (In January he was in
the air for twenty out of the thirty-one days.) And then it was time.
From the monthly squadron report: "Thirty-seven (37) flying offi-

cers, two (2) air corps administrative officers, and forty nine (49) air corps enlisted men, constituting the air echelon, departed for the forward area by air on 15 February 1945." Such dry militarese. There were sixteen Widows in the convoy, plus a B-25 and a Navy twin-engine fighter. (Two more Widows would come behind; the squadron's main body, which is to say all the ground support, would shortly leave Hawaii on the USS *Hyde*.) My father once told me that, on takeoff from Kipapa, he and Jack Kerr had crammed *The Rita B* with as many cases of Hawaiian beer as they could get aboard and still "make weight." Every Widow in the convoy was fairly groaning with beer, he said.

The destination was Saipan, south of Iwo Jima, and they'd get there by flying in a kind of lazy U or lower half of a circle through vast stretches of ocean. The squadron couldn't go due westward (with an overnight and refueling stop at Wake Island) because the Widow didn't have that kind of range. So the plan was to island-hop in a southerly and then westerly direction through the Pacific via some coral-ringed specks that had already entered American mythology because of what had happened there. They flew roughly 1,000 miles a day. The first leg was Palmyra, almost due south of Hawaii. From there it was Canton Island. The next day the convoy cut west for Tarawa in the Gilbert Islands. (They left Canton on the morning of February 17, crossing the International Date Line, thus making the 17th instantly the 18th.) On the 19th, it was up to Eniwetok in the Marshall Islands. And the next morning it was another 1,134 miles to Saipan in the Marianas—where they would end up holding for a full month, doing nightly combat patrol work, while the Battle of Iwo Jima raged. The brilliant military minds had counted on a quick taking of Iwo. I will soon say something about that bitter irony.

I'll end this part of the story with the idea of distance, distance alone. "Make it a story of great distances, and starlight," wrote Robert Penn Warren in his beautiful poem.

From Bakersfield to Oahu is something like 2,535 miles. In their sort of lazy U to Saipan from Oahu, the flyers of the 549th traveled approximately 5,242 miles. If you add the two numbers together, that's nearly 8,000 miles (it's more, really, because they didn't travel straight from Bakersfield to Hawaii, of course, but rather via Seattle). A month onward from Saipan, it would be another 726 miles before getting to South Field at Iwo Jima. One of Charles Lindbergh's biographers wrote that what stirred the world most about his story was the idea of a "single, lonely boy" crossing an ocean alone in the dark in a single-engine monoplane. I've already said my father was never Charles Lindbergh (and thank God for it). Set against Lindbergh's feat, my father's daylight journey with his comrades through the Pacific to get to war in a sleek black two-engine plane with my mother's name glinting behind its bullet-shaped nose wouldn't even compare. But who cares about comparing? The boy from Morganfield was still going so far out. And he was still so young. And all he wanted to do, I know in my heart, was go there, get there, to Iwo, not be an American hero, just follow orders and do what he was supposed to do, and then navigate himself safely back home to his family.

Really, I didn't do all that much in the war, Paul.

But you were there, Dad.

Yes, I suppose that's so.

PART TWO

THERE

"A few years ago at a dinner party I was asked by a woman what on earth I had ever seen in military life. I couldn't answer her, of course. I couldn't summon it all, the distant places, the comradeship, the idealism, the youth. I couldn't tell about flying over the islands long ago, seeing them rise in the blue distance wreathed in legend, the ring of white surf around them. . . . I couldn't tell about Mahurin being shot down and not a soul seeing him go, or George Davis, or DeArmond who used to jump up on a table in the club and recite 'Gunga Din'—the drunken pilots thought he was making it up. I couldn't tell her about brilliant group commanders or flying with men who later died . . . the days and days of boredom and moments of pure ecstasy, of walking out to the big, sleek machines in the early morning or coming in at dusk when the wind had died to make the last landing of the day and the mobile-control officer giving two quick clicks of the mike to confirm: grease job. To fly with the thirty-year-old veterans and finally earn the right to lead yourself, flights, squadrons, and a few times the entire group. The great days of youth when you are mispronouncing foreign words and believing dreams."

—JAMES SALTER, "The Captain's Wife," *Esquire* magazine, June 1986

"Was it possible that they were there and not haunted? No, not possible, not a chance."

—MICHAEL HERR, *Dispatches*

MY MOTHER, the great archivist in our family—until she wasn't—once told me she wrote to my father nearly every day that he was overseas, and that he wrote to her, if not daily, then at least a couple of times a week. I've never been able to locate even one of those letters. Were they destroyed in later decades when things were going very bad in our family? It's possible, but something in me doubts it. Maybe the explanation is simpler—and far more banal.

Maybe, on my dad's side, he read my mom's letters on his cot in his officer's tent on Iwo and let go of them as they came in (did they arrive in small batches?) or maybe saved handfuls here and there but, in any case, either forgot to pack them up (or didn't bother to) when it was time to come home. My father was never much of a preservationist, much less a sentimentalist, but he did, throughout his life, keep things that meant something to him—spottily.

For his part, I picture my dad writing to my mom at wobbly tables under bare bulbs in the Ready Room on the flight line before a mission. He told me once he played a lot of poker with fellow officers in that large tented space, before briefings from the intelligence officer. He said he won a handy pile of cash from those hot games of draw and stud. Like letters home, poker would have helped eat some of the tension. There's a poet I love, Richard Hugo. He was a bombardier on a B-24 in Italy. He writes of choking down the powdered eggs at midnight and "always the phlegm before the engines warmed."

On my mom's side, it's impossible for me to believe that she wouldn't have kept every one of my dad's letters, which she told me were almost always love letters. I picture her placing them in a box in Pop and Nonna's home on Mechanic Street in Xenia. After she's put Marty and me to bed, she rereads the latest one. Then she puts the lid on the box and turns out the light.

But where is that box? What happened to that box?

I own a few letters from my father, maybe not even two dozen. I keep them in a red folder not far from my writing desk. You wouldn't call them love letters. You would hardly call them letters. Somehow, by the time he got to middle and late age, the great talkative Morganfield boy, so gifted with language, had leached out of his anemic letter-writing habit almost anything resembling vulnerability and affection. He had all that in him, along with everything else that was opposite and scary and eruptive in him, but he almost never showed the vulnerability and affection in his letters, at least in his letters to his second-born. They read more like Western Unions. It's as if a man behind a counter were waiting to charge him not by the word but by the number of characters in the word. And my dad, formed by the Depression, was nothing if not a lifelong frugal man.

Here is a not-untypical letter from my father to me in his late years. It's dated "4/5/00." He wrote it on a half sheet of white paper, which he folded in the middle, using only the top quarter. The heck with Dear, *heck with commas. He wrote it in his odd combination of printing and Palmer Method and quirky capitalization, the lettering slanting rigidly rightward. This was three years and a month before he died. He wanted me to know his latest whereabouts.*

Paul
*   I'll be leaving tomorrow driving to Chi & Flying back to Fl on Fri.—Ret. To woods the Following wk*
*   Hope this finds everyone well & happy—*

Love
Dad

My mom told me that my father, every now and then, in his three- and four-page love letters to her, would include separate pieces of paper with notes addressed to Marty and me. She told me that on my first birthday— April 29, 1945—he wrote me a letter (probably it was about two or three lines) safety-pinned to a big, brown teddy bear. I keep wondering how a night fighter pilot on Iwo Jima got hold of a teddy bear. A few months before, from Hawaii, for Christmas, when I was about to turn eight months old, he had sent me a black teddy bear, along with a tiny blue rocking chair. My mom documented the fact in one of my two baby books.

Even if it's sentimental, I wish to believe that my parents' letters from the war, which must have numbered in the low hundreds all told, just fell through the cracks of time and circumstance and various relocations. In the first half dozen years after the war, we moved five times. Our young family packed up and went from Ohio to Florida to three rented houses in the greater downstate Chicago area as my father pursued his copiloting career at Eastern.

In any case, they're gone.

In 2006, Clint Eastwood—an iconic director and movie star and also a puzzling man who for a long time now has seemed on a campaign to revise himself in terms of the great American male hero myth—released a black-and-white small masterpiece of a film with an all-Japanese cast entitled Letters from Iwo Jima. *It wasn't hard for me to want to go see it, not with a title like that, even before I knew the two most important things about the movie: namely, that it was telling the story from the so-called faceless other side, and that the central figure and main letter writer of the story—which is a fictional treatment but rooted deeply in historical and biographical fact—was the commander-in-chief of the doomed Japanese forces. Among other gifts, this man possessed an uncanny knack for projecting himself into the mind of a child. He even illustrated his letters with deft, playful strokes in soft pencil that any child—or grown-up—would adore. In another life, Lieutenant General Tadamichi Kuribayashi might have been an illustrator for a big Tokyo daily. Or half a dozen other things, for that matter.*

Clear Pictures

Midmorning, March 26, 1945. A scene in the near-vicinity of my father's eight-man officer's tent, six days after landing on Iwo Jima.

UNTIL I STARTED READING for the first time in a serious way about the Battle of Iwo Jima, I had no clear sense of what the dying on the ground was like in the place where my father risked his life at night in the air in the last five and a half months of World War II. After, I had a further understanding of why he seemed disinclined to talk much about the war, to shrug off whatever things he had done in it. He knew what had gone on at Iwo in the days and weeks before he and his squadron landed there. It was as if, by comparison, his own risks were nothing, when, in fact, they were a very great thing, not least to his family.

About the dying on the ground: Listen to former Marine William Manchester in his magisterial Pacific war memoir, *Goodbye, Darkness:* "The deaths on Iwo were extraordinarily violent. There seemed to be no clean wounds; just fragments of corpses. . . . Often the only way to distinguish between Japanese and Marine dead was by the legs; Marines wore canvas leggings and Nips khaki puttees. . . . You tripped over strings of viscera fifteen feet long, over bodies which had been cut in half at the waist. Legs and arms, and heads bearing only necks, lay fifteen feet from the closest torsos. As night fell the beachhead reeked with the stench of burning flesh."

The island itself reeked, like rotten eggs, even before there was any burning flesh. The word "Iwo" is Japanese for sulfur.

Almost a third of all the United States Marines who died in World War II died on the speck of earth known as Iwo Jima. Hell in a very small place, as a famous Indochina war correspondent, Bernard Fall, said much later about Vietnam. There were almost three times as many combat deaths on the Japanese side, and yet Iwo Jima was the only battle in the Pacific war where the Americans suffered more casualties than their enemy. Twenty-seven Americans won the Medal of Honor for bravery on Iwo—more than in any other battle in U.S. history.

The place is barely eight square miles of landmass—about four miles in length at its longest point, about two and a half miles at its widest. "An ugly, smelly glob of cold lava squatting in a surly ocean"—this again is Manchester. By dusk of the first day, February 19, 1945, 2,400 of the roughly 30,000 ground forces, Navy and Marine and Coast Guard, who'd participated in the landings and beachhead, were either wounded or gone. Before it was over, there were 27,000 American casualties. An armada of 435 ships had brought three Marine divisions to this dot in the far Pacific that's 760 miles almost due south of Tokyo. If you were watching from six miles up, what would 435 American warships, converging on something so tiny, look like? Maybe like Gulliver and his Lilliputians, only in reverse? We were the swarming Gullivers, Iwo the Lilliputian.

Not to even speak of the U.S. airpower and tonnage of bombs trying to pulverize the place beyond the sulfurous dust and twisted rock it already was. That's not entirely accurate. Iwo once had small sugarcane and vegetable farms hard wrung from the seemingly untillable soil. There were once five villages on the island. There was a Buddhist temple. There were sulfur mills. Japanese families lived in small frame houses covered with paper and woven leaves. They'd produced turnips, carrots, tomatoes, mangoes, bananas, coconuts. They'd had goats and pigs and milk cows.

February 19, D-Day on Iwo, was the day when my dad and his fellow flyers of the 549th were on the last island-hopping leg of their five-day journey to Saipan from Hawaii.

In his fifteen-volume account of naval operations in the war, in a section titled "D-day at Iwo Jima," the great sea historian Samuel Eliot Morison wrote: "The operation looked like a pushover. Optimists predicted that the island would be secured in four days." Some thought it would be a matter of hours.

The Japanese defenders, wildly outnumbered, ended up holding out not for forty-eight or seventy-two hours, but for five weeks, thirty-six days, to be exact, and not the least of the reasons why was because they were burrowed into bunkers, caves, and tunnels. They let the enemy come to them. There may have been as many as 5,000 caves, and as many as 13,000 miles of underground tunnels. Some of the concrete bunkers went twenty-two yards deep. "The Japs weren't on Iwo Jima," one Marine officer said. "They were in Iwo Jima." Little wonder that the American forces regarded their enemy as rats who needed to be flamethrowered from their holes. "Rodent Exterminator" was stenciled on uncounted numbers of American helmets.

At the southwest tip of the island lay 554-foot-high Mount Suribachi. In Japanese, the word means "cone-shaped bowl." Under Suribachi lay a galley that may have gone as deep as four floors. There was a hospital down there. Suribachi alone was said to be fortified with something like 1,000 installations, including 642 pillboxes, blockhouses, and other gunnery positions.

As was said earlier, it was not quite in the literal shadow of this cratered mountain that my dad and the 549th NFS landed on what the Americans called South Field. That was on March 20. By then it was thought the fighting on the ground was largely over, that there would be no more tripping over fifteen-foot-long strings of viscera. That turned out to be wrong, and for evidence I'll refer you to the photograph at the top of this chapter. In a way, that picture drives everything I'll have to say here.

There was also a Central Field on Iwo, smaller than South Field. And farther up, an uncompleted third airfield. The black-sand landing beaches on Iwo, beneath and along Suribachi's eastern side, weren't so much beaches as "volcanic pumice" (once again, Manchester). They consisted of something like flour mixed in with fine-grained cinder. These beaches rose in a series of terraces and ledges. On D-Day, the Marines came ashore in waves in their landing craft (LSTs) only to sink up to their ankles with every seeming crawl and step. They tried to dig foxholes only to have the sides cave in. The going forward was literally by inches. The Japanese let them come, in eerie quiet. And then, from their hidden fortifications, they let loose.

On February 23, 1945, four days from D-Day, while my dad was engaged in patrols on Saipan, waiting for Iwo to be secured, Joe Rosenthal of the Associated Press captured what is arguably the most famous photograph of the entire war: the Americans raising the flag on Suribachi's conquered summit. But the rest of the island was far from conquered.

Iwo Jima is one of the Japanese Volcano Islands, a part of what is known as the Ogasawara Archipelago. It wasn't one of the islands strewn through the Pacific that the Japanese had overcome at the outset of the war and then tried to hold on to; no, Iwo was Japanese soil. It had a Tokyo mailing address. It was part of the homeland's inner ring. If the Stars and Stripes got planted there, the message metaphorically to the world was that Japan's ultimate defeat was no longer in question. Really, by February 1945, it hadn't been in question for some while.

But why, militarily and strategically, was the taking of this foul spit in the surly sea so important in the first place? The received answer in the history books has to do with geography—and the B-29 Superfortress. Saipan, which is about six times larger than Iwo, where my dad and his fellow flyers held while the taking was going badly, had been won back by our side in the previous summer—on July 9, 1944. Saipan is in the Mariana chain, about 1,460 miles south of Tokyo. Little Iwo sits directly in the middle of the two. Since the fall of 1944, waves of "Superforts," based on Saipan, had been making bombing runs on the Japanese home islands. They had the range to do it, to fly 2,900 miles round-trip, but they were also highly vulnerable. Japanese Zeros, based on Iwo, could go after the huge bombers, with their crews of eleven, on their way up from the Marianas, or on their way back down, when some of them were limping home, wounded by flak. There was also the warning problem: Iwo's radar equipment could give Tokyo at least two hours' notice that the latest wave of B-29s were on their way. Thus, Iwo had to be taken. And after it was taken, Iwo's airfields could provide an emergency landing site for the crippled bombers. All of that was true, although it remains a matter of great debate, even now, whether the human taking cost was even remotely worth the strategic gain.

About those miles of gaseous and suffocating caves and bunkers and underground tunnels: They existed in the first place because of the will of one man, a lieutenant general, who had to go against the strategic wishes of all of his superiors on the mainland. He was the commander-in-chief of the approximately 20,000 Japanese forces dug into Iwo (against a full American force of something like 110,000). In a sense, he was ever the samurai who wasn't, the soldier who loved Shakespeare and who once had many friends in America and who was capable of writing such tender, witty, fatherly, spousal, and altogether *human* letters to his family on the mainland. Tadamichi Kuribayashi is the core reason why it took the Americans five weeks to win. He was aware that he and his forces couldn't last (nearly all died, save for the few hundred taken prisoner), but his aim was to try to inflict so many casualties that the Americans might postpone or maybe even think again about a ground invasion of the home islands. The emperor's reluctant warrior, as *The Japan Times* described him in a beautiful 2006 retrospective piece, had pledged himself to fight to the end, even though he longed for another destiny. "I was at the point in my life when I was ready to make my family happy, as a husband and father, when this enormous war erupted and I was assigned to protect this strategic island," Kuribayashi wrote to his family in June 1944, right after he had taken up command on Iwo. "So be it—this is my duty."

I can't prove it for a fact, but I'm almost positive that this immensely contradictory military man—whose tensions of character so appealed to Clint Eastwood not quite two decades ago when he set out to make a movie about the faceless other side—had once traveled on some of the same roads, exact roads, that my own prewar parents traveled when they crisscrossed America, not knowing where the future was going to take them.

Let's pick him up here for a moment, the fanatic who wasn't, thirteen years before Pearl Harbor, this small, cultured figure from the Far East with the brush mustache and erect bearing and beautiful manners and dress, not to say his quite passable English. It's a late-summer day in America in 1928. Thirty-seven-year-old Tadamichi Kuribayashi, graduate of his country's best war colleges and army universities, is reclining with a book under a tree in the Harvard Yard. He's reclining, but he has on a dress shirt and tie. And his hair is combed. With part in place.

He's reading a book and he's also writing a letter to his family, specifically to his first child, whom he misses terribly. He writes the characters in his delicate hand, but, as is his way, he also draws himself onto the page, in his tie and groomed hair, cooling himself with a foldout paper-and-wood Japanese fan. His suit jacket is off, and his sleeves are rolled, and his legs are crossed in an almost fey manner. His book and letter-writing materials are at his right elbow.

"Oh, it is very hot," he writes. "I went to the grounds of Harvard University to lie down."

He works a squirrel into his illustration. "A squirrel visits," he writes beneath the image. The squirrel seems to be paying him no mind and is busy with a nut. He must figure Taro will laugh at this. Taro is his baby boy, three and a half, back home with his mom. Her name is Yoshii, and she's expecting again in three months, a fact that makes husband and father sad and joyful both. He won't be there for the birth. (They'll name their baby girl Yoko.)

The cavalry captain has been in America since April. He's a military attaché assigned to the Japanese embassy in Washington. But his superiors wish him to travel through the country, to get a sense of her vastness, not to say industrial might, not to say military capabilities. This pleases him greatly. Really, it's a lifelong dream, to be able to tour America and see her wonders.

Four months ago, nearly the first thing he did on arriving in San Francisco on a steamship from Yokohama, via Hawaii, was to visit Yosemite National Park. Ever since he was a kid he'd heard about Half Dome and those giant Sequoias. Then he went down to Los Angeles. Then he came across the country by Greyhound, stopping over in Chicago to look at that magnificent sky-blue great lake on which the city sits. Always, the jottings and drawings in his journal.

In these next three years, by train, bus, and automobile, the intensely curious traveler from the East, with his poetic turn of mind, will be in Buffalo; Kansas City; Fort Riley, Kansas; Fort Bliss, Texas—and he will pass through uncounted other towns and cities in between. (He'll also get to Mexico and Canada.) He'll become deeply aware that America is the last nation on earth Japan should ever engage in combat. In some places, there will be extended stays, and he'll form beautiful friendships. Fort Bliss (it's outside El Paso), in early 1929, is where he'll buy himself an American car, the better to enable his travels. It's a new Chevy. Naturally, he has to tell his son all about it. "Dear Taro," he writes. "I've just bought this fabulous car. . . . If you were here I'd drive you around all you want. How about it? Fancy a ride?"

Because his art is so good, he could have easily drawn the Chevy into the letter. This time, though, he has scissored an illustration of the car from an advertisement in a glossy magazine and glued it onto the sheet. He draws himself in his full Imperial Japanese Army dress uniform standing next to the auto, one hand touching the hood, as if mystified by its power.

From Buffalo, where his landlady is perhaps a little more solicitous than he would prefer (although he would be horrified to let on): "Here I am taking a walk. Should I step it up? And sing a song? The leaves have started to fall."

From Kansas: "It makes no sense to me. Why do men have to stop eating and stand every time a woman comes in?" (He draws several wives of American officers seated at a dinner table. Above them, like a cartoon bubble, this caption: "Blah, blah, blah, blah.")

On the eve of a major trip, studying his maps: "Mmmmm. There are exactly 1,246 miles. This is going to be a big undertaking. And there are a lot of uninhabited deserts along the way."

Although childlike whimsy is nearly always in them, the attaché's prolific dispatches home often have their serious notes. "Be kind to others, it is the most important thing in life," he says in one letter. "Taro, be sure to eat well and play nicely with your friends," he says in another. "Keep your tummy warm while you sleep so you won't get sick. Wrap a flannel cloth around your stomach when you go to bed," he urges in still another.

That one's on July 20, 1929, from Texas. Almost sixteen years hence, in early February 1945, from his concrete bunker on a piece of odiferous rock that the barbaric Americans are trying to blast back into the Stone Age before commencing their all-out ground invasion, a commanding general, facing his destiny, will write a similar plea to his wife of twenty-one years: "Take a hot water bottle and keep your waist and stomach warm." Yoshii and the three children, the older two of whom are not quite adults, are hiding in a Tokyo air-raid shelter, terrified of "Mr. B."

That would be one of the fiendish B-29s.

I wonder what my father thought, in the forenoon of March 20, 1945, when he circled the island for his first approach and saw the wrecked ships and other broken landing craft listing in the surf, littering the black sand to his immediate left and right. The bodies, and pieces of bodies, would have long been cleared away. Mostly.

Four days before, the American military powers that be had declared the island secure. Would that it had been true.

The sixteen Widows in the convoy landed, each in turn, perhaps having circled the island three or four times. The ground support troops of the squadron, who had come ashore from their combat transport six days before, on March 14, had already begun setting up the 549th's new home. The bivouac wasn't located at South Field, but a bit farther up, maybe a mile and a half away. The squadron's assigned area was on the west side of the island, close to what the Americans called Central Field and which the Japanese had named Motoyama #2 Airfield. The large olive-colored tents just going up were known as squad tents. They almost looked like circus tents, in the way that they were tent-poled in their middle and staked into the sand and secured with heavy ropes. The compound was practically at the water's edge. Quoting from the March 1945 squadron report: "This area was located on the west beach in black sand a few hundred feet from the shore." Squeezed in and around the same general area were the bivouacs of other military units. The large 21st Fighter Group—these were primarily P-51 Mustang fighter pilots and their ground crews—was located just above the 549th, on a plateau, a bit more exposed. Next to the 21st FG was a Signal Corps unit. Just south of the tents of the 549th was the camp of a large Navy Seabees unit. (The nickname Seabee comes from the letters "CB," which stands for Construction Battalion.) Not too far away was an antiaircraft battalion. Each of these units, and there were more than I have named, was now in the process of establishing its own little village.

The 549th arranged itself in three rows of tents. On one side were the quarters for the enlisted men. These twenty-two large tents were split into two rows of eleven tents each. On the other side, across a space of perhaps thirty yards, if that, were six tents for the officer corps, lined in a single row, with approximately eight men to a tent. Each officer had been assigned a cot, kerosene lantern, canvas stool, makeshift nightstand, small wooden locker, a Bunsen burner for making late-night cups of coffee without needing to go to the Mess.

The common area was located between the tent rows. From the squadron report: "A large tent was hoisted for the mess hall and table tops were set on barrels which afforded standing places for eating." A headquarters tent—where the commanding officer and his two lieutenants worked and slept—had been set up at the top of the common area, and also a tent for the chief medical officer (he was a surgeon) and his team. Down at the bottom of the common space was the motor pool, and a little bit north of that, the toilets—for the entire squadron. Again from the monthly report: "Since no latrine facilities were available, a temporary straddle trench was constructed. . . . Wash and shower water was obtained from salt water and sulfur wells." Showers were permitted between 4 p.m. and 5:30 p.m. each day. The showers were rigged up in the common space on platforms with overhead drop tanks holding the smelly and sticky water.

Do I seem too focused on the physical layout of the camp? In some real and not figurative sense, that physical layout was about to save my father's life, in what I can only think of as the awful randomness of chance.

Two nights after his arrival, my dad flew his first mission—actually two. This was in the overnight of March 21–22. The flight line where the Widows of the 549th were parked was down at South Field. He and his crew would have gone to the flight line in a jeep parked in the motor pool. Perhaps they stepped out of their tents in their flight gear about nine or ten on the 21st—they were now anxious men at work. It took about ten minutes to get to the flight line. My dad and Jack Kerr would have gone into the briefing tent, close to the edge of the runway.

And then *The Rita B* went up. I don't know the time.

It was patrol work, officially known as CAP, for "combat air patrol," circling the island, going northward for forty or fifty miles, doing the same in the other direction, on the lookout for enemy invaders, loaded to the oarlocks with armor. The first "hop" (I can dimly hear him using this word once or twice when I grew up) lasted an hour and thirty minutes. *The Rita B* touched down and the two officers went into the briefing tent again. Maybe they were down for about two hours. Maybe there were snatches of sleep, or poker, or the start of letters home. They climbed back in and went up for another two hours and twenty minutes. I know the lengths of the two missions because they're written in my dad's official flight record of the night. My guess is that nothing terrifying happened to my dad and his crew on that first night.

The terrifying, what I'll call the *first terrifying,* and which was something I believe stayed with my father for the rest of his life, happened four nights later, on March 26, a few hours before dawn. It didn't happen in the air. It happened, or began happening, about 4 a.m. in the living quarters of the 549th. My father and his fellow officers were asleep in their tents, on the right side of the camp (if you were looking to the north), as the others of the squadron were in their own tents, sleeping or trying to. (A contingent of the unit, assigned to fly missions that night, along with their ground support, would have been down at South Field, either in the air or resting between hops.)

The tents on either side of the bivouac—the two rows on the enlisted side, the single row on the officer side—had been laced shut at their front; it was a regulation. The moon had set early. Suddenly, the camp was brought jolt awake. People were screaming, and the screams were not in English, or at least not initially. The canvas entry flaps were being slashed open with knives and swords. Grenades were being rolled in from the front and also the back. People were dying or getting grievously wounded. Some were being shot at point-blank range.

An enemy force, out from the caves and bunkers, was making its last-ditch suicide stand. The stand was happening not quite simultaneously in the half dozen other compounds located on the western beach, near Central Field. My dad's squadron was in the middle of it all.

This night has been described in many books and articles. One of the better accounts is entitled "Final Spasm on Sulfur Island," published in March 2006 in *World War II* magazine by Ivan E. Prall, who lived through that night. (He was not in the 549th.) One of the things Prall came to believe is that there may have been far more than 300 attackers, which is the number historians have generally cited through the years. There may have been as many as 600 Japanese troops. How many came running through the 549th is impossible to know.

I used the word "suicide." It was that, yes. But this was not a *sake*-fueled *banzai* charge, as has been commonly repeated through the decades. This was a *kirikomi* attack. If the one is wild and des-

perate and dervish-seeming, the other, from the start, is something
that has been strategically thought out. The root meaning of the
word *"kirikomi"* has to do with cutting, severing.

The commander-in-chief of the Japanese forces on Iwo despised
the concept of *banzai*.

He had fairly despised it for his entire military life. Such a waste
of humanity. It was just one of many things that separated him
from the warrior tradition he had grown up in—at a career cost.

The central objective of the *kirikomi* was to slip into the various
compounds and "sever" as many flyers as possible. They were the
biggest threat to the homeland.

Nine nights before the attack that cut (literally) right through
my father's squadron, fifty-three-year-old Tadimichi Kuribayashi,
from deep inside his bunker at the north end of the island, had sent
a farewell telegram to the Imperial General Headquarters in Tokyo.
He radioed it at midnight on March 17 (so he must have begun
composing it in the late hours of the 16th). It was an eloquent message of almost a thousand words. "The battle is entering its final
chapter," the general wrote. "I must disappoint your expectations
and yield this important place to the hands of the enemy. With
humility and sincerity, I offer my repeated apologies," he said. He
signed his name and then offered a three-stanza death poem he
had composed, the ending of which was: "When ugly weeds run
riot over this island / My only thought will be the Imperial Land."

At midnight on March 17, my father was still three days and
some hours from landing with his convoy at South Field. Five
hours after the general's first telegram (at 0500, or zero five hundred, in military-speak), he wrote again to his superiors on the
mainland—or at least he addressed the cable to the General Headquarters. In this one, he kept his words to a minimum. He was
really issuing an order to all the remaining and half-starved forces
left under his command. He repeated that the final stage had been
reached. After dark that night—the 17th—the entire corps would
attack the enemy and give up their lives for their country.

The last of his four points: "I will at all times be at your head."

But the *kirikomi* didn't take place on the night of March 17. Nine
more days and nights went by. By which time, my father, know-

ing none of this, had set down *The Rita B* on South Field and had already flown a handful of missions.

The onslaught of March 26 lasted for approximately four hours—from roughly 4 a.m. until eight o'clock. An hour later, there was something like the start of calm on the western beach. Early on, the Marines had come rushing in with their flamethrowers—they, not the airmen, did the bulk of the fighting. I have read many oral history accounts of that night, and I have studied a lot of the photographs. Here is a softer remembrance from an officer in the 72nd Squadron:

> The carnage was terrible. In the hole behind our tent we counted thirty-three dead Japanese. Most of the American casualties had been removed or covered with blankets. I remember seeing a shivering cocker spaniel lying on the end of a stretcher which had a blanket-covered body on it. I knew the dog's owner, and lifting a corner of the blanket, I sadly confirmed that Major Whitely was indeed there, shot through the neck.

And this, typed in its officialese by the historical officer in my dad's squadron and filed a few days later in the 549th's monthly report: "One (1) Officer reported seeing two (2) and one half (2½) ton truck loads of dead Japanese being hauled away from the vicinity."

Take a look again at the image at the top of this chapter. There seem to have been four or five such pits in the common area of the 549th. Again, I've studied the photographs. Unless my father tied a bandanna around his eyes, it would have been impossible for him not to have seen, and possibly looked into, one or more of those ditches that morning. I am not saying he saw this exact one. I don't know that. What I do know is that until I started this book, I knew nothing of such scenes or photographs. My father never spoke of them.

Among the mysteries: Somehow, when the Japanese came through the 549th, they ended up—in the main—concentrating their fury on the left side of the compound. To repeat: There isn't doubt they were out primarily to get the flyers. I know this to be true from the historical accounts I have read and from the experts whom I have consulted and indeed even from studying some declassified command papers that were found on the bodies of Japanese officers who had participated in the attack. Logic might have said that the pilots and the radar officers of the 549th, who were far fewer in number than the ground support troops, would have been asleep in the smaller line of tents. But somehow fate saw to it that the attackers ended up screaming and running through the middle of my father's camp and then making a pivot to the side where the two tight rows of twenty-two enlisted tents were pitched.

The way I have come to view this story is that the literal and spiritual distance between the possibility of my father getting killed but instead being allowed to live, six nights after he had come to Iwo Jima, was about thirty yards. The awful randomness of chance.

Something else I can't quite explain: I *knew* about this night, at least in its broadest outline, more than forty years ago, but somehow its full emotional force went right past me until just lately, when I began studying March 26, 1945, in close-up ways—and consulting some old handwritten notes. Not to say looking at some awful photographs.

The background: Earlier, I told in brief of accompanying my father to a night fighter reunion in Orlando. It was over the Labor Day weekend in 1982. My dad, who was recently retired from Eastern Air Lines, didn't want to go, but I talked him into it. I understand more clearly now that he was doing me a substantial favor. My parents were not in a good place, to say it wanly. My mom's drinking had lately come back, and not in a small way. My dad flew to Florida from Chicago and I came down from Washington, D.C. We met at the airport on a Friday afternoon and took a cab to the hotel where the reunion was being held. Many old night fighters from various squadrons had come, both enlisted men and officers, but the 549th was well represented—maybe two dozen men, along with some spouses. I couldn't take notes fast enough. There was so much disguised and undisguised emotion in the room, and often enough the "room" was the lobby bar, where big ghostly images of Black Widows played silently in a loop on a portable movie screen.

My father knew what I was doing: mining a story. I didn't know the when or the where of this story, only that I had to try to get everything down. "This is my son. He's a writer. He works for *The Washington Post*. Never tell a damn thing to a writer," he said, in the Morganfield cackle, introducing me to guys called Pinky and Lit and Geronimo. He introduced me to a man named George Hayden. He was from Paducah, Kentucky, seventy miles southwest of Union County, at the confluence of the Ohio and the Tennessee Rivers. He and my dad hadn't seen each other since the war. "Good ol' Ken-tuck, me and your dad, how could we dare get hurt over there with them Japs?" he said, bear-hugging me. I didn't buy a drink all weekend. No one would let me.

I'm looking at some of those old notes now. The night of March 26 comes up in several places, and not obliquely. My dad said he could hear the strange yelling outside his tent. He had been sound asleep. He said that his own tent did, in fact, get slashed down the middle, and that bullets did come whistling through, but that no grenade rolled in. He said he jumped up from his cot and reached for his .45 shoulder-strap Luger, which was the only firearm he had. He threw himself on the canvas flooring. The other seven men in the tent were doing much the same. He pointed the gun toward the opening, holding it straight out with both hands, thinking that, at any second, he'd see a maniacal face a few feet from his own face. It didn't happen.

"What did I know about hand-to-hand, Paul? We weren't trained for that." He said there was an officer in the tent, junior to him, who started firing through the ripped opening. My dad said he kept jerking his arm down. "Jesus, are you trying to draw their fire?"

After what seemed like hours, he crept over and peered out through the opening. Four figures in early light were running in circles trying to set fire to fuel drums. They were about ten feet away. He heard a Marine yell: "The saber's mine!" What the American meant was that he personally intended to kill an enemy who must have been an officer, because he was wielding an ornate sword. The Marine wanted the saber as a souvenir.

My dad said other things about the attack, which he kept calling "the raid," and I have them in my notes, but I am drawn to something else entirely from those notes. I think I wrote it on the plane home, after we'd been at the reunion for the better part of three days.

He was so tired after the banquet Sat. night—packed it in together by 9:30, only I had to go pick up a rental car & when came back at 10:30, he was half in, half out of sleep, in his Budweiser nightshirt, hiked up, with big moon of cheek exposed. Mumbled to me. Seemed old, fragile. Almost dead or dying, comatose. I wanted to pick him up & was repelled too. The night before, we lay in dark at 1 o'clock & he was really depressed. "Well, it's over for your mother & me. After 40 years it's over. I'm a problem-solver, and I can't solve this one." He turned over. "If you have kids, if you have family, you're going to have heartache." He said it to the wall, going off. Fifteen minutes later, I heard him say: "Home and family." He was dreaming.

From another page of the notes: *I kept having this fantasy he was going to die in the banquet hall—have an MI & I would be weeping in his mouth, trying to remember CPR. I kept trying to remember the CPR steps. "If it gets too hot, you can go right out that door, Paul."*

Is this why my mind refused to let the emotional weight of March 26, 1945, hit me full force forty-odd years ago, because visions and fantasies and terrors right in front of me were crowding them out? Was I, too, haunted by an old and dying man (in reality, my dad was only sixty-three and still vigorous as hell and had another two decades yet to live), turned to the wall, in the bed opposite, in his Budweiser-themed nightshirt that had gotten twisted and rucked up over his smooth and pearly rear end, mumbling things to me and to himself in his half sleep?

It's all I can think. And, really, I don't wish to examine it more.

Home and family. Forty-one of Tadimichi Kuribayashi's letters from Iwo Jima survive. They run from late June 1944 to early February 1945. In 2005, when excerpts of the letters appeared in Japan in a Kuribayashi quasi-biography, they were a literary sensation. The book became an overnight bestseller and won prizes. A first-time author named Kumiko Kakehashi told the general's story, bleeding the letters movingly through. She located two of his children, found people who had known him. In America, the book appeared under the title *So Sad to Fall in Battle*. As the author noted, it was as if a lifelong military man, writing from his foreordained doom, wished to speak of the homely things of home. Of the minutiae, the loving mundane. Well, not entirely.

A note to his baby girl, third child of the family, who is almost ten, whose name is Takako, but whom he calls "Tako-chan": "In my mind's eye, I can still see you and Mother standing by the gate to see me off on the day I left." He signed it, "Daddy at the front." This was June 25, 1944—in his first dispatch. He had written a much longer one to the whole family that day. He didn't hold back. "I fear that my chances for survival are less than one percent."

Two months after his arrival on the island, August 25, 1944: "I have made up my mind to think of my life as something I have today, but will not have tomorrow." That sounds like Robert Jordan, the hero of Hemingway's *For Whom the Bell Tolls*.

December 8, 1944, to Yoshii, who is thirteen years younger and whom he married when she was nineteen: "You'll get cold sometimes when you're in the air-raid shelter, so you need to prepare a small foot warmer or a hot water bottle. You'll need a blanket, too. And make sure you've got straw matting."

October 4, 1944, again to his wife: "Perhaps I'm just worrying too much, but recently I had a dream in which you looked terribly gaunt and your eyes were shining feverishly. Are you getting the massage lady to come? Make sure to take a bath about twice a week to improve your circulation and avoid hardening of the arteries."

November 17, 1944: "Tako-chan, do you have any cavities? You musn't forget to brush regularly."

December 15, 1944, to his spouse: "Now, let's talk about clothes. In my previous letter, I recommended tie-up straw sandals, but what do you think about my old lace-up boots?"

January 18, 1945, to Tako-chan: "Your mother wrote the other day, informing me that you had made straight A's in school. It has made me very happy."

October 10, 1944, to his boy, Taro, who is almost twenty and the man of the house: "When you're at home, always make pleasant conversation with your mother and your younger sisters; make the odd joke from time to time. It's important to make the whole house cheerful." (A month later, the day after his son's birthday, he'll send a letter home with drawings and diagrams on how to fix a draft in the kitchen.)

January 21, 1945, to Yoshii: "If I have a soul, it will stay near you and the children."

December 23, 1944: "Tako-chan, a little while ago Daddy had another dream with you in it."

And from the final surviving letter, February 3, 1945, addressed to all four, Yoshii, Taro, Yoko, and Tako-chan: "Please take good care of yourselves. Don't catch cold and try to stay well. . . . Don't let Taro oversleep in the mornings or steal a nap in the kotatsu [hot table or other such heartwarming object or space]. . . . I must stop now as the plane is leaving. Goodbye."

I couldn't read that without thinking of my own parents, not even five months before, early on September 20, 1944, in an Amarillo motor court yard. Kissing goodbye. And doubtless crying.

Sixteen days from that last letter, the first waves of Americans waded into the black sand.

Six enlisted men in my father's squadron died before and after dawn on March 26, 1945. Quoting again from the formal but not quite emotionless monthly squadron report:

> On the morning of 26 March 1945, the infiltration of Japanese caused six (6) men to be killed in action and nine (9) men to be evacuated. Four (4) of these evacuated were severely wounded. During the attack, the Medical men of this Squadron handled themselves with a valor that merits great esteem and commendation from all. Captain Gehl was summoned from his tent, on the opposite side of the area where the injuries occurred, and was seen crawling on his stomach to aid the wounded and dying.

Corporal Donald S. Freyer died. He was twenty-two, barely. Before the war he had worked at Pacific Fruit & Produce at King and Occidental Streets in Seattle. On his enlistment card someone had written: "Semi-skilled occupations in production of bakery products." He had a twin brother, Lyle, who was in another branch of service and at that moment was recuperating from wounds at a military hospital in the Philippines. (He was going to live a fairly long life.) They had both graduated from the same high school in 1942, and afterward one twin had stood up for the other at his wedding.

Corporal Max D. Rowe died. He was twenty-one. Carved into his tombstone in Pioneer Cemetery in Rigby, Idaho, is a Black Widow with this inscription: "Killed in action by Attacking Japanese at Iwo Jima Island."

Sergeant Donald J. Cramer, of Malta, New York, died. He was a radar technician, a month from turning twenty-two. He was also a talented graphic artist who had just lately designed the 549th's unit insignia (fearsome-looking bat, wings spread, with bolts of fire streaming from both nostrils, and .50-caliber machine guns in its claws). A day or two before, the technicolor insignia had been stuck up on a tripod at the southern end of the compound. Back at Waterford-Halfmoon High School, Cramer had been president of the art club and star of the chess team.

One more thumb-note about someone who'd been asleep on the enlisted side. Several years ago, I located an old 549er named Ralph J. Carrington. He was ninety-four and one of the last six or seven still alive from the squadron. (Now, none is alive.) He'd been in ordnance supply. He was from Wilmington, Delaware. He'd come home from the war and had gotten married to Bernadine Rucinski (she could almost pass for my mom in her classic forties good looks) and had a large career in the business world. In 2011, when her dad was eighty-seven, Carrington's daughter, Cyndy Carrington Miller, who worked in public relations and marketing, got him to sit down and talk out some of his wartime memories. She found old letters and news clippings. She produced a privately printed book, *Iwo Jima Album: Photographs and Memories of Staff Sgt. Ralph J. Carrington, U.S. Army Air Force 1943–1945*. I have a signed copy of this beautiful and moving softcover work, with its dozens of brown-toned photographs. I say "beautiful," even if there are in *Iwo Jima Album* eleven very-hard-to-look-at photographs (some made by her dad with his box Brownie) of the Japanese bodies and half bodies and sometimes almost no bodies at all. They're in the trenches, they are lying out on the open ground, in and around the tents of the 549th. They're the same kind of photographs as the one at the top of this chapter.

On Veterans Day 2018, I talked to Ralph Carrington on the phone for about half an hour. It wasn't until afterward that I fully realized it *was* Veterans Day. He seemed such an unassuming man. He remembered my dad's name, of course, but they hadn't really known each other. (Sergeant Carrington had been assigned to the armament supply of another Widow.) He was in hospice care in a high-end senior living community in Pittsburgh. His daughter, the last alive in the family save for himself, was in the room. She had arranged our talk. The early morning of March 26, 1945, had been seventy-three years before. I edged into it, worried about tiring her father.

"I can see them flying up into the air," he said softly. I wasn't entirely sure what he meant. Then it hit me: He meant the Japanese bodies. Blown up into the air by the Marines, who'd come in with their satchel charges and flamethrowers. The clear picture was still in there.

Ralph Carrington died a month later.

The faceless other side. In an essay about Clint Eastwood's career, entitled "God/Country/Family," a cinema scholar named Lester D. Friedman has written: "Who but Clint Eastwood, despite being the most well-known conservative in Hollywood, would even consider making a two-hour-and-twenty-one-minute film that contains dialogue spoken mostly in Japanese (with English subtitles), that is shot in black and white, that possesses no familiar American actors, and that presents a sympathetic, essentially heroic, portrait of Japanese military men? Indeed, no one else in the history of the American cinema provides audiences with such a relentless positive portrait of America's Pacific World War II enemy, not to mention back-to-back movies focusing on the men fighting each other during the same battle."

Students of film history are doubtless aware that *Letters from Iwo Jima* is the companion movie to Eastwood's better known and more widely distributed and much more expensively made *Flags of Our Fathers*. But I wonder if they know that Eastwood considers *Letters* to be one of his two favorite films of the roughly three dozen which he has directed over more than half a century. (The other is *The Bridges of Madison County*.) Eastwood is thought to be the first director in the history of the movies to have made two films, one after the other, about the same event.

His twin pieces came out in late 2006. *Flags of Our Fathers,* which tells the battle from the American side, is based on the 2000 best-selling book of the same name, by James Bradley and Ron Powers. It's the complicated story about the five Marines and one Navy corpsman who were involved in raising the flag on Suribachi, and what became of their lives afterward. *Flags* failed at the box office; *Letters* didn't. Much of it was shot on the extreme cheap on sound-stages in Hollywood, although there were scenes done in Malibu and out in the California desert. There were one or two days of filming on Iwo Jima. Since 99 percent of his cast spoke little or no English, as director he had to work through interpreters, using his hands and body to try to communicate the action and emotion he was proposing to his actors. The movie earned out in ways other than financial. It was nominated for four Academy Awards. It is one of those strange movies with a strange afterlife, known, and not known.

Eastwood has said in interviews (indeed he says it in the bonus tracks accompanying the compact disc of the film that I own) that it was Tadamichi Kuribayashi's letters that took him over. The letters made him go to Steven Spielberg, one of the major supporters of the film and one of its producers, and insist that he needed to make a movie about the other side, and about the general in particular. It was something about the quality of those forty-one letters.

The main scriptwriter of the film, a Japanese American, is Iris Yamashita. She is a modest person who had never before had a script produced. When her agent told her that she was being con-sidered, she thought to herself: *Oh, yes, I see, this is going to be an extra thing. It won't be in theaters.* She was told, actually, no. "You mean in real theaters? In America? You mean a feature?" Yes. She went feverishly to work. On the internet, she found an oral history of a Japanese survivor of the battle. Every day, during the thirty-six-day siege, this ordinary soldier had said prayers to himself and for his family back home and then said aloud, "Today is the day I am going to die." At that point, she understood her movie.

She went to see the megawatt star himself at his office in Burbank. She was shaking. There was a piano in the room, where Eastwood composed his jazz. "The most essential thing I remember," Yamashita told me on the phone, "was how kind and calm he was. As if he somehow knew that it was all determined, that this movie had to be made, that this movie was going to be made, that nothing was going to stop this movie from being made, and that I was going to be involved. It was kind of surreal, being in that room."

Eastwood had had a complex relationship with his father, who had died of a heart attack at sixty-three. Several friends felt that the relatively early death was a turning point in Eastwood's life. As if he was determined to look more deeply into himself through his films.

I spoke by phone to Tim Moore, a producer, who has worked closely with Eastwood on every film Eastwood has made since 2002.

"Why was it so important to him to make this movie?"

"Well, I think a lot of things," Moore said. "You're not supposed to like the people you're fighting against. These were young kids who had no say in determining what was going to happen to them. That's what he's interested in. Ordinary people get put into heroic situations. You have to perform in impossible situations. He's always for the underdog. Just normal guys who get thrown into something that's way beyond them. I mean, even the general, Kuribayashi, in a sense isn't he just this ordinary guy, this home guy, this very human guy, this brilliant guy, who wants desperately to be anywhere but here? But he can't be. Destiny has stuck him here."

"Do you think there could have been anything autobiographical going on?" It was my stumbling way of trying to ask whether Eastwood might have recognized anything of his father in the general.

"I wouldn't want to analyze that," Moore said, not at all in an unfriendly way, but closing the door on the question.

No one knows the circumstances of Kuribayashi's death. His body was never recovered or identified. It's a large part of his myth. There are many theories. Some feel he fell into a stupor toward the last, almost catatonic in anxiety over his family, the more so after March 9–10, 1945. That's the overnight date when 279 Superfortresses firebombed much of Tokyo, using napalm. Maybe as many as 100,000 died—women, children, the elderly. It is considered the single-most destructive bombing attack in recorded history. Some have said that, after learning of the firebombing by transmitted radio code to his bunker, the general gave up. Others have hotly disputed this, insisting that he was with his defeated forces until the very end. On the other hand, could he have committed ritual suicide in that cave in the final moments, after issuing the orders for the final stand, and then have been secretly buried? In *So Sad to Fall in Battle,* Kumiko Kakehashi hedges, with a double negative, "It does not seem impossible that he might have plunged into sudden despondency at the final stage." Except she doesn't quite seem to believe it. She quotes a study from Japan's Ground Self-Defense Force Officer School: "There is no other example in the history of the Japanese army where a division commander (army corps commander) led the charge himself." But she seems to think this is what happened. So do other historians whom I've consulted. That he tore off his epaulets. That he stripped the stars from his general's cap. That he put on an ordinary infantryman's steel helmet. That he said aloud, perhaps screamed aloud, drawing his saber, the words he had written in point four of his cable nine nights before, on March 17: "I will at all times be at your head."

In the closing minutes of *Letters from Iwo Jima,* you can see a flickering glimpse of some circuslike squad tents sticking up from the western beaches. I told both Tim Moore and Iris Yamashita that in real life my dad had been sleeping in one of those tents at 4 a.m. on the 26th.

In Yamashita's movie—which is to say in *Eastwood's* movie—

Kuribayashi (played by the great Japanese film star Ken Watanabe) shoots himself in the chest by early light with his own pearl-handled pistol. He is lying injured in the sand. He's on his back. He draws the revolver from his belt and closes his eyes and fires. Way back, years before, that prized pistol had been presented to him in a beautiful case by some friends in America, at a full-dress military dinner. One of the general's lowliest troops (he's a fictional character named Saigo, a minor star of the film) then drags off his body and buries him behind boulders just before the Americans close in.

"But that, of course, was made up," Yamashita told me, with an awkward laugh. "We had no idea. Nobody has any idea."

I have an idea. I believe that the emperor's reluctant warrior, the samurai who both was and wasn't, the man who revealed his humanity so utterly in the letters to his family that didn't go missing, is lying facedown with his troops in the photograph at the start of this chapter. Or perhaps lying facedown in one of the other very similar photographs that I've seen of that day, perhaps in one of the images sealed in a box Brownie by an ordnance man from my dad's squadron. I wish to believe that the general, with all his insignia torn off, was right outside my dad's tent, ten or fifteen yards away, somewhere in the common space, this faceless and horrid enemy who wished my horrid and faceless father dead. In any event, why did it take me so long to grasp such an obvious truth: that my trying to know the humanness of Tadamichi Kuribayashi was only another way of trying to know my unknowable father?

That night, the 26th, the clock having wound around once, into Iwo's darkness, my dad and his R/O and gunner were in the air for two tours for a total of five hours and fifty minutes. Looking for the enemy.

YES, I HAD MET GEORGE HAYDEN, from Paducah, Kentucky, at that night fighter reunion in Florida in 1982. He was a radar operator in the 549th and had flown in another P-61—not The Rita B. *I'm not clear on how close he and my father were on Iwo Jima. But they were Kentuckians, fellow western Kentuckians, and that meant all the difference. I was Joe Hendrickson's boy. It was enough. I almost felt I could ask him anything on earth.*

At one point he said, gently: "I was a little psycho after the war. I was hospitalized on and off. I guess I didn't know who I was. I did some bad things. I was too rough on my sons."

He said he'd gone to Murray State University on the G.I. Bill, and that he'd earned a teaching degree, but that he didn't really make use of it for a good while. He did shift work at Union Carbide. He worked for the government at Oak Ridge, Tennessee. He was a county health inspector. Eventually, he got a master's degree and started working in school systems.

Hayden also said something else, and it is what sticks with me most: "I saw one come over the house about ten years ago. Oh, I don't know, maybe it was twenty years ago. It scared me. I thought I must be dreaming. I look up and here's this Widow coming over real low. I never found out why. Got me all upset. I thought, 'Am I dying?' I know it was a Widow. I don't know where it came from or what it was doing in Kentucky."

Was this some false, far-back dream in a war-damaged man?

Through the years I have sporadically kept journals. Probably I have eight or ten leatherbound journals lying around. Most have been connected to whatever book project I was working on at the time, with so many of the scribbles just trying to calm my late-night anxieties.

Recently, I went looking for a note in one of these journals. I started this journal in the eighties and abandoned it a few years later. But I have been gold-panning things from it related to what you have been reading in this book. My parents' voices are in this journal.

The entry I was looking for was about an abandoned Black Widow, into the cockpit of which I had climbed at the former Hammer Field in Fresno in the early seventies. In the early seventies, when I wasn't yet thirty, I was working at my first big-city newspaper job in Detroit. I had taken a two-week vacation to the West Coast, touring myself around. I had gone to Fresno—I hadn't been there since my infancy—to see where my folks had lived when my dad's squadron got formed. I had gone out to the municipal airport, built on the site of the old Hammer. I had driven around to the back end of the airport. There, sitting up against a fence, in weeds, was a half-rusted-out P-61. No one was around, so, with heart thumping, I had gotten out of my rental car and climbed the fence. I circled the machine. And then I clambered up and climbed in.

Except I am now convinced, utterly, that this never happened, that there had been no Widow against a Fresno fence. It was a false, far-back dream. Okay, maybe some other old rusted-out plane sitting in a corner of what had once been Hammer. But not a P-61. And, in any case, no climbing in. All I can think is that a decade and a half removed from that California trip, making a journal notation about a supposed "fact," I must have alchemized my Widow fantasies without even realizing I was doing so. I wanted the story to be true. It's embarrassing to admit this. Another reminder that the past can be another place, memory can have another pattern.

Which is why I'm almost giddy to report something unexpected that happened to me only last week, as I am writing. (It's the reason I had gone back and searched for my old journal entry.) I got to experience, at point-blank range, at a modest-sized air museum and restoration facility in Reading, Pennsylvania, the inside of a P-61. For more than three decades, some World War II warbirds have been putting this Widow under a loving and costly rehabilitation.

"You want to look in the cockpit? Go ahead," the president and owner of the Mid-Atlantic Air Museum had said. His name is Russ Strine. He's a quirky and generous fellow with many flying hours under his belt. It was a slow tour day. He had led me into the museum hangar where the Widow was on display, even as she was being rebuilt. Suddenly, he offered. This time, my heart was thumping for real.

I stood on the top rung of a small yellow stepladder, with my head and shoulder blades sticking up through the floorboard of the fuselage. Somebody had been working on the plane that morning. I was standing spit-close to all those knobs and dials and levers and gauges which my dad would have known in his sleep. I was at eye-level with the control wheel. I could see the firing switch for the 20-millimeter cannons on the upper right side of the wheel. I could see the gunsight mounted on the cowl in the middle of the windshield above the instrument panel. I could see the push-pull rods for the ailerons and spoilers.

This P-61 was rescued in the late eighties from the side of a jungle-green mountain in New Guinea. She'd belonged to the 550th NFS. That is, she had belonged to the squadron at Hammer formed right behind my dad's. (The 550th got activated on June 1, 1944, a month after the activation of the 549th.) This P-61 was in the "B" series, meaning she was the same version which my dad piloted. She had crashed on Mount Cyclops on January 10, 1945, having never flown in combat. Through the decades, she'd survived in her jungle nest almost miraculously intact, while the snakes and lizards crawled through. There was even air in her tires. If she wasn't The Rita B, she seemed about the nearest thing that I'd ever encounter in this life.

I noted earlier that there are just four Black Widows known to exist worldwide. Three are on display in national, governmental museums: at the Beijing Air and Space Museum; at Wright-Patterson Air Force Base in Dayton; at a suburban Virginia annex of the National Air and Space Museum in Washington. But these are museum pieces, not meant to fly again. The fourth known Widow, with a different dream up its sleeve, is at Reading Regional Airport, no more than an hour from my home. I had long known about her. The museum was shut during COVID. For some reason, I kept delaying. Last week, I drove over—and took notes and pictures.

More than four decades ago, Russ Strine, and his now deceased father, a World War II naval aviation veteran, started their museum in order to recover and restore Black Widow #42-39445. Having an air museum gave them credibility with officialdom. After endless delays and undreamed-of costs, the father-and-son team secured the plane from the Indonesian government and brought her to America in crates. Their small-city museum has by now built up an impressive collection of more than 120 aircraft, military and civilian. But the Widow from the 550th remains the jewel. They're getting closer to the finish line— maybe another three or four years, Strine hopes—that is, if the donations keep coming, if the skilled volunteers can keep facing down the technical problems. The quixotic dream, from all the way back, is to paint a name on her nose, open the hangar door, roll her out onto the tarmac, fire up her Double Wasp 18-cylinder air-cooled piston engines, and sail her in her glossy blackness up above the Pennsylvania cornfields. A vision.

I could have peered in at the cockpit all afternoon. But the man who says he hopes to take off in her—and, like me, Russ Strine isn't young anymore—was now standing beneath the yellow ladder, clearing his throat. He had let me keep my head in for about fifteen minutes. As I was climbing down, I twisted around and looked for a moment at the plexi bubble behind me.

Mmmm, *I thought,* that's where Leo E sat.

Where Leo E Sat

Jack Kerr, my father, Leo E. Vough

I LOVE THE WAY MY DAD, the boss of this tiny orchestra, is dangling his rimless aviator shades against his pant leg and the way his other arm is tucked behind him, as if half consciously posing for a portrait. To his right, with about three inches of Iwo Jima air between their elbows, is Jack Kerr. I love the way my godfather's Luger is holstered in his armpit, and the way he has *both* arms behind his back, as if standing at a loose kind of parade rest. The R/O could almost be a Texas lawman looking for Bonnie and Clyde. His shoulders seem a tiny bit more squared off and thrust forward than my dad's. (In late midlife the ex–radar operator will develop a barrel chest and put on a bit of weight to support the barrel. He can scare the hell out of kids in the New Jersey school where he's the top-kick disciplinarian.) The prop tip from the engine on the right side of *The Rita B* is nearly touching the side of Officer Kerr's head. These two poker-faced airmen, who've been with each other as pilot and navigator since back in Florida almost two years ago, so reliant on each other's skills and split-second judgments, the one a first looey, the other a second, have to know, as they all do, that they're participating in something way beyond them. They're far too young to be here, but here they are, semi-squinting into the tropical sun, and in another way, their own history.

But look at the third figure in the frame. Who seems about seventeen.

His name is Leo E. Vough. He seldom omits his middle initial, to the extent that later in life his family and friends will take to calling him "Leo E." They'll decorate his cakes that way: "Happy Birthday Leo E" (skipping the period). Kids will address him on the street, "Hey, there goes Leo E." (Sometimes they hail him as "Uncle Leo.") Ditto at church and the union hall and on Friday nights at the VFW: almost always "Leo E." Funny thing, though: As the years go on, no one will seem quite sure what the "E" stands for. It's almost as if Leo E himself has forgotten.

He's the enlisted man of the crew. He's the gunner. He's relatively new to *The Rita B,* in fact, relatively new to the 549th itself. He wasn't with the squadron when it got formed back in Fresno. (He was getting his Aerial Gunnery Diploma at Hickam Field on Oahu.) Best I've been able to determine, he joined up with the P-61s in Hawaii somewhere around Christmastime, and then got assigned to the 549th, and then to *The Rita B* in the third week of January.

He's twenty-three—barely. There's no date on this print, but I believe it was taken within the first month or two of the arrival on Iwo, possibly in mid-April. If that is so, then Staff Sergeant Vough's birthday was just days ago. Maybe they had a "Leo E" cake waiting for him in his tent on the enlisted side of the compound when he came in from work on the 13th.

My dad and Leo E haven't begun to know each other in the way my dad and his R/O do. But they can't fly together without an implicit trust, without the gears meshing.

He's out of the deeply ethnic and anthracite coal regions of northeastern Pennsylvania, specifically a little burg named Avoca (you pronounce it Ah-VO-cuh). Other than Main Street, there aren't too many streets, at least big streets, in Avoca, which sits not quite midway between Scranton and Wilkes-Barre. One little town or borough or township in the narrow and whale-humped Wyoming Valley bleeds right into the next. Most have their own Main Street. An outsider can go from Main Street in Avoca to Main Street in Dupont without quite realizing he's on two different Mains in two different municipalities.

Another line from one of Richard Hugo's poems: "Home. Home. I knew it entering." It's a poem about the only bar in a gritty-looking place called Dixon, Montana. There's more than one bar in Leo E's hometown—in fact, Leo and his older sister, Louise, owned one of them for a while after the war—but Hugo would have recognized, and loved, Avoca's Main Street. Home.

He's first-generation Polish. His hometown is full of Poles and Irish. The Poles go to Saints Peter and Paul Catholic Church, the Irish go to Saint Mary's. (Years from now, when the diocese consolidates, and Saints Peter and Paul is forced to close, some of the Polish faithful of Avoca will never get over it and refuse to worship where the Irish worship.)

The Airplane Armorer Gunner (his official duty description) is five-foot-four-and-a-half. He barely makes the top of my dad's life preserver. Maybe he reaches five-foot-four-and-a-half (the *half,* like the "E," is nearly always there on his government paperwork, from his draft registration card to his honorable discharge form) because of his luxurious upsweep of thick, dark hair. I love the hair, which he will manage to keep for his whole life, if not in a black sheen. I also love the studly way he's got his jumpsuit unzipped down his front, not quite to the top of the high-waisted canvas belt. He's got on a white T-shirt, like Jack and my father.

On his sleeve-rolled right wrist is a bracelet of some kind. It looks like it has tiny stones set into it. That seems to go with the studliness. And on his other wrist, that's a watch with a thin and almost ladylike leather band. He's wearing the face of the watch on the underside of his arm. His whole life, my dad wore his own plainspoken wristwatch with the leather band outside and the face underneath. I can picture him to this minute flicking his left wrist outward to check the time on his Timex. "See, you wear it on the inside of your wrist, you won't crack the crystal, Paul," I can hear him instructing me. Just one more piece of advice I never took. I've noticed that a lot of old aviators, at least of a certain era, tend to wear their watch face on the inside.

My father watched time the way he watched weather: a pilot thing. He loved his fifty-dollar Timex. He used to singsong the ad jingle: the "watch that takes a licking and keeps on ticking."

But Leo E: Where does my dad's gunner sit? Immediately above and behind my dad, in his own narrow and claustrophobic-seeming greenhouse. It's his job, when he's aboard, to man the four fearsome .50-caliber M2 Browning machine guns (able to fire simultaneously) mounted in a turret atop the fuselage. The dorsal turret, as it's known, can rotate 360 degrees, to try to intercept the enemy ahead or behind (or to either side of you, for that matter).

The gunner's glassed-in and exposed compartment is "made up of molded Lucite sheets within extruded metal framing." That semi-techie description is from an amazingly in-depth book on the Black Widow, by Jeff Kolln, entitled *Northrop's Night Hunter: P-61 Black Widow.* I've learned oceans from it. It's practically a manual, even as it's full of myth and lore. Kolln lives in the Pacific Northwest and has written much on aviation and World War II history. I've been the beneficiary of his large generosity. A week after I introduced myself to him on the phone and said I was trying to write about my father and the 549th, Kolln sent me a clutch of valuable documents, including photographs.

Like my dad's station, the gunner's has forward windshield panels made of thick, bullet-resistant glass as well as armor plates at its bulkhead to try to deflect incoming fire. Looking through his 5.8-power sighting binoculars, with bicycle-like handles on a pull-down track, Leo E can swivel his leather seat and lock it into place in either the forward or aft position. Then, from either vantage point, he's able to fire off his "fifties," as I've heard them called. But not before the pilot has relinquished control of the guns from the cockpit, has depressed the proper release mechanism. If there's no gunner on board, the pilot himself has the capacity to fire the .50-calibers, along with everything else that he's trying simultaneously to do. From his own glassed-in station in the rear, the R/O also has the capacity to fire the fifties. Of the "twenties," however, which is to say the four 20-millmeter cannons recessed on the underside of *The Rita B:* Only my dad in the cockpit has control of these. A couple of years before, when Northrop introduced the plane, its slightly overheated PR department in Hawthorne, California, put out an illustrated brochure that said: "In the belly of the crew nacelle are 4 forward-firing 20-millimeter cannon operated by a button on the pilot's control wheel. A single burst from the fifties or the twenties can destroy anything that flies."

Where Leo E sat. From what I can determine, after the war Leo Vough was in a place of not very much emotional darkness. He apparently didn't come home with the Iwo demons in him, or at least not so many. And even as I'm suggesting a seeming lack of after-dread, I want quickly to reference again Michael Herr's unforgettable Vietnam memoir, *Dispatches:* "Was it possible that they were there and not haunted? No, not possible, not a chance."

If Leo E had managed to live eight and a half more years he would have made 100. Aside from the three and a half years he gave over to Uncle Sam between March 1942 and September 1945 he spent the entirety of his ninety and a half years in Avoca and the Wyoming Valley. I doubt he ever thought of it as gritty.

Snapshot of that life:

After his discharge, the youngest son (of four) in the family moved into his old bedroom at 1034 Plane Street and tended his parents until the end. In his immigrant dad's case, that was only five years: the black shale of the mines got George Vough early—in 1950. For the next forty-two years, Leo E took care of and lived with his widowed mom, until Frances Rodejewski Vough died in 1992 at ninety-seven.

The family name used to be Wolch. Then it changed to Voke. Then it became Vough. No one seems to have an explanation of the reason for the changes. Maybe Leo's folks thought the last sounded the most Americanized.

Something else that moves me about his life: The last child, who never married or had children, bought his first and only house almost twenty years to the day from his discharge. It cost $5,300.

There was a notice of the purchase in the *Wilkes-Barre Record*. He and his mom moved to 540 Main from 1034 Plane. The two houses are an eighth of a mile apart.

He put a wooden swing on the back porch. That's how Avocans who knew him casually seem to remember him now, or the seven or eight to whom I spoke: rocking softly on his back porch swing on summer evenings. Sometimes, after retirement, he'd swing all afternoon. Sometimes with a can or cans of Genesee Cream Ale. He liked pouring it into seven-ounce glasses. To make it last.

He had gotten discharged at Fort Dix, New Jersey, on September 13, 1945, although he had left the Western Pacific in the beginning of summer. He had earned enough service points to go home early, but not quite enough to get out of the Army Air Forces. He landed stateside and scored a furlough to Avoca. In his pocket was an engagement ring for an Avoca girl named Frieda. He wrote to Joe Baumbach, one of his 549 buddies from Iwo, that he was going home to propose. Baumbach had also built up enough service points to leave the war early. On August 24, 1945, Baumbach wrote to his pal from his own home at 3026 North 38th Street in Milwaukee: "Having yourself quite a furlough I see. and [*sic*] that is the way it should be. Having quite a time myself tho I haven't tied myself down to one gal yet. Still playing the field and I do mean playing." He closed: "Give my best to the gal fella. I'd like to meet her someday. Hope its everything you want and I'm wishing you both a whole lot of the best of everything."*

---

* Baumbach's letters could be straight out of *The Best Years of Our Lives*. September 26, 1945: "Hi fella—Don't remember whether I wrote you to congratulate you on making civilian or not." April 18, 1946 (so seven months after he's back): "I haven't heard from any of the gang for a long time. And it was swell to get your letter. . . . Had a lot of ideas about what I was going to do when I became a civilian again, damn few of them have panned out. Haven't been able to get a car yet. . . . Yeah fella—I found a gal, or maybe she found me—could be. And she's working on the settleing [*sic*] down idea. So far I've been able to duck but I'm slowing down a little and maybe one of these days she'll ring the bell, and then I'll be doing my damndest to ring the bell and maybe we'll be raising a few G.I's for the next war. . . . I'm thinking it's worth taking a chance. She's big, blond and almost beautiful, stacked like we want em, and seems to like having me around. I'd send along a snap but I don't have any right now."

Frieda jilted him. For something like the next forty years, Leo E would keep that ring in a drawer. If the bitterness was there, he kept it tamped down, or so say those who loved him.

He joined the local Wyoming Valley chapter (it's up in Scranton) of the United Brotherhood of Carpenters and Joiners of America. For the next sixty-one years, he was a UBC dues-paying member in faithful standing. The late, great folksinger John Prine once wrote a rollicky tune about his maternal grandfather called, "Grandpa Was a Carpenter." It goes: "[He] hammered nails in planks / He was level on the level." That sounds to me like Leo E.

Who earned his forty-year pin from the brotherhood. His fifty-year pin. His sixty-year pin. At the UBC sixty-year banquet in October 2009, three years before he died, there's a photo of Leo E looking natty in a button-down shirt and sneakers and a light gray cardigan with all five buttons buttoned. He still has a good head of hair, albeit gray now. All these decades, he's kept himself fit. Besides himself, only two other Scranton-area carpenters and joiners have endured so long.

At some point after coming home he joined the Polish Citizens Progressive Club of Scranton. The Progressive, everybody called it. The initiation fee was a few bucks, annual membership the same. Yuengling on tap was something like 50 cents. There were good dances on weekends. You could meet the ladies. Problem was, so many of them were taller than he was.

As the years went on, he became a man increasingly set in his ways: dinner at five on the nose and preferably with peas on the plate. (This went for holidays, too.) A glass of water set out on the nightstand before bed so that, first thing in the morning, swinging his short legs to the floor, he could sit on the edge of his bed and drain the contents without taking a breath. Good for the constitution. Setting the water out overnight warmed it the way he liked it.

One Friday night in the late seventies (he would have been in his mid-fifties now) confirmed bachelor Leo E went to a polka dance at the DAV: the Disabled American Veterans up in Dickson City. (It's six or seven miles above Scranton.) Rose Borgna and her teenage daughter, Michele, were there. They lived in Moosic, a town or two up from Avoca. The band was playing a tricky and lively polka known as the Oberek. Leo E knew his steps. He saw the teenager and invited her to go around the floor with him. After the dance, the teenager pulled in her mom, who was sitting over at a table. Rose, divorced, was interested in meeting eligible men.

Soon enough, Rose and Leo were a pair. She was sixteen years younger. She was also about two inches taller, which made it tough on Leo E's ego whenever she wore heels. Soon enough mother and daughter left their own place in Moosic and moved down to 540 Main Street in Avoca. Not that Rose moved in with her boyfriend, exactly. She and Michele lived upstairs and Leo and his mom kept their quarters downstairs. Now the townsfolk often saw two people swinging away the weekend Avoca summer afternoons on the back porch. Leo was still driving nails into planks—big construction jobs, little ones.

Rose and Leo loved going for polka weekends in the Poconos and the Catskills. And to the slots at Atlantic City. There was a trip or two to Las Vegas. Mostly, the Wyoming Valley was fine by them. As for dining, to Leo E there was nothing like the Big King XL burger and a sack of fries at Burger King. When he and Rose were putting on the dog, they'd go for dinner at the Dough Company down in Wilkes-Barre, famed for its Stromboli and garlic knots.

One day, he brought out and gave unceremoniously to Rose the engagement ring that had been meant for Frieda all those years ago. Not that they were going to get hitched. He just wanted her to have it.

Once, on a vacation, the two got locked inside their hotel room. The door wouldn't open. That did it. After that, Leo E never went on a trip out of town with Rose without packing a hammer and a screwdriver.

I'm sitting with Michele McGowan. We're in her dining room. Leo E has been dead for a decade. Rose has now passed on, too. Michele McGowan, in late middle age, grew up to get advanced degrees. She's a respected professor at a local Catholic university. She's Polish through and through, and still loves to polka, but somehow, as she likes to joke, she had the bad form to marry a local Irish American, Leo McGowan. She and Leo have three grown children, all with Irish names. "Where did I go wrong?" she says.

"I married an Irishman and somebody also named Leo." Her son, Aidan, knew Leo E when he, Aidan, was a kid. Leo E taught him to pitch pennies, taught him to play rummy. Leo E loved that kid. He'd walk him down the block to Cwikla's Quality Bakery for the peanut butter cookies.

This is my third or fourth extended talk with Michele. We're comfortable with each other now. She has dropped on me a precious old grocery sack of Leo E documents—photograph albums, official papers from the war, letters (Joe Baumbach's, for instance), laundry receipts. She is the daughter Leo E never had. In effect, she was his common-law child. It's safe to say she knew him better, remembers him better, than anyone currently living. She knew him for almost half a century.

"Oh, he could be a terrific pain in the ass," she says, the affection unmistakable. "He was rigid. He could hold a grudge. Everything had to be just so. If there was a piece of lint on the carpet, it drove him nuts."

She's remembering something. "I never knew anybody to love the back of an envelope the way Leo did," she says. "He could do complex figuring on the backs of envelopes."

Michele's husband, Leo: "Holding grudges? You know the old joke about Irish Alzheimer's? You forget everything but the grudge. That was Leo E. He told me once a couple years before he died that he was pissed off at somebody from something the guy had done to him in 1974. Nineteen seventy-four?"

"But still a good guy?"

"Oh, yeah," says Michele's husband. "No question."

"Actually, I miss him terribly," says Michele. "What a pain in the ass."

"What about PTSD from the war, from Iwo Jima?"

"No, I don't think so. Or if it was there, I never really saw it," Michele says. "If it was there, he kept it hidden. He was just kind of this simple man. And then he died."

"Do you ever remember him saying anything about my father? *The Rita B*?"

"Truthfully, I can't remember him speaking much about the war at all," she says.

Five years before he died, Leo E wrote to the National Personnel Records Center in St. Louis to request a copy of his service file. There were some ribbons and medals and one Bronze Service Star that he'd earned for his time overseas but had never received, even though he had the proper paperwork. The center wrote back and said that most of Leo's record had been destroyed in the huge 1973 fire at their former premises.

In his last few years, Rose and Leo moved to a house in Moosic. The McGowans had bought Rose her own place, so that she could be closer to them. Leo E didn't want to leave Avoca, but at the same time he didn't want to leave Rose. You can get to Moosic in about ten minutes. But it wasn't Avoca.

He stayed mentally sharp, while his kidneys and his heart and other things began to go.

"He knew. I think he knew," says Michele. "He'd say, 'I can't figure numbers like I used to. I can't do my figures.' Toward the end, he kept thanking me. I had to take a business trip. He said he wanted my son Aidan to get a tux so he could be a pallbearer. He made me promise."

On the morning he died, my dad's old Airplane Armorer Gunner awoke and swung his weary legs to the side of the bed and drained his seven-ounce glass of room-temperature bathroom water. He got dressed and went into the kitchen and had pancakes, eggs, bacon, toast, black coffee. Winter was coming. He was scheduled to see his doctor. Rose was going to go with him. He walked out the kitchen door to the garage and turned the handle on the side door and went into the garage and put his hand on the door handle of his sedan and turned and said to Rose, "I don't feel so good." Rose told him to lie down right there on the floor of the garage. He slid slowly down the side of the car door and onto the cool concrete while she ran to the house for the phone. Soon the sirens were marrying her panicked cries.

The funeral Mass was at a Polish parish down in Dupont. Michele saw to all the arrangements, including the funeral breakfast at one of the valley's larger VFWs. His burial was at Saints Peter and Paul Cemetery on the north end of Avoca in the Vough family plot, surrounded by other World War II veterans and other

Avoca families with names like Sledgeski, Skowronski, Saktowski, Koniszewski. If you go there now, you'll see his bronze veteran's marker, flat to the ground. There's a small flag flying from a dowel rod. The dowel is punched into the earth. Next to the flag is a paper carnation attached to a pinwheel. The stone marker with its gold lettering reads: *Leo E Vough. S Sgt US Army Air Forces World War II April 13, 1922, Oct 29, 2012.*

SOMETIMES I think that almost half my family's coded history could be conveyed in three coded words: getting back down.

Forget Iwo for a moment, and what those words would have constantly conveyed. I'm thinking of when I was a kid, and my dad was an airline pilot, and of the unspoken tension cutting our lives. Again, as I wrote many years ago: "In Kankakee, in the early fifties, while I swam to consciousness, my mother waited for phones to ring from the field in the middle of bad winter nights. None of us talked about this tension, though once I recall asking my father if he worried about all those lives lined behind him in rows of twos and threes. 'Yes, but you don't let yourself think about them, son,' he said. 'What you concentrate on is getting yourself back down and they'll be fine.' "

Once, years later, long after I was on my own, and married, I witnessed the tension of those three words working themselves out before my eyes and not in coded ways. Only, my dad wasn't the one trying to bring in a plane in threatening weather. It was my kid brother, Mark. And my little sister, Jeannie, seated beside him in my father's Beech Debonair, with aeronautical maps spread out on her lap. My father was the one having to watch from down below.

It was the 4th of July 1980. Mark was only twenty-two, but already a skilled pilot, a recent graduate of the Institute of Aviation at the University of Illinois. My father trusted implicitly in his ability to fly, which is why I don't think he had second thoughts about turning over the Deb's ignition key to his fourth son to fly himself and his kid sis up to the woods.

Jeannie was twenty, still in college. You've possibly already picked up that, in so many senses, Mark and Jeannie represented for my parents a deep try at starting over. There were two rungs of children in our family: Marty and I and Ric, born in the forties, at the upper end; and the doted-on Mark and Jeannie, born in the late fifties, down below. When I went off to the seminary in 1958 at age fourteen, Jeannie hadn't yet been born and Mark was five months old.

My wife and I had come to the family cabin in northern Wisconsin to spend the holiday weekend with my parents. Mark and Jeannie had summer jobs down in the Chicago suburbs, and so couldn't get away until late on the afternoon of the 4th. A line of thunderstorms was rolling across the Midwest. I think they must have delayed their takeoff time for a couple of hours.

We—my parents and my wife, Ceil, and I—had gone to an early dinner and had then dawdled around, waiting for fireworks on Chequamegon Bay, which is an inlet of Lake Superior at the port of Ashland. Ashland, by far the biggest town in those parts, had an airport with two runways and asphalt surfaces. There was no operating tower. Pilots had to fork their way in, on instruments, if it was dark, and the more so if the weather was turning sour and the ceilings low.

Up there, in the land of the northern lights, it doesn't get dark in the early part of summer until well past nine. Even after the sun sets, the light will linger. Then it gets pitch.

All through our dinner at a local restaurant, my father was jumpy. He could read incoming weather better than anyone I ever knew. If we all grew up around flying, in another way we all grew up around an awareness of weather. I don't think he ate much of his dinner. He was just as itchy during the fireworks, which didn't get delayed because of the threatening weather, after all. I think he may not have even watched the fireworks, but instead sat in the car trying to get reports on the radio.

The rain kept holding off, but the wind coming off the big lake was howling. Finally, the four of us got into the car and he took the wheel—he always took the wheel—and sped us toward the airport on the south end of town. "C'mon, c'mon," he had commanded.

My mom and my wife and I sat in the car in the empty parking lot, while my dad paced along a chain-link fence at the runway's edge. A small front passed through. Heavy rain and then things seemed to calm. But the clouds were socked in. Out on the big lake we could hear low rumblings and see flashes from stray forks of lightning. I bet the visibility at the airport wasn't much more than 100 feet.

It must now have been close to 10 or 10:30. It was very dark. No sign of my kid siblings.

From my notes: He's wandering around out by gate <u>w</u> jacket on. Suddenly runs back to car. "Airplane coming." Is it Mark or not? Might be the Deb. Looks like the light on top. It is. Catharsis. I have goosebumps as this little winking thing seems to hang out there in the black.

We could hear the Deb before we could see her. Mark seemed to drop her down out of nowhere. That's when I saw the nose-landing light. Suddenly he and Jeannie were on the ground. He rolled the plane to the end of the runway, pivoted her around, pulled right up in front of us smart as you please. He cut the prop and climbed out with a big grin, as if he were Lucky Lindy landing at Le Bourget in Paris. He was wearing a Washington Post *T-shirt which I had given him a year or two before.*

My dad, sixty-one then, seemed about two feet off the ground. He was laughing loudly. I was laughing loudly, too.

"How in the hell did you do that?" I remember asking Mark. Mark grinned and shrugged.

The other day (as I write this), forty-two years after the fact, I asked my gifted little brother, his father's protégé, the only one of us who ever wanted to do it, the same question. We were on the phone. I was reading him some of my notes from that night, which I had scribbled on a yellow-lined pad and had put away for years.

"I'll tell you what I remember," Mark said. "All the way up from Chicago, dodging thunderheads, going in and out of the clouds, Jeannie and I kept looking down and seeing fireworks going off in all the little Wisconsin towns. Kinda beautiful."

"I'll tell you what I remember, and you had no way of knowing it, not then," I said. "How incredibly nervous Dad was until you got back down. He couldn't sit still. There was nothing he could control. It almost felt as if he were willing you down."

Eighty-Three Years Later, Not Quite to the Day

My father's airplane on the flight line at South Field, the hatch of her greenhouse propped open. That's not a bomb beneath The Rita B's *right wing. It's a 165-gallon drop tank of auxiliary fuel. There's one under her other wing, too. Once they've served their purpose, the "drops" can be dropped. In the background, on the lip of the cliff that goes down to the sea, are the briefing tents, more commonly known by the flyers as the Ready Room. In the monthly squadron reports, the name is nearly always capitalized. Something quick about it, tense, and then, too, the alliterative effect.* Ready, *even if you're not.*

TWENTY-TWO DAYS after he was on Iwo Jima, my father flew his first intruder mission. I wonder how ready he was. The date was April 11, 1945. It was sixteen days since General Kuribayashi's *kirikomi* suicide forces knifed and saber-slashed through the living quarters of the 549th. I have to think he was still trembling a bit from what had occurred in the predawn of March 26, and from the scenes he saw, they all saw, when the sun was up.

Until now, my dad and his two crew members had flown combat air patrols. CAP missions had their own implicit lurk of danger, even if Japan was much on the run. On CAPs there were almost always two crews in the air, one Widow patrolling at 10,000 feet, the other at 15,000. Quoting from the March squadron report: "These patrols were alternated nightly between the 549th Night Fighter Squadron and the 548th Night Fighter Squadron, located across the taxi-way." Since arriving on Iwo, late in the month (on the 20th, as previously said), my father's squadron had flown patrols on the 22nd, 24th, 26th, 28th, and 30th. *The Rita B* had been up for four out of five of those nights. (On the 24th, they had let the ship and her crew have a rest.) At least twice in that first week of their missions off Iwo, 549th crews had had sightings of the enemy, or what must have been the enemy. Again, this sentence from the monthly squadron report: "A chase was made, with slight radar contact on the airborne set, and then the object pulled out of sight."

Before each patrol mission, there was a briefing in the Ready Room. Again, from the official unit history:

> The briefing covered Operations—areas of patrol, altitudes, times of take-off, the crews to fly that night, duration of patrol, and friendly aircraft that would be airborne that night; Intelligence—the geography of the surrounding islands. . . . Tactics were covered using the latest that were experienced by the other Night Fighter Squadron. The briefing ended with coverage of the weather.

But an intruder mission carried a different magnitude of fear and risk—everyone knew it going in—and that's because it was offensive in nature, rather than defensive. Again, from the unit history: "The primary purpose of these missions was to: first, hit enemy aircraft; second, sink enemy shipping; and last, to harass the enemy." And a few sentences onward: "For these intruder missions the Intelligence Officer of the Squadron drew up target charts containing a tracing of the island area, a pin point of the target, prominent mountains which would aid the Radar Observer, bombing tables, and routes to, over and from the target."

My dad's orders on the 11th were to fly northward, to bomb

and strafe a fortified little place in the Bonin Islands named Chichi Jima. (It is now more commonly referred to as Chichijima.) The island was roughly 165 miles from Iwo, in the same archipelago.

About an hour before takeoff that Wednesday night, in the Ready Room, the briefers must have told my dad and Jack Kerr there weren't any searchlights to worry about up there.

"I could have read a newspaper in the cockpit, Paul," my father said the only time he ever talked about it to me.

"I was making these intensive evasive actions," he said, his right arm jerked out in front of him, doing dips and sine waves.

"The ack-ack is everywhere," he said. His voice had a high timbre. "I can't get out of the lights. They've caught me in the lights. The only thing I can think is they were radar controlled. I redlined it at above 425 and tore straight out to sea, diving very low to the water. When we got back down, soon as I had her parked, I practically ran into the Ready and started screaming at the head intelligence officer. 'You better get your damn act together before you get some of your pilots killed.' That guy was superior to me, too. I don't think I stopped shaking for a week."

The emotion is so stark, undisguised. And yet I don't remember feeling this starkness back then, exactly. This was one of just four or five or six times—at most—in which my father was opening himself up about the war. I longed for such openings up, or thought I did.

It wasn't until after I began trying to piece together the full story of April 11, 1945, and to think through my own responses to it, that I could feel a tincture of the fright and rage which must have been inside my dad (and Jack and Leo E, too) when night suddenly turned into day. And what brought me to that feeling was a typed, one-page piece of old declassified government paper with the word CONFIDENTIAL written at the top. It was my dad's mission report from April 11, 1945. He didn't write it—the unit historian and the intelligence officers did. Once I saw its minimizing language— I'll call it a papering-over language, and I will quote it later in this chapter—my own rage and fright just followed.

———

On April 12, 1945, at about 1:15 in the afternoon, the president of the United States was sitting in an armchair in the living room of his beloved Little White House in Warm Springs, Georgia. With him were his terrier, Fala, his two cousins, and his lover, Lucy Mercer. He was getting his portrait painted. He said he had a tremendous pain in the back of his head. He fell into unconsciousness. In about two hours, the presidential doctors declared Franklin Roosevelt dead at sixty-three. At 7:09 p.m., Harry S. Truman was sworn in as the new president in the West Wing of the White House.

The day before this global-rattling moment, there was another pivot point of history, albeit narrower and far less noted but hugely significant in its own way, the more so if you were in the Army Air Forces and had anything to do with night fighters. It happened in the European Theater of the war. The Eighth Air Force and the Ninth Air Force pounded something like 2,900 bombers and fighters against Germany in daytime and nighttime attacks. Several night fighter units, stationed in France and elsewhere, participated in these strategic and tactical missions. According to aviation historian Stephen Joiner, the Black Widows "strafed German locomotives and convoys attempting to retreat under cover of darkness from the onslaught of General Patton's Third Army." In the "most productive single night shift of the war," to again quote Joiner, "P-61 intruders took down fourteen Luftwaffe airplanes, most of them Junkers transports attempting to bring supplies to surrounded German troops."

On the other side of the world, that same night, my father was not taking down any Mitsubishi Zeros or bombers or transports or any other kind of airplane. (Japan and its islands were seven hours ahead of Germany. But the date I'm writing about was still April 11.) On what would turn out to be the night of the Black Widow's greatest military glory, *The Rita B,* across a different ocean, was just trying ingloriously to get out of some supposedly pissant searchlights that must have seemed to her pilot and crew as bright as the lights in a hospital operating room. And I'm willing to bet that, for the remainder of his life, my dad never knew anything about that European glory. And if he did, I can't imagine him much caring. My father wasn't a man for irony and paradox. He tended to see things in straight lines.

Still, I have to believe he would have been a little bowled over to learn that his Civil War ancestor, Private George Hendrickson (whose name, as I earlier said, I don't think he ever knew, much less on whose side he fought), of Company C, Thirteenth Kentucky Volunteers, at the Battle of Shiloh, suffered the rebel bullets singing over his head, in the morning rain of April 7, 1862, in his first testing under fire: which is to say, eighty-three years and four days before his *own* first serious testing in the air under fire. And neither the private in Tennessee nor the lieutenant in the Pacific turning tail to run.

As I said, the mission was to a fortified little place called Chichi Jima, another Japanese speck, although it was the largest island in the Ogasawara Archipelago. It was a square mile larger than Iwo Jima—and about a hundred times more beautiful. It almost looked like an island in the Caribbean—if you could see past its fortifications and bombing ruins. It had (and has) deep-water coves and palm-fringed beaches and small mountains and steep rocky cliffs and clear coral waters and thick stands of subtropical forest. It lay not quite due south of Tokyo by about 612 miles. As far back as 1880, the volcanic island had been officially incorporated into the Tokyo Metropolis. In 1914, the Japanese navy had established a small base there. In the late part of the war, most of its one-time civilian population of 7,000 had been evacuated to the home islands, but as many as 25,000 Japanese military were garrisoned there. The island was a vital signal point for long-range radio contact to the mainland, as well as a central shipping and supply port for the various islands in the Ogasawara Archipelago. Likely no one was going snorkeling for pleasure on Chichi Jima in 1944, but it was almost perfect snorkeling water, with uncounted varieties of fish species.

The whole point of these intruder missions, my dad said, was to keep the islands isolated from the Tokyo decision makers.

Some seven months before my dad ever got near Chichi Jima,

something barbaric had happened on it. Had fate tilted in another direction, it might have happened to him. In September 1944, the planes of at least eleven Navy flyers got shot down in the waters off Chichi Jima. Nine aviators survived and eight were captured and tortured. The tortures included being beaten with clubs and then getting bayoneted or sliced through with bamboo spears. There were beheadings; and four of the flyers were cannibalized, their livers served at a formally set table for officers, including an admiral and a general. The cannibalization wasn't about starvation; it was about contempt. At a secret American postwar war crimes tribunal, a former Japanese medical orderly testified to what a Japanese surgeon had done: "Dr. Teraki cut open the chest and took out the liver. I removed a piece of flesh from the flyer's thigh, weighing about six pounds and measuring four inches wide, about a foot long."

Of the eleven aviators whose planes were shot down, and of the eight aviators who were captured and tortured, and of the four whose remains got eaten, only one escaped this hell, although in a deeper sense he escaped nothing. He was twenty. He was a lieutenant, junior grade. He came from a pedigreed East Coast family. He was already mildly famed for having become one of the youngest pilots to serve in the Navy. In 1944, flying against Chichi Jima, he commanded a three-man Grumman TBF Avenger: a torpedo bomber able to take off from and land on aircraft carriers. When his Avenger got hit and caught fire, the lieutenant bailed out, his parachute opening cleanly. One of his crew got stuck inside the plane and crashed with her into the sea. The chute of his other crewman never opened. But the lieutenant, as if divinely protected because he had another destiny awaiting him, bobbed in the choppy waters off the island until sailors on a suddenly surfaced Navy sub roped him to safety. His name was George H. W. Bush.

For years the U.S. government and the Navy referred to the atrocity as "The Chichijima Incident." The truth of what happened didn't get fully out until 2003, with the publication of James Bradley's best-selling *Flyboys: A True Story of Courage*. The book was published in September; my dad died four months before, in May. My father was not much a reader of books, not even of his son's, but I've always let a small part of me wonder if, in that spring of his dying, when he was drawing more and more into himself, his eye might not have caught a small feature or a news item in a Florida paper about the coming book, with the words "Chichi Jima" in the story. And if so, did it call him back?

Imagine it like this: Two suited-up officers and an enlisted man, all in their twenties, one from a town called Morganfield, one from the Scranton–Wilkes-Barre area, one from the New Jersey exurbs of New York City, are exiting their squadron tents in late-afternoon light. It must be about 5:30. The two officers have walked out the front flap-door of the same eight-man tent. As I've already said, my dad was one of the 549th's flight commanders. He and my godfather shared the same living space, as did the three other flyers and their radar observers who served under my dad in Flight C.

Leo E would have come out of his tent on the other side of the compound.

Did they meet in the middle? Did they nod and walk in silence toward the motor pool? Did a private or a corporal drive them in a jeep on the ten-minute trip to South Field? I can see my father, the ranking guy, seated in the front, his right foot propped up with nonchalance. *The Rita B,* stolid and black and loaded with armor, was waiting for them in a row with her sister P-61s.

Takeoff tonight is scheduled for 6:50. That's pretty early. The dark will just be gathering when they go up. The weather at South Field is clear.

I'm guessing the two officers entered the Ready Room at about six o'clock. They took their briefings. Maybe thirty minutes later, the three airmen would have walked down the line to the ship with my mother's name on her. They would have entered her on the drop-down ladders in her belly—my dad and his gunner via the ladder at the front, behind the nose-wheel strut, the R/O via the one at the rear. When they were in, the ladders would have gotten pulled up behind them and locked flush to the outer skin of the ship.

Strapped into their seats, each airman is going about his preflight rituals, the most elaborate ritual taking place in the cockpit.

I'm pretty sure my dad had a photograph of my mom taped somewhere on his control panel. I faintly remember him saying this once. If so, maybe it's that one of her taken in Yuma, wearing his wings, on graduation day, with that white bib of lace around the collar of her fringed and buttoned-up and so beautifully fitting dress.

It took about thirty-five minutes to get in range. My dad remembered it when he told me of that night, and it checks with the documents, and it further checks with my own calculations about cruising speed vis-à-vis distance. It was dark by the time they were in Chichi's vicinity. My dad said he had the ship blacked out—lights turned off, no radio communication with his R/O and gunner.

He approached the island from the east, keeping ten to fifteen miles from shore. Immediately north of and adjacent to Chichi are two satellite islands—Ani Jima and Ototo Jima. (I'm spelling the names in the way they appear in the wartime documents; the more common spelling today tends to make them one word: Anijima and Ototojima.) Apparently, he flew past Ani and kept going northward, rounding Ototo, and then coming back down on the western side of the island group, pulling up close to the southern end of Ani. There was a village down there named Takinoura, sitting on a small bay of the same name. Takinoura Bay and a narrow channel of water next to it—on maps it almost looks like a canal—divide the much smaller Ani from the much larger Chichi.

This is when my father did something foolhardy—by his own description. "I decided to fly down the island lengthwise," he told me. It was about 7:45 p.m.

Which is when the lights came bathing on.

Against his blacked-out ship.

With the ack-ack puffs exploding on every side.

He had intended to strafe and bomb from north to south. Now he was just trying to save his life. The lights kept tracking him as he dipped and weaved wildly. He said the tracking may have lasted half a minute or more, easy. Miraculously, the ship didn't take a direct hit. He redlined *The Rita B* straight out to sea, diving toward the water. He went maybe fifty miles out and pulled back on the throttles. He was trembling. He turned on the ship's radio but kept all the external and interior lights off. Jack Kerr came on the radio from his station in the rear.

"Holy shit, Joe, what was that?"

I can hear my dad answering (although I don't have him saying this in my notes): "The bastards screwed us on their intelligence, Jack."

What I do have in my notes is my dad saying: "I'm going back around."

But according to the documents, this didn't happen for at least another thirty-five minutes. My dad must have kept making circles out in the sea. I don't know what Jack and Leo E had to say about the coming back around.

What my dad could remember was that he headed back and tore across the narrowest neck of land that was detectable on the scopes. He dropped down below 7,000 feet. He released the bombs and turned for home. He said he never even saw what he was doing. This time, night hadn't turned into day.

Thirty or so minutes later, he would have found South Field. The documents have him touching down at 9:10 p.m., so I'm thinking he might have circled a time or two before he got clearance from the ground control operators. He would have taxied to the flight line. Would have parked her, cut the switches. I can see him whipping off his headgear, lowering the ladder behind the nose strut, not climbing down but almost leaping down, then taking off in a half sprint and a full rage through the prop wash and across the unlit tarmac to the tent-flapped Ready Room, strung with its low-wattage bare bulbs, where he started screaming at the head intelligence officer, who almost got some pilots killed.

I wonder if, in that thirty-five or so minutes between 7:50 and 8:25, when my father's plane hung in the ocean's darkness, he was stoking his nerve to come back around to strafe and bomb. His crew must have been stoking theirs as well. Things had gone grotesquely wrong. But my dad was not going to come home with his 500-pounders still dangling in the bomb racks beneath *The Rita B*'s wings. That would have been humiliating, added to the fright and rage. Was this in his mind? I don't know.

In the early summer of 2020, I set out to try to corroborate in any way I could what took place on the night of April 11, 1945. I knew the documents were housed at the Air Force Historical Research Agency at Maxwell Air Force Base in Montgomery, Alabama. But it was the pitch of the pandemic. I couldn't travel to Alabama. For close to four months I kept calling the agency's reference desk from my home in Philadelphia. No one ever picked up. There wasn't even a recorded message. Then one afternoon in late September, someone answered. I sputtered, trying to get out who I was and what I was trying to do. "I know. I know," the voice said, as if to cut me off kindly. "We've only shortly been back to work. The reading room isn't open. We don't have that much to do. Maybe I can help you. Do you have any document numbers handy?"

Yes, I had them, or at least the basic ones. I had long ago looked up the 549th Night Fighter Squadron at airforcehistoryindex.org. There were all kinds of hits.

At 4:56 p.m., the reference assistant sent by email and via something called DOD SAFE (the "DOD" stands for Department of Defense) about 500 pages of the 549th's declassified monthly squadron reports. I could hardly believe it. In less than an hour, I had gone from no paper to mounds of paper, at least digitized paper.

Over the next several months, this same reference assistant kept sending via DOD SAFE thousands of digitized pages related to the 549th NFS, and to the much larger VII Fighter Command, and to the gigantic Seventh Air Force.

I've agreed to omit from this account the name and gender of the reference assistant. This is at his/her request. This person's dedication and generosity are one of the luckiest strokes of archival fortune I've ever had, and I'm still not exactly sure why and how we connected so quickly. We just did. To this day, we've never met.

That initial document-drop, 500 pages, was so exhilarating and simultaneously disheartening. The first thing I did—on the same evening the batch had come through—was to search for the monthly squadron summary of April 1945. The after-action reports for intruder missions, along with supplementary material, such as photographs and maps, were supposed to be at the back of the respective thirty-day monthly reports. But the mission report for April 11, the one I desperately wished to see, wasn't at the back. The reports didn't begin until the 12th. Ahead of the first attached mission report, there was a small card. On the computer screen it looked to be about the size of an index card. Written on it in a neat hand was this: "549 Night Fighter Sq'n Mission Reports with drawn to complete VII Fighter Command historical files of mission reports." ("Withdrawn" was spelled as two words.)

Why would they have done that, whoever "they" were: lopped off the mission reports for the first eleven days of April and filed them somewhere else?

The reference assistant didn't know.

Every squadron and unit and flying group had its own historical officer—sometimes more than one. Think of it as a series of ever-expanding organizing principles. The 549th was a relatively small military thing. Administratively, the squadron operated under the wing of the much larger military thing, the VII Fighter Command. The VII Fighter Command, in turn, operated, administratively, under the mammoth military thing, the Seventh Air Force.

If my dad's intruder mission on April 11 hadn't been preserved by the unit historian in the monthly squadron files of the 549th, presumably it must have been archived (from what the card seemed to suggest) in the files of the VII Fighter Command.

The problem was, there were so many pages, and so many were extremely hard to read, typed on old government typewriters with worn-out ribbons. Some of the pages looked like third-layer carbon copies. One of the DOD drops the reference assistant had sent was 1,229 pages. Another reel was 1,430 pages.

I couldn't find my dad's report. The reference assistant couldn't find it.

In the meantime, something else was becoming raggedly clear, and in this I was beginning to feel a little less self-righteous and conspiracy-minded: The pilots from various squadrons and fighter groups, who had flown intruder missions to the Bonin Islands ahead of my dad, seemed to be reporting, back at base, the fact of minimal searchlights and antiaircraft fire up there. For instance, the commanding officer of my dad's own squadron, Major Joseph Payne, had flown the first intruder to Chichi Jima. This was on March 29, nine days after the flyers had arrived on Iwo. That report was right where it was supposed to be: attached to the end of the squadron's monthly summary. The CO had strafed and bombed Chichi and gotten back safe. In the mission report, this sentence: "Encountered no A/A fire or searchlights." He must have reported it that way to the intelligence officers when he came back in, and they wrote it up as such. That same night, one of my dad's fellow flyers, indeed a fellow Kentuckian, Captain Larry Garland (you're going to hear a whole lot more about him later on), had also bombed and strafed Chichi and gotten back safe. In his mission report, there was this sentence: "No shipping, no A/A, no S/L." (The "A/A" stood for antiaircraft; the "S/L" for searchlights.)

From a mission report of another squadron on the overnight of April 8 and 9: "Five extremely inaccurate searchlights were encountered at Chichi. There was no flak and no shipping was observed."

Weren't the so-called brainy guys in the briefing tent just putting down what their flyers had informed them, so that the "true gen" could be given to the next crews going up? Weren't they only going on the information they had, what they knew, or thought they knew?

Some months went by. The reference assistant and I had exchanged many emails and had talked six or seven times on the phone. We had sent things back and forth related to our searches. I had turned to other parts of my research. The reference assistant and I kept puzzling over the "with drawn" statement on the index card.

One day, the assistant wrote: "I just carved out time to review the flight records you sent me. I also reviewed what I've already sent you. . . . [I]t sounds like the 549th NFS historian either sent the missing reports to the VII Fighter Command historian or set them aside to complete relevant paperwork to send to the VII Fighter Command historian. That seems to be a likely reason why the April mission reports don't start until April 12, 1945 (in the 549th history). That makes me very curious if the reports ever made it to the VII Fighter Command historian."

The next day—March 4, 2021—my phone rang. The assistant said, "You have to stop whatever you're doing right now and get on your computer and go to frame 543 on reel A7593. I found it."

I was staring at it on my screen as the assistant was staring at it in Montgomery: "549th NIGHT FIGHTER SQUADRON MISSION REPORT NUMBER 4-9 VII Fighter Command Mission #105."

There was my dad's name: "PILOT: Lt. Joseph P. Hendrickson." The line below: "RADAR OBSERVER: Lt. Jack H. Kerr." The line below that: "GUNNER: S/Sgt. Leo E. Vough."

It turns out that the report was in the files of the VII Fighter Command after all. It wasn't in the most logical or chronological place, but it was there. The other reports from the other missions, flown by my dad's fellow flyers of the squadron, in the first eleven days of April, were there, too. The reference assistant had been searching on and off, whenever there was time, through several thousand pages, from four or five digitized film reels, and while he/she never said so, I am convinced that some of the searching had taken place during nonwork hours.

"I'm not going to interpret it for you. I'll leave that part to you," the assistant said.

The next morning, I began to read with a terrible sinking feeling, and at the same time a rising rage. The report, entirely legible, spoke of how the "light tracked the aircraft for a few seconds." It said that the pilot "saw lights in the area of Takinoura Town." It spoke of how the pilot saw a light "at 1945 K [7:45 p.m.] behind him and to port but close to aircraft." It spoke of how "One light tracked again." At the bottom the report said that the "Radar Observer counted six lights pointing straight upward in a horseshoe shape around harbor," and that these lights had "remained on after the crew left island."

Left island?

Tracked for a few seconds?

There's no way my father would have described it to them like that, not from what he told me. And when he told me, he was hardly boasting. He was telling me how scared he was, even if I couldn't hear it, or not hear it enough.

Later that morning I wrote to the assistant: "I know you could never answer this, and you don't even have to reply, but . . . here's my thesis, or at least my question, which *will never be answered:* is it possible the two unit historians—the one for the 549 squadron and the one tasked up above with the much greater authority at the VII FC—were protecting each other for history? They knew these reports were going to go to the higher echelons of the whole 7th Air Force and eventually to Washington and eventually to the national archives. . . . I realize I should never even be posing such things to a reference/archivist at AFHRA whose job is to just help furnish the documents, which you have done a thousand times beyond my imaginings."

The reference assistant didn't reply. Which to me was its own reply.

Let's assume for a moment the worst scenario: My father had come in screaming at them, maybe cursing at them, his superiors suffered it, and the next day (or shortly thereafter) they deliberately wrote up their own pale version of events. And then, at some later point, they decided to up the ante and shuffle the decks a little: See to it that the report itself would get "with drawn" (along with the other reports from the first eleven days of April) and stored at the next level up, in and amid thousands of pieces of paper, so many of which had nothing whatever to do with intruder missions, and many of which were almost impossible to read. Why would they have done this? Well, a plausible answer, not necessarily the gospel answer, is that they did it so that Mission Report #105 might be hard to locate on the ten-million-to-one chance that someone might someday care enough to come looking for it.

If I've got things even a quarter right, then shouldn't I be grateful "they" did this, at my father's expense? Because it allowed me in a circuitous way to feel a fractional equivalent of what he had felt. In that sense, they did me an enormous favor, unwittingly.

But let's assume, for the sake of argument, another scenario entirely: That even though they decided to downplay severely what he had told the officers, my father was flat wrong about the actual time. It hadn't been fifteen or twenty seconds, much less half a minute, before he had managed to get free and redline out to sea. It was only, just as they stated in the after-action report (but not for the truth's sake), a "few seconds." Okay. But wouldn't a few seconds, if they were the right kinds of seconds, which is to say extremely bad seconds, be enough? For the truth of that emotion, let me quote Ernest Hemingway, who once wrote that "It is not the duration of a sensation but its intensity that counts. If it is of enough intensity it lasts forever no matter what the actual time was." But Hemingway was only talking in that instance about trout fishing, as a child, in its cruder and more innocent forms, in that instant of spray and light and force and chaos when the hooked thing has broken the surface of the pool and you, standing on the bank with your buck-fifty hardware-store pole, are trying to horse him out of the water and swing him over your head and into the cool wet ferns somewhere behind you, where he'll flop and thrash until you set him lovingly in the wicker basket roped to your five-year-old waist.

What I now believe is that, for however long the searchlight-trapping lasted, whether three seconds or thirty-three seconds or even much longer than that, it was of enough terrifying intensity to last *The Rita B*'s pilot "forever." For the rest of his stay on Iwo Jima, which was only another five months, my father must have had to summon a fantastic nerve every time he suited up and walked toward his airplane. Jack and Leo E, too.

WHAT IF YOU WERE SEATED in the cockpit of your P-61 and one of the two propellers came slicing through the glass, skinning down the rim of your back, from nearly nape of neck to belt buckle, in the way of a very sharp peeler cutting away the thinnest outer skin of a potato?

Even if your thick flying suit had absorbed the brunt of it, so that your injuries turned out to be almost miraculously minor, might not the experience be so traumatic that afterward you'd go to your superiors and say something to the effect of, "I won't fly again. I don't care what you do to me. Go ahead and court-martial me. I'm not going up."

This happened in the 549th, or a close enough version did. It happened to one of my dad's friends and fellow officers. My dad never mentioned the story, although there's no way he wouldn't have known of it. The squadron was too small, the cadre of pilots in the squadron too small.

The problem was and is the documentation. All the parties who were directly involved are dead. I have enough documentation to convince me, absolutely, that the incident did happen. But the paperwork I've been able to find concerns the accident itself—not its psychological aftermath. There are just too many details which I don't know—before, after, and in the middle. For this reason, I have decided to omit the name of the person to whom it happened, out of regard for his family, whom I got up the courage to ask about the incident, and its aftermath. It's important to say, however, that they didn't ask that I omit the name.

Why am I telling it at all? Because of the humanity in the story.

It happened on Saipan on May 5, 1945. The flyer, who'd been with the 549th from its activation back in Fresno, hadn't gone on with the unit to Iwo Jima on March 20. He and several other officers—pilots and R/O's—had been told to stay behind on Oahu. They were going to bring several additional Widows to Iwo after the first wave of flyers had made its island-hops.

In late April, the pilot had come to Saipan from Eniwetok in the Marshalls. His R/O and gunner were with him. Coming into Saipan, there had been some minor engine trouble. It got fixed. The pilot and his crew had held at Saipan for not quite two weeks. They'd run some routes and patrols. On May 5, they had gotten the orders to go to the front.

On takeoff, the plane—named for the pilot's wife, who was an RN—seized up. The Widow was about forty feet in the air off the end of the runway, her landing gear up. The right engine quit. Because the pilot couldn't stabilize her, she tilted downward and hit the runway. (One of the descriptions I've read is that she "mushed back down.") She skidded along before coming to a stop against a small rise in the runway. Her external wing tanks burst into flame. Her nose wheel collapsed and the fuselage folded inward on itself—which caused the left engine to buckle. The propeller, turning at very high RPMs, cut through the cockpit like a chain saw. If the pilot, who was strapped in, had been leaned back in his seat, his life would have been over. But he was hunched forward, gripping the wheel with all his might. And this two or three inches of leaning-forward panic saved his life.

They all got out safe. Much of the pilot's flying suit was in ribbons down his back side. Seventeen days went by. The pilot was apparently in sick bay for a while. On May 22, he left for Iwo—but he wasn't in the pilot's seat. He hitched a ride on another plane. (It may have been a transport.) On landing, he went to the 549th's CO and said he wouldn't go up again. They didn't put him in the stockade. They didn't file paperwork on him, none that I can find. Rather, they allowed him to remain on the ground and to use his considerable skills as a builder and an artist and designer. Before the war, he had studied architecture for three years. He designed and built the officer's club out of scavenged lumber. He worked on the outdoor theater that USO comedy and singing acts would soon be using to entertain the troops. That theater, with its dressing room, proscenium stage, big draping curtains (where in the world did they get those?), and a large THE FORTY-NINER'S styled across its top, became the envy of almost every other squadron and unit and fighter group on the island. When they'd run the nightly movies, troops from all along the western beaches would turn up at THE FORTY-NINER'S theater.

When did the twenty-seven-year-old get his nerve back and start to fly again? I've never been able to find a mission report with the pilot's name on it. *What I think may have happened is that, until the war was over, he flew CAPs. For most of those nightly patrols, not many reports got saved.*

He survived the war. He got home. He served six years on active duty and twenty-four years in the Air Force Reserve. He made lieutenant colonel. He and his wife raised two daughters. (They'd gotten married, stateside, on September 18, 1944, less than a month before he went overseas to Hawaii with the unit. When I was looking into his life, the date bumped right out at me: It was two days before my parents said their Amarillo goodbye.)

For the next forty years he worked as a builder and site inspector for the U.S. Department of Housing and Urban Development. Most Sundays, he showed up at his local Presbyterian church in South Texas to help usher and pass out the collection baskets. (His wife was the real and devout member of the congregation, but he was there.) He died surrounded by his family on December 12, 2007. He'd almost made ninety-one. He'd been married happily for sixty-three years. He had four grandchildren and three great-grandchildren.

A while ago, I called up and spoke to several members of his family, but most especially to his older daughter, who was my approximate age. I was trying not to let on how nervous I was, but I suspect she saw right through that. She disarmed me with her generosity and openness. "He didn't talk about his feelings. That kind of talk just didn't happen with my dad," she said. "He just didn't go on about it. Well, it was a house of three women. I guess we weren't so interested. I feel kind of horrible about that now. He didn't have another male to talk to about the war, not until I got married in '68. He wouldn't have talked about it so much, anyway, even though my husband was very curious to know."

At length, I asked if she knew anything about the propeller incident. I told her what I knew. She said, yes, she could vaguely remember hearing something about it as a kid. She didn't understand it then and didn't know any details now. She called to her husband in the other room and asked if he knew anything. He said he didn't, other than it was something about a propeller that had missed slicing into his father-in-law by a couple of inches.

I cleared my throat. "Do you know anything about him refusing to fly afterward?"

"I never heard about that. But I can kind of believe it." I asked why. She

said, "Well, wouldn't anybody feel that? You come that close, wouldn't it kind of change your life? At least for a time? See, I don't think my father ever saw himself as a big war hero."

At the end of our talk, she said it again. "He just didn't go on about it."

Formulate the parable like this: An ordinary man (except weren't they all extraordinary?) had to suffer some public shame for losing his flying nerve, at least for a time, so that he could help build the coolest entertainment venue on the island, so that his comrades might get a momentary reprieve from their own deep anxieties, taking in a movie or a showgirl's legs.

Of James Dickey and My Father

Cockpit of The Rita B

ANOTHER PARABLE—about truth and lies. But to tell it I'll need to color a bit outside the lines of Iwo Jima and my dad's squadron. But his airplane is still at the center of the frame. Indeed, her cockpit is at the center of the frame. It's where some of the key truths and lies converge.

Here he is, twenty-six, forever young, in either the spring or summer of 1945—there's no date on the back—half turned, gazing straight at whoever is documenting the moment. Is he going up tonight? I don't know. My siblings and I share a fair number of pictures of our dad in the war, but insofar as I know this is the only one that we possess in which we're able to see him so clearly sitting in his "glass treasure-hole of blue light."

That's one of the many indelible images pouring forth from James Dickey's magnificent and morally fraught stream-of-consciousness free verse poem, "The Firebombing." The airplane isn't named, but to P-61 esthetes it is unmistakably the Widow. The thrilling fact that it was my father's airplane is what first drew me to the poem close to half a century ago, when I was preparing to spend what turned out to be almost an entire—and entirely overwhelming—day with James Dickey for a profile I was writing of him for a newspaper.

Once inside the poem, which is to say the reading experience of it, it was almost as if I could not but be hypnotized by the language itself, no matter what disquieting messages were being signaled to me, no matter what I felt later when I found out how Dickey had deceived me.

The "moon-metal shine of propellers."

The "silver night-sea."

The "nightgrass of mountains billowing softly."

That instant "when the moon sails in between / The tail-booms."

That feeling of the "greatest sense of power in one's life."

That moment when you swing "directly over the heart / The *heart* of the fire."

How one is so "cool and enthralled in the cockpit."

That coolness perhaps aided by "Combat booze by my side in a cratered canteen."

How you can find yourself "Turned blue by the power of beauty."

On and on, image after image.

Near the start of the roughly 280-line mini-epic, this image, this line:

"Snap, a bulb is tricked on in the cockpit."

"Tricked," it turns out, is a laden word. To my reading, it's as if the narrator, the "I" of the poem, the speaker, the persona, the poetic genius behind all this, is letting us know that, *snap,* a bulb has tricked on, almost as if by its own will, in the searchlights and cockpits and moral quandaries of a long-ago Pacific night war.

I remember my own dad using the same words: his "long-ago Pacific night war." Did they all say it that way?

The only trouble, or at least the only trouble for me, is that the poetic genius in question built his masterwork on an autobiographical lie. On that mid-November day in 1976, which in its own way was indelible, James Dickey told me, straight to my teeth, as he apparently told hundreds of people throughout his life, that he was the pilot of his particular P-61. It isn't true. And literary critics would doubtless shrug and say: Who cares? We have the poem.

I care. I remember him telling me how tricky she was to fly. "You had to be right on the stick," he said, miming the act with his hands. Our interview wasn't five minutes old and he was spooling up the lie. We were still in the hall of his handsome lakeside South Carolina ranch-styled home. I had blurted out that my dad, too, had once been an old P-61er, and that even though they were in different squadrons, I was pretty sure that their paths would have crossed, must have in some sense collided, in the spring and early summer of 1944, at Hammer in Fresno.

Their paths did cross at Hammer Field. Which is to say they both were in training there at the same time, not that they necessarily knew each other. (I've never been able to determine that.) Probably they didn't. The P-61 unit which Dickey eventually joined was the 418th NFS, and he ended up with it on Okinawa. Dickey wasn't a famous American poet in Fresno; he was just another guy at a very crowded airfield, getting set to go over—to Europe or the Pacific.

The poetic genius told me a lot of other bilge, too, that day, I would later find out, but I was more than willing to swallow it all then, be snowed. Unwittingly, I put some of the bilge and snow into the story I wrote.

It wasn't until almost twenty-five years later that I discovered that Officer Dickey had never sat in the pilot's glass treasure hole of blue light—not on a mission anyway. (Maybe he sat in there posing for a photograph.) That the creator of this wonderwork—which, if there is any justice, will be read by lovers of language from here to eternity—was actually the R/O of his aircraft. He had washed out of flight school on his first try at soloing as an aviation cadet. That was before Fresno.

James Dickey, the famous American poet who grew into the famous American alcoholic poet, was never shot down in the jungle, as he used to tell his firstborn son. He never fought his way out with a knife. He didn't go on a hundred missions. He went on thirty-eight. Still, that means thirty-eight potential risks to your life, even when some of the missions, or even many of them, might have turned out routine and fairly boring.

In real life, a poetic Southern genius, for whom being the radar guy in the back of the plane just wasn't enough, needed to construct a different myth about himself to compensate for the ignominy of having nearly cracked up a two-seater biplane on his first solo try (after about five minutes aloft), in the fall of 1943 at an Army Air Corps Field in Camden, South Carolina. But it needs to be stressed that although the poet lied repeatedly in real life about having sat in the cockpit of his particular Widow, there were other times, in other poems and novels, when Dickey the artist explored reasonably accurate if disguised versions of the truth, of his soloing trauma, his washing-out trauma.

Not for nothing is the definitive Dickey biography entitled *James Dickey: The World as a Lie*. It's a 750-page astute and almost relentless vivisection. The biographer's name is Henry Hart, and I've come to know and admire him. To read his book, which took eight years of research, is to learn that Dickey was not a prize pro football prospect, as he often claimed; that he didn't fly over Nagasaki hours after the atomic bomb was dropped; that he was never awarded a Purple Heart; that he didn't play guitar for the famous Western swing band the Brazos Valley Boys. Et cetera and et cetera. From an entry by Professor Hart in the *Oxford Research Encyclopedia of Literature*: "Because he washed out of flight training as an Air Corps cadet . . . he told everyone he was a decorated combat pilot who had shot down enemy planes over the Pacific and had been shot down by them. . . . He lied to advertise himself, to make his life seem glamorous, to sell his books, to put down his rivals. . . . He lied because he was an alcoholic, adept at the art of denial, of blurring fact and fiction." Hart, a fine poet himself, once went to a reunion and met some of Dickey's old squadron mates. "They couldn't forgive the lying," Hart told me in an email.

But isn't this what poets do in their poems, are supposed to do: mold and shape reality, like a potter at his wheel, so that we can glimpse greater truths? Ernest Hemingway, who glamorized his own extremely short-lived experience in World War I, used to say that all that fiction amounted to was making up beautiful lies about things you deeply know.

It didn't matter. I couldn't help taking it all personally. For years after I knew the truth, and long after Dickey was dead (he died in January 1997, at almost seventy-four, three years before Hart's biography appeared), I continued to be enthralled by the language in the poem even as I harbored my small, keen, and perhaps illogical resentment against it and him. Maybe it isn't so illogical, though. It wasn't that Dickey had lied to my face—I could take that okay. It was that by doing so he had seemed to dishonor and disrespect my father, to cheapen the risks, however great, however small, he'd taken.

Just lately, though, I have experienced a change of heart about all this. To my surprise, I have arrived at a softer feeling; I'll call it a softer landing. Why? Primarily because of Dickey's own eldest child, Christopher Dickey, who was a fellow journalist and my casual friend for more than forty years, and who died, in July 2020, way too soon, of a heart attack at his home in Paris, at age sixty-eight. We had always meant to sit down and talk about our fathers and about the Black Widow in much greater depth than the several times we did talk about them, mostly in passing, mostly in a kind of nodding code. (We once worked together at *The Washington Post,* and we would have our peremptory talks in the hallways or the lunchroom.) And then Chris Dickey, who was known as a decent and mentoring journalist to a whole generation of foreign correspondents behind him, whose reporting career ended up going in a much different direction than mine, was dead. But he still bequeathed me a few things, especially one obscure piece of writing that I am grateful to say has helped to landing-light the way.

Snap, a bulb is tricking on.

"The Firebombing" is about an old flyer, twenty years after the war, twenty pounds overweight, thinking about purloining a daytime snack from the pantry of his suburban tract house, and somehow, in the same instant, remembering everything there is to remember about what it was like to go up into the midnight dark to do terrible things against unglimpsed human beings with those "300-gallon drop tanks / Filled with napalm and gasoline" suspended tremulously "on thin bomb-shackles" that were hanging "under the undeodorized arms" of your aircraft's wings.

It's all there, jumbled up, the brilliant cockpit myth. He's thinking about the hedge clippers he'll borrow from a neighbor, about the new scoutmaster for the kids, about the hammock in the backyard where he can have his erotic Sunday afternoon dreams after church. And in the same instant he recalls raining napalm fire upon a fast-asleep lush resort town on the southern edge of Japan called Beppu. He can't really see, so he is imagining what is happening down there. How "All leashes of dogs / Break under the first bomb." How "the low tables / Catch fire from the floor mats." How the blasts are "kicking / The small cattle off their feet." My God, he thinks to himself, Beppu in the Ryukyus is "burning with all / American fire." My God, "My hat should crawl on my head / In streetcars, thinking of it, / The fat on my body should pale."

After the bombing is done, "O then I knock it off / And turn for home," which is to say to home base, in Okinawa.

The moral condemnation which has rained down on "The Firebombing" from certain critics through the years seems chiefly to lie in this: Although this semi-overweight ex-pilot in his tract house and banal suburban life may suddenly be sweating about what he once did, he's not sweating enough. The poet Robert Bly, a contemporary of Dickey's (and subsequent mortal enemy), once famously wrote that the poem was "teaching us that our way of dealing with military brutality is right: do it, later talk about it, and take two teaspoonsful of remorse every seventh year."

No matter the narrator's "cold / Grinning sweat," is he simultaneously exulting in the memory? It seems hard not to read some of the poem that way. At a minimum, he is proud to be an American. That is where the poem ends up: "nothing I haven't lived with / For twenty years, still nothing not as / American as I am, and proud of it." These are the final two lines: "Absolution? Sentence? No matter; / The thing itself is in that."

The year before I traveled to South Carolina to talk to James Dickey, he had told journalist Bill Moyers on public television: "You never saw what you did. You never saw the families burned alive in their homes. You never saw the children mutilated. All you saw was this Godlike explosion of flames that you caused."

In real life, as opposed to poetic life, did the fabulist James Dickey, in the closing months and weeks and days of World War II, which, of course, were exactly my own father's time frame of service, ever witness, from his rear bubble as the R/O, anything close to what fictively happens in "The Firebombing"? It's a grainy question, his biographer reports. Safe to say, not to the extent the poem wants you to believe. Safe also to say: James Dickey, in real life, was never the guy up front firing the 20-millimeter cannons, depressing the bomb release on the control wheel.

Dickey published "The Firebombing" in May 1964 in *Poetry* magazine. The next year the poem appeared as the lead work in a new volume of his verse entitled *Buckdancer's Choice.* It was his fourth book of poetry and won the 1966 National Book Award. He was appointed Consultant in Poetry at the Library of Congress. He had gained the first rungs on the fame ladder he had so long craved. More climbing and greater fame were on the way, not least a few years later, in 1970, after the publication of his gothic Southern backwoods novel, *Deliverance,* a mega bestseller and an even larger hit at the box office. (It starred Burt Reynolds and Jon Voight; Dickey himself managed an unforgettable cameo as a cracker North Georgia sheriff.) All of this, and more, would lead in its winding way over the next three decades to a slow alcoholic unraveling. In essence, as the literary quality grew lesser, the boasting and insufferableness grew louder. The great (and now increasingly forgotten) twentieth-century poet Archibald MacLeish once wrote in a poem about Hemingway, whom he had known when they were both practically boys pedaling bicycles together through the Jardin du Luxembourg in Paris in 1924: "Veteran out of the wars before he was twenty: / Famous at twenty-five: thirty a master—" but also saying, in the devastating line immediately above: "And what became of him? Fame became of him." In large measure, that is the James Dickey story, even if it isn't nearly as fixed in our

national cultural consciousness as is the generally understood—
and misunderstood—myth of Hemingway's self-destruction. The
old curse could come in here: Be careful of what you wish for.

As I said, it was in the middle fall of 1976, so roughly twelve years
after he had first published the poem, and had become as close to a
household literary name as a poet can be in America—perhaps not
a name on the level of, say, Norman Mailer or Truman Capote, but
outsized all the same. I didn't know when I sought the interview
that, only days before, Dickey's wife of almost twenty-eight years
had died. Maxine Syerson Dickey had died of alcoholism. When I
found out (I didn't yet know about the alcoholism part), I figured
I'd better call it off. No, no, he had said on the phone, come down
anyway. "It'll be a distraction, and I need distractions right now."

My editors had reluctantly agreed to let me do the piece—I had
been the one angling. Dickey had a new book coming out, so it
would be timely, I argued. As things developed, there was a greater
timeliness than we knew. Jimmy Carter had just been elected president, and the president-elect was in the semi-secret process of
deciding whether to invite his ego-devouring fellow native Geor-
gian to come to Washington to read an original poem at his inauguration, in a kind of imitation of John F. Kennedy's celebrated
invitation to Robert Frost to recite a poem at his bitterly cold inauguration in 1961. Dickey got the invite (the word is he had been
working all the back channels) and called his commissioned work
"The Strength of Fields." It's a pretty good poem—which he ended
up delivering not on the podium at the Capitol but at the Kennedy
Center on the night before the inauguration.

"Two Jimbos from Georgia," Dickey crowed to me about Carter's election. "How do you like it? I mean, when will the stars be
this way again?"

I was ready to talk to him about almost anything, including the
new poetic work (it was titled *The Zodiac,* which turned out to be
a critical and commercial disappointment to him), but I knew the
real reason why I so badly wanted to be there: fathers and Black
Widows. My dad was fifty-eight then; Dickey was fifty-three. As it

turned out, I didn't get much about the war or the Widow into the piece, even though we talked a fair amount about both. The editors wanted other things.

He was so outrageous that day. He was so hilarious, so wickedly cruel. It was as if it was all one big performance for the benefit of one. Everything about him was gargantuan, Brobdingnagian, not least his head, which he kept bringing perilously close to my own. He had all these keys jangling from his pockets. He wore four large watches—two on each wrist—set to different times. He had on khakis, a blue pullover, a belt with the letters C.S.A. on the buckle. He kept sucking air through his teeth, flaring his nostrils, wiping his tongue across his gums, bugging his eyes, snorting whenever he got off a good line, which was about every two minutes.

Although not at first. "Well, welcome to our home," he had said with a kind of detached weariness when he had opened the door. "We're here alone now."

I remember how he went over to a table in the hall and took a small model of a Black Widow off its clear plastic pedestal. He wiped the dust off the fuselage. "If you write any of this up," he said, "don't make me look like one of these guys still living it all thirty years later."

Soon enough, Dickey became Dickey. Frank Sinatra got into the conversation. Sinatra, with his "pleasant little supper-club voice." Allen Ginsberg? "If you can really write poetry, you don't need to dress up funny." Folksinger Bobbie Gentry? "The debasement of all folk styles that have ever existed in the world come to a culmination in Bobbie Gentry. What the appeal of that little rat-faced woman is, I cannot imagine."

He drove us in some huge old car to a restaurant. There were noontime diners all around us. He started talking very loudly about poets and suicide. "You're *supposed* to be miserable if you're an artist." It felt like the whole room was staring at us. "People are always so disappointed when you have the money and means to do yourself in, and don't. One *wants* to be DOOMED. *America* wants one to be DOOMED."

On the way back to his home, we passed a roadside massage parlor with a neon sign out front. I had looked over. "Don't you go in there, boy, after you leave," he said. "You'll get the clap in that place." But the way he said it, I had the feeling he would have gladly accompanied me, had I gone.

Later that day he told me how Maxine had died of massive internal hemorrhages, had bled out right in his arms. He told me about the alcoholism. "The senseless grief. I mean, it's like trying to walk around dragging a Caterpillar tractor. You can't move. But I insist on doing my grieving privately." I asked if he believed in an afterlife. "No," he said. "I saw Maxine lying there, and it could have just been a dead dog in the road." It came out with a small savagery.

My God, I remember thinking to myself as I kept scribbling notes in my skinny reporter's notebook: *What would it be like to be this guy's son?*

The piece was published on December 4, 1976. Three and a half weeks later—which was two months after Maxine Dickey's death—Dickey married a student from one of his poetry seminars at the University of South Carolina. She was less than half his age. She was younger than Chris Dickey, who found out about it in *People* magazine. (It would end up a Vesuvius of a marriage.) The next year I joined *The Washington Post,* and Chris and I met. "Uh, you spent time with my father, I see," he said one day in the men's room, letting it go.

The thing itself, as he puts it in "The Firebombing."

I am staring at another of my dad's old mission reports from Iwo Jima. In fact, it was his second intruder mission, only eight days after the first. It was the overnight of April 19–20. This time he and his crew were going to another fortified outpost in the Bonin Islands called Haha Jima. It was smaller than Chichi, and about twenty-seven miles south of it, but, like Chichi, it had supported clots of Japanese life and culture for decades, a verdant little prewar place with coral-blue coves and beautiful beaches and mountains and forests full of banyan trees and rare species of birds. (Today, Hahajima—the preferred spelling, meaning "Mother Island" in Japanese—has a population of about 500. I'd give a lot to see it—or Chichi Jima—before I die and know I won't. I'd give far more to be able to see Iwo itself, any remains of South Field itself.)

There was a quarter moon out. Liftoff was at 10:55 p.m. on the 19th. (It was a Thursday.) There was sufficient fuel on board—325 gallons. On the way north, my dad cruised her at 8,000 feet. The enemy dot came in sight on Jack Kerr's scopes. They searched for shipping vessels in the coves and ports. They couldn't find any. What I think happened is that my dad swung out to either the east or the west of the skinny landmass. He was up at 11,500 feet, came down to 4,500, climbed back up to 7,500, made an arc, passed over a little village on a cove at the northern end. It was called Kitamura Town. He dropped two 500-pound bombs at 11:35 p.m. It seems that he and his gunner never fired a round.

They turned for home, but I am thinking not right away because of the time frames in the report. He probably headed out to sea, and maybe he swallowed his spit and arced back across the island one more time to look for vessels. The bombs were gone but they had their fierce fifties and twenties. Nothing again. So I conclude they headed back south through the overcast, touching down on South Field at forty-five minutes after midnight.

In the six-line, sixty-three-word mission report, written by an assistant intelligence officer in the 549th, there are four words that stab me: "saw flashes through overcast." The report writer, a first lieutenant, was referring to the bomb drop on Kitamura Town at 11:35 p.m. I have seen that same description in other mission reports, but it still sounds to my ear exactly like something my father would have reported and which was written down some hours later: He was low enough to see the flashes, but not low enough to see what or whom the flashes hit.

Take a look.

I have tried hard to find out who might have been down there that midnight in Kitamura Town. I've consulted scholars of the war, two of whom are Americans based in Japan. The consensus is that there was almost certainly not a single female civilian down there. The year before, the small civilian population of Haha had been forcibly evacuated to the Japanese home islands. Apparently some teenage boys, perhaps no more than two dozen, were ordered to stay behind. They were put to work in the service of the Japanese defense garrisons. I have found recent photographs of old, rusted-out remnants of the antiaircraft arsenals and the big search-

CONFIDENTIAL

1 - Hist 6
2 - Ken S

FROM: COMITFITERRON FIVE FOUR NINE   20 April 1945
TO : COMFITERCOM SEVEN
ATTN: A-2

549TH NIGHT FIGHTER SQUADRON MISSION REPORT NUMBER 4-32

1. A. One (1) P-61-B
    B. None

2. A. None
    B. None

3. Intruder (Night) (Haha Jima - Kitamura Town)

4. PILOT: Lt. J. P. Hendrickson (Laughing Boy Snooper 4)
    RADAR OBSERVER: Lt. J. H. Kerr
    GUNNER: Sgt. L. E. Vough

          TAKE-OFF: 2255K   LAND: 0045K

    From Base to Haha Jima at 8,000 feet and searched area for shipping.
Results negative so made bomb run at Kitamura Town on Haha Jima. Started
run on 260 degree heading from 11,500 feet and continued to 4,500 feet.
Dropped bombs at 7,500 feet at 2335 K and saw flashes through overcast.
No further activity during additional search so proceeded to base and
pancaked.

5. WEATHER: Overcast, tops at 9,500, bases unknown.

    COMMUNICATIONS: Good.

6. Unknown.

7. No Ammo; 2 X 500 lb. GP Bombs; 325 gallons of gasoline.

8. No enemy activity noted except very definite radar interference in
    vicinity of Haha Jima.

                              ARCHIE BEATTIE,
                              1st Lt., Air Corps,
                              Asst. Intelligence Officer.

lights and some old junked military vehicles. I've also found photographs of the ruins of an old elementary school that was once in
the heart of Kitamura. The blog posting is entitled, "The Long Lost
Kitamura Village." You can see the entrance pillars and the remains
of a staircase. There is an overhang of banyan trees. It looks like a
tropical rainforest. It feels peaceful.

Did my father's two 500-pounders end up "kicking" any "small
cattle off their feet / In a red costly blast / Flinging jelly over the

walls" that night? Well, firstly these weren't napalm bombs, at least there's nothing in the mission report indicating that. But bombs are bombs. They do what they are meant to do. Did "low tables," left behind in thatched huts, where extended families had once sat on their haunches eating from their rice bowls, "Catch fire from the floor mats" and "Blaze up in gas around their heads / Like a dream"? That is from "The Firebombing."

Flashes through overcast.

Could one of the teenagers who'd been ordered to stay behind have been asleep on a pallet in his parental home? I would not rule out the possibility.

While I'm at it, did some left-behind books and pencil cases from the Kitamura elementary school get blown to smithereens? What I do know, and am so grateful for, is that *The Rita B* and her crew didn't get blown to smithereens from an antiaircraft gun scoring a direct hit. What I also know is that to hold this one-page document in my sometimes trembling hand feels . . . *enough.* It needn't be anything larger than it is, which is just some old yellowed piece of government paper that survived the war and came into my possession three-quarters of a century after it got typed out: certifiable proof, as if I needed any, that my twenty-six-year-old hard dad had steered himself and two companions safely through the dark of an ocean so far from home, so long ago. I think the reason why I am showing it here is because it's *not* the kind of epic after-action report that James Dickey might have wished to carry around in his back pocket. For me, though, it's enough, more than enough. My father went to the war, and he did some brave things, and he would keep on doing some brave things. He wasn't going to come back to the States and turn into an alcoholic or a serial fabricator or a big-time celebrity or someone capable of writing a poem for the ages, although he'd carry back other things. Let it be.

And so Chris Dickey, and the converse lessons he taught, or at least reminded me of.

In 1998 (two years before *James Dickey: The World as a Lie* appeared), James Dickey's eldest child published a father-son memoir entitled *Summer of Deliverance.* I didn't read it at the time, although I did follow its reception. Probably I was envious that he had been able to get it done. The book was widely and favorably reviewed, but it was as if many of the reviewers didn't truly get it—as I now can say with conviction, since I have read it with great admiration. It is a book about love and reconciliation and a coming back together, about acceptance in spite of all. Too many reviewers seemed to want to quote from the first page, in which the author says: "For most of 20 years I did not see him, couldn't talk to him, could not bear to be around him. I believed—I *knew*—that he had killed my mother. He belittled and betrayed her, humiliated her and forgot about her. . . . My father was a great poet, a famous novelist, and a powerful intellect, and a son of a bitch I hated." And it's as if the rest of the book is saying: Okay, all that is true. But he is mine. And finally, I love him.

A handful of years ago, Chris and I rekindled our friendship. He was in Paris, I was in Philadelphia. I told him I was thinking of trying to write a book about my father and his time in the war—at long last. We traded some pieces of writing. I invited him to the university where I teach. I asked if we could talk, and not least about the awkward business of having aggrandized yourself, in real life, into the cockpit of a P-61. "Ah, the Black Widow," he said.

In our exchange of renewing emails, Chris had sent me a small essay he had written a couple of years after the publication of *Summer of Deliverance.* He asked if I would read it. Of course, I said. The essay is probably not 1,500 words. He titled it "The Poet's Family Album." It's about finding the key, among so many of his father's keys, to the closet between the kitchen and the laundry in the lake house in South Carolina. It's the week after his father has died. Chris goes in and rummages around. On a high shelf is his father's baby book—except that the book, kept so carefully by James Dickey's mom, hadn't stopped at the end of babyhood. It had kept right on going, documenting in photographs and news clippings a boy's all-American life through elementary school and high school and into his young adulthood. Football player, captain of the high school track team, young cadet on his way to the war.

Chris took the book down and started to leaf through it. The heavy black construction paper was crumbling. An overwhelming feeling of sorrow came over him, not that his father had just died, not because his father had become a man "destroyed by drink and gasping for breath at the end of his 74th year." But because his father had seemed to spend his whole adult life trying to live up to the effortless and golden child he once had been in that crumbling album. Chris closed the book. He took it home and put it in a box under his desk. "I couldn't bring myself to look at those friable pages," he says. "No key was needed, but I didn't have the heart."

Several years went by. One day he opened the box and started looking at the album again—and suddenly it was as if "that boy who haunted James Dickey, and who haunted me, was no longer a threat, and no longer a stranger." It was all gone. What was left was love.

Recently, I read the essay again, and this time there was a line in it that seemed to be vectoring me down all the right runways of anything I might be seeking to do: "I hadn't forgotten anything, but I'd forgiven everything," Chris so beautifully wrote.*

---

* I have lately come to know and admire Chris's little sister, Bronwen Dickey. She is a respected journalist and author and university teacher and the only child of Dickey's second marriage. She is in her early forties, so a whole generation younger than her late half-brother. I never knew her while Chris was alive. I have found her to be sensitive and kind—and someone who has spent a lifetime trying to get out from under the shadow of the words "James Dickey," even as she insists on honoring those words, evidenced not least, perhaps, by the profession she has chosen. Like Chris, Bronwen has attempted to direct me toward another kind of Dickey light, and she has largely done it by the power of *in*direction. Yes, the ego and boorishness and ceaseless fabrications and even the objective misery of the second marriage, which is very hard for her to acknowledge. But Bronwen also wants to bear witness to the beauty of an alcoholic and aging father struggling to be a father to his baby girl when she was growing up in her volcanic South Carolina home. That's the Dickey the world doesn't want to know about, she insists. "Whatever will make your life bigger—that's what he, and my mother, too, as a pair, both of them, were trying to convey to me," she told me. She and I have shared long emails in the last few years. In one of our first exchanges, Bronwen said: "[He was] the only person in my life who would spend hours talking about books or science or travel or history with me—the man who made up fairy-tales for me when I couldn't sleep, who helped me memorize Hector's death scene from *The Iliad* for a fifth-grade declamation assignment (you can imagine how well that went over in my SC public school!)." They'd spend whole nights or afternoons with a globe and an atlas, just the two of them, time-traveling the world, buccaneers of their own private seas. It isn't a mystery she followed her father into words.

Nine days after my dad went on Night Fighter Squadron Mission Number 4-32 on Iwo Jima, I, my mom and brother Marty and my maternal grandparents celebrated my first birthday in the backyard of 8 Mechanic Street in Xenia. I have a picture of that event, me propped in a high chair, a lone candle stuck up in the middle of a cake on the table in front of us, the shrubs and the trees of the little Ohio farm town in bloom, my young mom looking so beautiful with her legs crossed and in her short-sleeved dress and white bib collar. I'm all full of baby fat. The one missing, the one I barely know—which is something I almost feel I could say right now, as I hit eighty and he so long gone—is 7,000 miles away, wanting only to get the hell out of there.

FEINTS AND SHADOWS.

That backyard birthday party, April 29, 1945, the three of us in the Xenia sun. Marty, in his big-boy chair, helped out a bit by that cushion beneath him. He's two years and four months and must be talking a blue streak. His whole life, my older brother was a talker. Something about that fixed set to his mouth is so instantly recognizable: the child already serving as the father to the man. In his roustabout life, Marty rarely ever had three dimes to rub together. We were so close in age, and radically different. We both entered religious life straight out of eighth grade, Marty first, me following two years later. I spoke of this in passing. Although there were many factors and reasons to go away from home at such a young age, I see now, as I said toward the start, that we were subconsciously trying in our separate ways to get away from our dad, whom we loved deeply and were scared of unqualifiedly.

Sometimes, the beveled mirror of memory is hard to stare into. He could come home from a trip and put down his bags and get a report from our mom that we had been bad. Sometimes he'd still be in his airline uniform. He'd jerk us upstairs by the shirt collar to the many-windowed sunroom at the back of the house at 230 South Harrison Avenue in Kankakee. He'd order us to take down our trousers and jockey underpants while the belt came off. He'd have us lie over the bed, facedown. It was the terror of waiting. Our crying and begging would begin before the whipping started. I remember trying to shield the back of my legs with my hands, promising I'd never sass our mom again. The attempted shielding only made his anger more lathered. In thirty minutes or so, the awful pain would subside. Marty and I would sniffle our way to sleep in the twin beds in that sunroom.

My mother never interfered, not in those years, in the late forties and early fifties.

Once, I vividly recall, a neighbor interfered. His name was Al Baron. He lived behind us, directly across the alley, on Chicago Avenue. Marty and I used to play with his sons. He must have heard the screams one too many times. It had to have taken considerable strength to come over and quietly confront my father. They were friends. The whippings subsided for a good while after that. Many years later, my mom and I talked of this. I didn't have to remind her that it happened. I asked her why she never tried to stop it. Her answer didn't satisfy.

All these decades later, I can never glimpse a belt out of its belt loops without shivering. And yet I have a deeper understanding, even a forgiveness, about that belt. Or I think I do.

But Marty. I almost never knew a greater reader of books. Paradise for Marty would have been a ten-dollar-a-week room over a good public library. In his last couple of decades, when he was living in subsidized government housing in the Tampa–St. Pete area, he would take a bus (vets and seniors could ride for free) to one of the largest municipal libraries in the area and spend most of the day there—chatting up the staff and patrons, playing online chess with people in Romania, reading five or six newspapers and magazines off the periodical racks: a blissful, impecunious man with a natural gift for making friends. And then, sooner or later, trying to use those friends for something or other, usually involving money.

He did some bad things in his life, and I don't feel like going into them. I'd rather remember the time he got off the school bus (we'd left Kankakee by then and moved up closer to Chicago) and fought the town bully in a culvert right on the side of the road. The bully had been bullying me. I was terrified of fighting. The bully, who was an eighth grader, used to make me cry. Marty followed the bully off the bus and threw down his books and got the kid in a headlock as they rolled into the culvert. Marty won easily. The bully never bothered me again.

When Marty was in the Coast Guard, he did a hitch as an MP at the foot of Manhattan. He used to tell me about the drunken, spoiling-for-a-fight Friday night sailors he was all but too happy to nightstick and hammerlock into the brig. I don't think he was boasting.

Growing up, I had always lived in his shadow—he was six or seven pounds heavier and two steps quicker and far more gifted in any kind of game involving a ball. But then, almost in the way that a sandbar can shift in the night, I began to surpass him. I did better in school as he did worse. I found sustained employment as Marty drifted from lousy job to lousy job. And his reaction when the tables seemed fully turned? He was so damn proud. I cannot remember him being resentful, not once. "This is my brother, Paul," he'd say in my presence almost to a perfect stranger. "I'm sure you know his books." That drove me crazy.

Did Marty's toughness and hard life descend from my father's anger? I wouldn't want to draw a straight line between the two, but I will say this much: Marty bore the brunt of things far more than I ever did. I got buffered. Later on, in our early adulthood, Marty officially took on the role of black sheep in our family. By then, my baby brother and sister were in the picture, and, as I have said, my parents were trying to set things anew. Here's something funny, though: No matter that my parents could never seem to straighten out their firstborn, to use their words, my father and Marty, especially in the last two or three decades of my dad's life, formed an odd kinship. My father had cleaned up so many of Marty's messes over money, which is to say other people's money (literally saving him from the hoosegow a time or two). And yet, as enraged as he could be over what he had to fix and shell out, he and Marty could still sit down on a weekend and drink Cutty Sark or a six-pack together and fairly laugh their asses off. Marty always knew how to have a good time, far better than I did. Marty had more of the wild Kentucky gene in him.

I said there was something almost eerily recognizable in the set to my brother's mouth, and if I look across the table, at my mom, who must go to sleep every night having prayed on her knees she won't become a widow at twenty-two, the feeling almost doubles over on itself. The namesake P-61 of Rita Bernardine is deep in the Pacific, and she is here, with her babies and her parents, at 8 Mechanic Street, catty-cornered across the alley from St. Brigid's, where she and The Rita B's pilot got married only three years before. So much change, so many thousands of miles crisscrossed. My mom is our one constant. I haven't a shred of doubt about how much they loved each other. And still, it all went wrong. Exactly when is impossible to say. They were woefully mismatched. By the middle of their sixty-one-year marriage it seemed a matter of twin titanic wills, and all the problems flowing outward. And yet there were always the reprieves, sometimes long reprieves, not to say the deep family loyalty, in spite of everything. And as I have said, when my mom and dad were good as parents, there seemed no parents better. On earth.

It's not the set of her mouth (although that, too, is recognizable), it's what I remember in her eyes. Probably you are seeing only the slender and beautiful and loving young mom squinting into the springtime sun. I see all that, but also the will and the control. I can spot them in that nail-painted right hand, the fingers perfectly splayed on the oilcloth-covered tabletop.

The late poet/critic Mark Strand has an essay entitled "On the Sadness of a Family Photograph." He's looking at a picture of his mom and his sister and himself. "I have stared and stared at this photograph," he writes, "and each time I have felt a deep and inexplicable rush of sadness." He tries to figure why. "Is it that the three of us are momentarily bound by the way the light distributes itself in identical ways over each of our faces, binding us together, proclaiming our unity for a moment?" He can't settle on a reason, although perhaps the sadness might have most to do with this realization: "Like childhood itself, it is innocent of the future." He means the moment of the photograph. It can't know all that's to come. It's just there, stopped in sepia.

The Short Unhappy Life of *The Merry Widow*

My dad, aside his plane, second from left, first row, with team members of Flight C, which he heads. My godfather, Jack Kerr, is standing behind him. Leo E's over on the far right in the second row.

ONCE AGAIN, the body language. Jack Kerr is still poker-faced and tight, but at least half of the others, including my dad, seem almost happy-go-lucky. It can't be true.

The paint-chipped tail of that plane behind *The Rita B* (it's visible just beyond Leo E's shoulder, maybe thirty feet away): Is it *The Merry Widow*? It can't be said. But this much can: Her regular pilot and crew were on my dad's flight team. It seems reasonable that the four P-61s assigned to "C" would be lined up next to one another on the flight line, just as the planes of the other flight groups in the squadron would be parked alongside one another. And why am I even wondering about this in the first place? Well, for one reason because my dad, and not her regular pilot, was in the cockpit of *The Merry Widow* on the night when she cracked up for the first time. The date was May 23, 1945, which was two months and three days after he'd arrived on Iwo Jima. The plane's second crack-up, which would take three lives, all of whom were new to the squadron, and which would splinter her into a thousand pieces, came not quite two months after, shortly before dawn on July 17. If ever there was a misnamed airplane in my dad's squadron, *The Merry Widow* seems it. This is her abbreviated story, but, of course, it's not really about the aircraft at all.

In May 1945, the personnel strength of the 549th NFS was roughly 56 officers and 245 enlisted men. The squadron was down an airplane and waiting for a replacement to get up to full strength of sixteen P-61s. Since January, the squadron had been organized into four flights: A Flight, B Flight, C Flight, and D Flight. Each flight had at least four crews. My dad was still in charge of Flight C. During May, the 549th flew 199 missions for a total of 328 hours and 35 minutes. To quote from the monthly squadron report, the "total combat or tactical hours flown as of 31 May 1945 is one thousand one hundred nineteen hours and ten minutes (1,119:10)." My dad was making his contribution to that number.

One Widow (not my dad's) got equipped to carry rockets that month.

A crash ambulance got assigned to the flight line that month, with the flight surgeon standing by. Eight Quonset huts were assembled in the living quarters, both on the officer side and the enlisted side. They served as mess halls and day rooms for writing letters. In one of the Quonsets, there was even a sandwich and coffee bar. Comforts of home.

Sick call was twice a day—at eight in the morning and right after lunch. Again, from the monthly report: "Eight (8) men were hospitalized for the following conditions: three (cases) dermatophytosis, one (1) case upper respiratory (infection), one (1) case sacro-iliitis, one (1) case anxiety neurosis, one (1) case temperature undetermined origin, and one (1) case ascending lymphangitis."

On the last day of the month, some enemy aircraft passed over the island. Some of the Widows in the 549th got scrambled to intercept. To quote from the squadron report: They "were unable to close." My dad was not in this chase.

Five flyers got promotions in May. From the squadron report: "Two (2) officers, First Lieutenant William R. Charlesworth, and First Lieutenant Joseph P. Hendrickson, were promoted to Captain." Captain is the nineteenth rank in the U.S. Air Force, right above first lieutenant, right below major. In a brief ceremony on May 22, in the middle of the living quarters, the CO of the squadron, Major Joe Payne, pinned the two silver bars on my dad.

And the next night, coming back in quickly souring weather from several hours of patrol, he damaged *The Merry Widow,* not irreversibly but serious enough to send her to the repair sheds for a couple weeks. Like his midnight taxiing accident in a P-70A back at Dunnellon Army Air Field in Florida a year and a half before, the incident must have been mortifying to my father, the more so since it had happened a little more than twenty-four hours after his promotion, the more so since he was such a highly regarded flyer and a flight leader in the squadron. The accident got written up and put in his official record. I never knew anything about it until I started the research for this book. And I never knew anything about the larger, darker history of *The Merry Widow.*

Her serial number was 42-39503, and like all the Widows in the squadron, the last six digits were painted in large white numerals on both her tails. She had come off the production line at Northrop in Hawthorne, California, on the same day—October 12, 1944— that the 549th had boarded a troop transport at Fort Lawton on Puget Sound for Oahu. She was delivered first to Sacramento and then down to Long Beach and then up to Oakland, where she was disassembled for transport to Hawaii. She left the States on December 16 and was formally accepted by the 549th on January 28 in the new year. She got assigned to Lieutenant Blois Merriman, who served under my dad. *The Merry Widow,* with Merriman at the controls, was among the sixteen P-61s which left Hawaii for the war on February 15 in convoy in tight formation, and she was also one of the same sixteen Widows which left Saipan for Iwo on the morning of March 20. Her name probably got painted on at Kipapa Airfield in Hawaii.

Four days after she was on Iwo, a naval cameraman recorded *The Merry Widow* in a one-minute-and-thirty-five-second film sequence. Why her? Maybe because she was just there, at the head of the line, closest to the film crew when they got out of their jeep. So far as I know, this is the only sixteen-millimeter film footage in existence that has anything to do with my father's squadron. Objectively, it's just a scrap of out-of-focus film, in primitive Technicolor. I've probably watched it two dozen times.

You can find the film clip on YouTube. There is no sound. The sequence starts with a wide-angle pan. There are seven or eight other P-61s lined up on the flight line, but you can't make out their names—not *Midnight Madonna* or *Little Joe* or *Sleepy Time Gal* or *Trigger Happy* or *Miss Jeanette* or *Blind Date* or *Old Black Magic* or *Swiftie* or *Hoof Hearted* or *Hop 'N Ditty* or, not least, *The Rita B.* No, *The Merry Widow* is the solo star of this minute-and-a-half show.

Several maintenance guys are walking on the tarmac, which is yellow and shimmery and dusty looking. The sky is glaringly blue. In the near distance, you can sense the ocean. The camera comes closer on *The Merry Widow.* The hatch on her greenhouse is propped open. The cones on her propellers are royal blue. A maintenance guy is standing on her wing. Now he's kneeling atop her fuselage, working with what looks like a screwdriver. He's fixing or tightening something on the rotating turret with the .50-caliber machine guns. He knows he's being filmed, so he turns and mugs. He's done. He gathers his oil can and rags and small bag of tools. He climbs down. He skinnies through the gunner's bubble and then the pilot's cockpit and gets back down on the ground via the drop-down ladder behind the nose wheel.

The camera goes wide again. A jeep rolls through the "set." The camera hangs for a few seconds on another plane. You can see the white script on her nose, but the footage is too blurred to read the name. I've convinced myself she's *The Rita B.*

———

Something I wondered about from the start: Why was my dad not in his *own* night fighter, but in Lieutenant Merriman's, on the socked-in night of the accident? I don't know the answer, but I'd guess *The Rita B* was undergoing maintenance on May 23. Since he was scheduled to go up that night, my dad took over one of the other planes in his flight, *The Merry Widow.*

It happened at 11 p.m. as he was trying to get back down. Once again, those three coded words in our family history.

On the first page of the five-page accident report, the word SECRET is stamped at the top. Next to that: "Army Air Forces. Report of a Major Accident."

The staff weather officer was tracking the weather not from South Field but from up toward the middle of the island, at Central Field. Fog and low clouds had come in at the north end of the runway at South Field, while Central Field remained clear. The weather guy let ground control at South know that conditions were safe to land, except they weren't. In trying to understand what it might have felt like, I searched around and came across this description written by the squadron's historical officer, not relating to that night, but to general operating procedures in such circumstances: "During extremely poor conditions the Ground Control Approach was supplemented with a radio jeep placed at the approach of the runway. As the landing plane passed over the jeep a flying officer in the radio jeep would tell the pilot to cut his throttles and land straight ahead. . . . Many landings were made with ceilings of from twenty five (25) to fifty (50) feet and visibility of one fourth (1/4) miles or less."

I don't know if there was a guy in a jeep with a radio at the end of the runway trying to help my dad get down. But all of it sounds so primitive, no matter that this was such a highly sophisticated airplane. (Was the guy standing on the jeep's hood, barking into the darkness on an intercom? I can't help picturing it like this.) And a ceiling of twenty-five feet? You might as well have been flying blindfolded.

I don't know what the ceiling was that night. From the accident report, I know that he circled for the approach. He couldn't see the field. He must have been searching for "the rabbits," which is what pilots call the sequenced flashing lights at the end of the runway. He pulled off and circled again and then approached from the other end. He was downwind and still couldn't see either the field or the landing lights. He might not have had enough fuel on board to keep circling. He decided to try to feather her in by feel. But there was too much turbulence. The ground smacked up to meet him. He hit with such force that he bent the left tail boom and broke both landing gear door rods and did some other damage before he skidded to a stop. Neither he nor his crew were injured, possibly because each was strapped in and braced for the collision. But I wonder if each of their jaws weren't aching badly for the next couple of days. Not to say their rear ends.

The weather officer made a statement for the file, in which he seemed to be assigning himself at least some of the blame: "Observations recorded at Central Field do not give true picture of conditions which existed at South Field. Low Stratus and light fog formations took place at north end of South Field before conditions became apparent at Central Field. This stratus and fog formation reduced visibility to such an extent that runway could not be seen on final approach, necessitating down-wind approach."

By daylight *The Merry Widow* got towed to the 490th Engineering Squadron on another part of the island. I'm not sure of the date when she was able to fly again. (The squadrons badly needed their planes, so there would have been no dilly-dallying.) I know only what happened to her—and to the three airmen who were inside her—seven weeks after her first accident. The story requires a jump-ahead in time.

They were so green. They were so young. Their names were Joseph T. Lamont and William V. Dexter and Leo B. Wolters. Joe Lamont, who was twenty, with his round, baby face, was an only child. He was a native of Providence, Rhode Island. He'd left Saint Raphael Academy in Pawtucket in April 1943, two months before his graduation. His mother had begged him to finish high school, but he had turned eighteen and said he was enlisting in the Army Air Forces. He wanted to serve his country, get in the war before it was over. He somehow got on a super-sped-up track for flight school. In thirteen months, he had his wings and his commission as a second lieutenant. His mom had pinned his wings on.

They hadn't sent him overseas until December 1944. In March 1945, he got attached to the 549th, but he didn't show up on Iwo until June. Compared to my father, he had so few hours in the air, never mind combat hours.

It was the same for the other two in the crew. The gunner, Leo Wolters, a corporal, was two years older than his officer pilot—that was a rarity. He'd arrived on Iwo on May 28. He was from Atchison County, Kansas. He's lying now in Fort Scott National Cemetery in Kansas.

I can't say for sure, but I have a strong feeling that Joe Lamont is the figure in the first row, second from the right, two over from my dad, in the picture at the top of this chapter. I think he'd been newly assigned to Flight C. So, of course, my father knew him, if not well.

The Merry Widow's regular pilot and crew were not operating her on the night of her second crash, and the explanation remains unclear. What's known from the documents is that Joe Lamont, trying to bring her in, got the okay to land at South Field. But then just as he was coming down, and just as the light was coming up, at 5:10 a.m., ground control radioed for him to abort. There were at least two P-51 Mustangs holding at the bottom of the runway, set to take off, with no communication equipment on board. The inexperienced twenty-year-old apparently yanked up too hard on his wheel—which caused his plane to stall out. She fell off to the left, losing altitude quickly. But he was able to get the ship out over the ocean, where she made a full circle. According to an eyewitness, who was standing guard duty and whose statement got put into the official record: The aircraft "was about 250 feet above the water and about one half mile out from [Mount] Suribachi, heading due North. Suddenly both engines seemed to quit and the plane pulled up slightly and then made a slow turn to the left. . . . When the plane had almost made a complete circle, it headed into the water in a direct dive, going beneath the surface."

Why did both engines seem to quit, after he had appeared to rescue her from the stall and gotten her out over the water? That part isn't clear.

From another line in the accident report: The plane "fell off to the left, completing one circle before striking the water." That word, *striking*.

From another line: "Pilot did not acknowledge last call."

There was a terrific explosion. Some debris later came to the surface. Rescue units could find no traces of the airmen, save bits of their clothing.

The day before, on the 16th, Joe Lamont had written home. Everything seemed to be shaping up just fine, the pilot told his folks.

It seems safe to say that there was no connection, mechanically speaking, between Lieutenant Lamont's fatal crash in *The Merry Widow* and the fact that my dad had had his own smaller crash in her two months before. What happened on July 17 seems clearly to have been a case of panicked pilot error—at least in terms of the initial stalling out. Still, I can't help wondering if my dad, once he'd heard, thought about a connection, and whether it unnerved him a little, even made him feel guilty in some vague, unarticulated way. Probably, I'm all wrong. The lifelong fatalist probably didn't let himself think about the coincidence, not consciously. He had cracked up in *The Merry Widow* and made his lucky escape. Joe Lamont had not.

I've had some good phone talks with the great-nephew of Joe Lamont, who, along with his crew, was posthumously awarded the Bronze Service Star and other medals. The great-nephew's name is Tim Lamont. Some years ago, through the Freedom of Information Act, he acquired much material related to the forebear whom he never knew. He worked hard to contact people in the government. He started a family blog partly devoted to Joe Lamont. The official accident report, along with several after-reports, are extremely hard to read. "I remember my Aunt Mary and I poring over them at her living room table sometimes trying to decipher a single letter," Tim wrote in an email. I asked him why he had given over so much devotion to trying to piece together what had happened to his great-uncle, aware I was asking a rhetorical question.

"Because he was this unknown entity," he said. "He'd never done anything with his life, except in another sense, he'd already done everything with his life. I wanted to honor that. He'll forever be twenty years old and unknown, just this white Catholic kid from the greater Providence area who couldn't even wait another two months to earn his high school diploma."

On the day of my dad's accident in the grievously misnamed *The Merry Widow,* the Third Reich was officially dissolved. Heinrich Himmler, mastermind of the gas chambers and concentration camps, swallowed a suicide pill. Albert Speer, minister of armaments, was found at the castle where he was cowering. "So now the end has come," he said. "That's good. It was all only kind of an opera anyway." Sixteen days earlier—on May 7, in a signing ceremony at 2:41 a.m. at Supreme Headquarters Allied Expeditionary Force, at Reims, in northeastern France—Germany had surrendered unconditionally. Eight days before that, on April 30, Hitler shot himself in the head in his bunker. In the Pacific war, on May 23, 1945, two B-29 raids of about 500 planes dropped about 6,000 bombs on Tokyo. Over half the city, something like fifty square miles, was now in ruin.

The Last Living Airman of the 549th

Lieutenant Ray Rudkin, in the middle, with his gunner on the left, his R/O on the right.

WHAT WERE THE ACTUARIAL CHANCES that even one old flyer from my dad's squadron was still alive? He'd have to be somewhere up near 100. Even if the gold got struck, he'd probably be too feeble to speak in anything more than hazy generalities—right?

Sacramento, California. June 2021. A Wisconsin farm boy got up at six this morning. Hauling yourself out of bed too much after six is just sloth. "'Course I go to bed at eight-thirty," he says. "If I'm awake before six, I'll just lie there and think about things." Often, he thinks about Anna Belle, love of his life. They had sixty-three years together. There were some heartache and family sorrows in it, naturally. She's been gone for the last fourteen.

It's 106 degrees outside, not even noon yet, but the last living airman of the 549th Night Fighter Squadron is wearing a cardigan sweater over a thick green polo shirt. There's a large cotton patch on the left side of his scalp—he recently got treated for melanoma. His hickory cane is leaning against the coffee table just to his right, next to the remote for the TV. His tan cotton socks are pulled up over his slightly swollen ankles. He's in his favorite place and chair: a reclining blue rocker in the sitting room off the living room. Ray Rudkin likes to watch golf in here, keep up on the news, go in and out of waking dreams and snatches of sleep.

"I played golf till I was eighty-six or eighty-seven," he says. "Best I ever was, I guess, was a nine-handicap."

"Eighteen holes at eighty-seven?"

"Well, we had a cart. That's kind of cheating."

Up until seven or eight years ago he used to mow his lawn, do the pruning on the hedges out front, sweep up the clippings. "The doctor told me I better stop the mowing," he says. "Said it was still okay to trim the bushes, just don't overdo it. He said I was getting too old for serious yardwork. I said, 'Oh, okay.' "

My brain can't help pivoting to my dad. He'd be into his second century if it were somehow possible for him to be in this overwarm room with us. So far as I know, my father never hired anybody to do his yardwork, but then again, he made it only into his mid-eighties. Once, about a year or so before he died, he got on a ladder and climbed up on our roof in suburban Maryland and cleaned out our gutters. He was up there before we could stop him. "You gotta make sure you get those leaves out of your gutters every spring, Paul," he instructed me. And, of course, the next spring, after he was dead, I didn't.

Ray Rudkin, who'll be ninety-seven in four months, still has his driver's license, along with every one of his marbles. "Oh, yeah," he says, in reference to the license. "No problem. I can drive across the freeway, to West Sacramento, to see my doctor. Do it any old day. I could drive over there right now. You and I could go for a ride after we finish talking. No problem. I don't go at high speeds. Well, I won't go downtown anymore."

He motors around his East Sacramento neighborhood and on

the access roads of the freeway in his 2010 Toyota Camry. It's in the garage, gassed up and good to go. Up until the pandemic hit, he loved getting up and going for donuts every morning at a little coffee joint down on the corner. The place opens at five. He tended to get into the parking lot by six-thirty. He and a buddy used to meet some widows at the donut joint—not Black Widows, but widow widows, as in elderly women who've lost their husbands.

Maybe the word "lost," which he just used, tripped thoughts of sweet Anna Belle. He met her and he married her—that seems to be about the story. The meeting was in the hurry-up wartime spring of 1944, not long after he got his wings at Luke Field in Phoenix. The hitching was a few months later, in July, not too far from the day when my own parents were kissing their goodbyes in Amarillo.

"We met at a dance place out here in California. I was transitioning on the A-20 in Salinas. Everybody went to dance places to meet people during the war. Boy, could she dance. Cab Calloway might have been on the bill. She was looking for another good dancer. I guess I passed the test. I was nineteen, almost twenty. She was two years older. Her people were from out here in California. I talked her into it. I was going for night fighters, but I hadn't trained on the Black Widow. I hadn't been sent to Fresno yet. I hadn't joined up with the 549th yet. Anyway, Anna Belle and I found a justice of the peace. I lied about my age. I just wanted to get it done with. So somewhere out here in California there must be a piece of paper that says I was twenty-one on the day I got married. Ha."

Ray Rudkin has lived in this comfortable rancher on this quiet street on the east side of town for the last fifty-eight years. He's a former junior high school teacher and counselor and principal. He's also a retired lieutenant colonel in the U.S. Air Force Reserve who got called up for service during the Korean War. He lives here with his daughter Connie, who's seventy-six and his firstborn. He looks out for her; she looks out for him. Connie is watching a game show on the TV in the other room. Every now and then, she pokes in her head and smiles.

Other than for his time in war, he and Connie have been together pretty much for their entire lives. She was born deaf. It was a botched delivery. She arrived in the world on April 13, 1945, when her father was on Iwo Jima. In fact, her father had landed at South Field only five or six days before. Lieutenant Rudkin hadn't departed Hawaii for the front with the regular air echelon of the 549th on February 19, 1945, as my dad did, in that sixteen-plane convoy of Widows which I've already described. Instead, Connie's father and three other flyers from the squadron had come behind with their R/O's and several escort planes. If you allowed for the time differences between California and Japan, Connie Ann Rudkin was born at almost the same moment that her father was flying his first mission on Iwo. Not that her father knew. He didn't learn he had a new daughter for a couple more weeks.

He was twenty and a half on that first mission. He was the youngest flyer in the squadron. Lieutenant Joe Lamont hadn't arrived yet. There was a significant difference between them, though: Ray Rudkin had had more flying time stateside before he went over.

On that first mission, which was in daylight, he witnessed a P-51 Mustang in trouble. The pilot was supposed to bail out but he couldn't get out in time. The Mustang went into the water. The last living airman remembers the way she went in. I have read the after-action report.

But he's talking about his eldest child, a few years from eighty. "Oh, hell, Connie helps *me* around here," he says. "She does all the laundry. I don't know how to do the damn dishwasher. Connie does that." She also makes sure he takes all his daily meds. Before COVID, father and daughter had their circuit of local restaurants and would dine out three or four times a week.

A little bit ago, Connie's dad and I had been studying the pilot's manual for the P-61. I bought the book on the internet and have carried it with me to Sacramento from the East Coast. I had told Ray—who, from our first telephone conversation onward, some seven or eight months back, had insisted I call him by his first name, and even though it made me feel awkward, I began doing it—that I had a surprise for him and that I would show it to him when we finally got to meet. The P-61 pilot manual isn't the real thing, which is to say the old Army Air Forces *official* thing, published by the U.S. government for pilots-in-training during the war. But it's a pretty impressive facsimile document all the same, with lots of schematics and diagrams and black-and-white illustrations, both of the interior and exterior of the airplane. It's the kind of detailed work that thrills aviation geeks, World War II geeks, Black Widow geeks. The same niche publishing company that put it out has also put out facsimile pilot editions for the P-38 Lightning and the AT-6 Texan and the P-47 Thunderbolt. But the Black Widow pilot's manual is apparently one of the perennial sellers, due once again, or so I can only think, to the highly stylized design of the shiny black machine, along with the fact of her lateness into the war, added also to the fact that there are only four Widows known to be in captivity—so to speak.

I had set the manual before Ray and then kind of held my breath. He'd leafed through it and stopped on Figure 20. The illustration on that page features the pilot's instrument panel. It's a combination photograph and diagram. Two dozen gizmos and gadgets and dials are identified by means of circles and numbers and drawn rules. For instance, number 1 in the image identifies the airspeed indicator, and there's a small circle and a rule pointing to it. Likewise, number 9: the radio altimeter. Likewise, number 5: the rate-of-climb indicator. Likewise, number 11: the tachometer. Likewise, number 17: the fuel pressure gauge.

He'd looked in silence at the illustration for a long minute. Then, "That's a little incomplete."

Beat.

"I don't think they've got the manifold pressure gauge lines identified here."

He'd traced his veined and slightly bruised fingers down the page. They were my father's hands. He had his head cocked sideways, like a cocker spaniel. My dad did that on occasion.

"Wait a minute. I take it back. Here they are. Yes, they've got this right. My damn memory must be playing tricks on me. For some reason, I always thought those pressure gauges were on the left side of the panel."

The last time the oldest living airman was reading pressure gauges in the cockpit of his Black Widow was three-quarters of a century ago. I say we should cut him some slack.

It was goosebumping to find him, naturally: the breathing link, near-centenarian link. But the added fact that a once-and-ever Midwest farm boy was *so* much alive—and reminded me in uncanny ways of my once-and-ever Kentucky dad—seemed the gift on top of the gift.

I just used the past tense: "*was* so much alive." Ray Rudkin has died in the time between my trip to California to meet him in the early summer of 2021 and the writing of this paragraph. I'll come to that sadness, which in another way I don't feel is a sadness at all.

There were never more than eighteen pilots in my dad's squadron of roughly three hundred men, and usually the number of active flyers was closer to fifteen or sixteen. At the reunion in Florida, I had met about a dozen of the men with whom my father had flown. (Rudkin wasn't one of them.) But that was forty years ago, and those conversations were mostly in passing. I knew that by the time I started searching in earnest, these decades later, my odds would be about slim to none.

One day, going down the "R's" on my roster lists, I dialed a Raymond Everett Rudkin in Sacramento, California. I knew he had been one of the flyers because I had seen his name in the documents. "Yep, it's me, I flew her, still here," he said. He said he was sitting in an easy chair out in the garage that the junk people hadn't yet hauled away. He said he was trimming his fingernails and passing the afternoon. He said that a couple feet away from him was an old trunk with letters and photographs and medals and news clippings and flight logs and other stuff from the war in it. "You might like to see some of it," he said.

We spoke about seven or eight times before I was able to go to California. I kept waiting for the pandemic to subside. I would call about once a month, saying my prayers every time I dialed that he would still pick up. Sometimes our conversations would last almost an hour.

"You've got to hold on," I blurted at one point.

"Don't worry, I don't think I'm going anywhere just yet," he said.

Through that winter and spring, I was continually amazed at the texture of his memory, never mind by his stamina. He was filling me in on a hundred things I hadn't even thought to wonder about. Sometimes he spoke elliptically, which made things more dreamlike, surreal. I couldn't help feeling that somehow my dad had arranged all this.

One time, he said: "Those four .50-calibers on the ball turret. You know, the thing was right above you. You couldn't believe the way flames would shoot out over top of your head. It didn't matter whether you were firing them, or the gunner was firing them—the flames were eight or ten inches wide and they're coming right over the top of your cockpit, and on either side of you, and they're firing simultaneously and you can't believe the noise."

Another time, he said: "Those Red Cross girls. They lived on the other side of the island. They'd come over in a jeep to our officer's club. We had one of the best officer's clubs of any unit. We built it out of scavengered plywood. We used to dance the legs off those durn Red Cross girls." (I had had no idea there were Red Cross girls on Iwo.)

Another time, he said: "You had a pee tube in the cockpit. That wasn't the exact name for it. I mean, you're going to be up there for a couple hours, and sometimes it's going to be cold, and other times hot, and you're rattling around, and what do you do, you've gotta take a pee. The tube had a spiral cup on top. It went down the cup and into the tube and down to the floor of the fuselage and out of a hatch and right out the bottom of the plane." He tacked on: "For the other business, you had to wait till you got back down."

He said: "You had a rifle by the head of your bed. That, and your .45." He meant in the squad tents on the nights you weren't going up.

He said: "There was canvas on the floor. Later, they laid down slats over top of them. You had about eight or nine feet between your cot and the next guy's cot."

He said: "You had a little ledge for your elbows in the cockpit, that's all. Once you got buckled in, you weren't going to move around. After a three-hour hop, you couldn't wait to get out of that damn harness. After a three-hour hop, you didn't have any trouble going to sleep."

He said: "Those tarpaper shacks we slept in on Kipapa in Hawaii. You could spit through a crack in the knotholes in the damn floorboards."

He said: "You had to be careful and latch that thing tight. It flew off on me once." He meant the hatch on the greenhouse.

He said: "You would get on your screen in the cockpit, he would get on his in the back. His scope was much larger. He could read the dark maybe sixteen miles out." He meant his R/O. He meant the radar screen linked to the antenna in the nose. *Reading the dark sixteen miles out:* The last airman was writing a poem.

He said: "I can still see them, scrounging in the garbage cans for scraps, on the perimeter of our compound." He was talking about the Japanese. He meant the enemy stragglers still hiding out in caves. They would come out at night, he said. He said he could remember hearing them from inside his tent, rattling the bins. He said he also remembered seeing a dozen or so Japanese prisoners who'd been taken on March 26. They were being held in a stockade not far from where the 549th was bivouacked. Ray hadn't arrived on Iwo until about ten days after General Kuribayashi's *kirikomi*. But he later saw some of the pictures.

He said, "I took a bottle of Black & White Scotch with me from Hawaii. I waited till I got to Saipan before I took the lid off."

Another time, he said, and I could hear the hesitation (I had been dying to know, but was waiting to let it arise in him organically): "Your dad. Well, I knew him, of course. All the flyers knew each other. But he was older. What was he—five or six years older?" Yes—almost exactly six, minus eight days. Ray was born on October 20, 1924; my dad on October 28, 1918. "See, over there that made a big difference. I mean, you take the poker games. I don't think I ever got invited into one of your dad's poker games in the Ready Room, and I certainly didn't invite myself in. He would have been playing poker with the CO and the operations officer and the other three flight team leaders. They were the top people in the organization. They knew it, too. They had their poker games on one side of the tent, we had our game on the other." He hedged a little more. "I wasn't one of the crews in his flight. But I kinda got the idea he ran a tight ship."

He had talked a lot about his boyhood back on the farm in Sparta, Wisconsin—and the leaving of the farm. Again, the echoes. He said he'd gone to a country elementary school—sixteen kids for all eight grades. The winters of the upper Midwest were a quantum worse than the winters of western Kentucky. "There was frost on your blanket when you breathed at night," he said. Sparta (it's in southwestern Wisconsin) was bigger than Morganfield, but it was a Depression farm town like Morganfield. His dad had a fifteen-head Holstein dairy operation. There were six kids in the Rudkin family, three boys and three girls. Ray was in the middle. They all took their turns at milking before the sun was up. At ten or twelve, he was driving a team with a twelve-foot-wide rake. His dad would plow and Ray would come along behind with the horses and the rake. Only, they didn't much call him Ray. In the family, he was "Red" (he once had a heck of a carrot top), just as his older brother, Ken Rudkin, was "Bud." Bud went to the war ahead of him. He, too, was a flyer: in a P-51 Mustang fighter in Europe. Bud got shot down and was a POW for something like eight months.

But on the farm, before all that happened, Ray and Bud were thick as thieves. The brothers formed a baseball team and found the money for flannel uniforms. They called themselves the Sparta Cataracts. They used to throw baseballs at a chalked strike zone on the side of the barn. They'd travel from county to county and play the other farm boys from the other towns. When he wasn't firing his fastball, Ray was boxing. He was a 147-pound welterweight Golden Glover. He graduated from Sparta High in 1942, turned eighteen, tried to join up. But they wouldn't take him. For one thing, he had bad teeth. He went up to Eau Claire (biggest town in those parts) and got two of them pulled. They still wouldn't take him, at least not into the Air Corps, which is what he wanted, in honor and imitation of his big brother. He went out to the Dakotas and threshed wheat. He went down to Racine, Wisconsin, and worked in a steel salvage yard. Finally, in the spring of 1943, a year out of high school, the Sparta boy got a letter informing him he could enlist in the Army Air Forces. (The Morganfield boy had been in for five and a half years; he was two months from earning his wings in Yuma.) Red's parents drove him to the train that took him down to Chicago for his swearing-in on May 3.

"I thought they were kind of accepting it," Ray said in one of our last phone talks before I flew to the West Coast. "When I went into the parlor to tell them, it was the first time I ever saw tears in my dad's eyes."

The patriarch of the family used to buy 100 chicks every spring, usually Leghorns. It was always a fresh start for the farm's growing season. But his second boy was going away to the war and the first one was already there. John and Mabel Rudkin, good country people, tough old English and German stock, stood on the rail platform and propped each other up as their son waved from the other side of the glass.

"My dad lived to be 103," he said. "He didn't turn in his license till he was ninety-nine. Hey, maybe I've got half a chance here."

Ray's son Derek has just come in with his wife, Jan. They've brought peanut butter cookies. It's my second day in his father's home. I still feel all of this is somehow not quite happening. The luck I've struck.

Derek Rudkin is the third-born in the family, not quite a decade younger than Connie. There was once another sibling between them: Rayna Lynn. She was born in late 1946, nine or ten months after Ray had come back from overseas. In July 1979, Rayna Rudkin McDonald and her eleven-year-old son, Bret, were on the way to a Little League game. Rayna lost control of the Bronco she was driving. It overturned. She was thirty-two. She died that day; her son seven days after, from massive brain swelling. Ray had spoken of this yesterday, elliptically, in the later part of the day, after I'd been in his home for close to five hours. (At noon, I'd gone to get a sandwich, so he could take a nap in his recliner.) I tried gently to ask a little more about it, but he'd sat there, looking off. He'd drummed his fingers on the armrests of his chair. Then he'd said his daughter's death, and the death of his grandchild, fairly killed Anna Belle. "Well, okay, me, too."

Derek and his wife live about half an hour away, up in the foot-hills of the Sierras. He checks on his dad and Connie every day by phone. He brings groceries, does odd jobs around the house. He's instantly friendly, the good son.

The blue veins running down the ridges of his father's hands today look like small rivers on a three-dimensional relief map. One of Ray's eyelids is drooping, and his other is watering. He dabs at it with his handkerchief, which is wadded in the back pocket of his khaki trousers. They're the kind you buy at Walmart.

"Hey, Dad," Derek says. "Did you open the trunk yet?"

All we've been doing is opening the trunk—but Derek means *the trunk:* the small locker out in the garage holding some of Ray's memorabilia from the war. I have been dying to see inside it.

Derek carries it into the sitting room.

Just the photographs. Here's one. It's of Ray and his crew—the gunner, Chris Christensen; the R/O, Jim Spellacy. It's not the picture at the top of this chapter, but it has the same feel. All three are in knotted silk scarves, projecting their stylish aviator man-hood, but the skipper seems to have a little more difficulty carry-ing off the look. He's still the meaty-faced farm boy from Sparta. After the war, Ray lost touch with Staff Sergeant Christensen, but he'd get together now and then with his fellow lieutenant Spellacy. The ex-R/O and his second wife made it big in the decades after the war in real estate in San Bernardino—apparently, millionaire-big. On Spellacy's simple government stone in Riverside National Cemetery in Riverside, California, the words "Dancing with Jim" are chinked in. If you look again at his picture up above, you can almost get a sense of that epitaph. Something insouciant and easy about the old radar guy.

My eye has caught another picture from the trunk: Ray and his wife on their wedding day. They may have driven hurriedly before a JP that July day in 1944, but they'd climbed into their best duds all the same: Ray in his full-dress uniform, Anna Belle in a broad pinstripe woolen suit and beautiful brooch. She's a knockout, with her high cheekbones, her intense eyes, her penciled brows, the full lipstick, the angled jaw, the great head of thick, curly dark hair. The farm boy must have pinched himself all the way to their honeymoon, which may have only been for an overnight or two, like that of my own folks.

There are letters in a beautifully preserved stationery box at the bottom of the trunk. Written atop the box in gold lettering is: "Army Air Forces." The drawn blades of a propeller are cutting through the middle of the "o" in "Forces."

Here's one from somebody named Hazel. It's before Anna Belle. It's summer 1943. Ray is in Preflight at Santa Ana, California (where my dad did his Preflight). He's only a couple months off the farm. Hazel lives with a gaggle of working girls at 48 1/2 Brooks Street in Venice, California. She dates the note: "Sat. Night." She'll send it special delivery (on Sunday morning), which will cost her 13 cents. She's writing as events unfold. You could almost make a soapbox script out of this and put it on coast-to-coast radio. Everything's in real time. Everything is *now,* extemporaneous, instant.

Dear Red,

    I surely was surprised to hear from you. I thought you had forgotten about me. Say Red there are five girls out here at the house wait a second the door bell is ringing. I'll have to answer it. Three more have come in so if I make lots of mistakes you can think why. They are all talking at once, they said to tell you hello. They are all crazy.

    Red I think all my girl friends are all filled up with dates for next week. Well Red I hope to hear from you soon. Oh yes I get off at twelve o'clock Saturday night. Will you meet me at the dance because it's so late when I come home but if you would rather come to my home you can.

    Well by for now and let me know your plans.

Love,
Hazel

Another: This one's written about six months later. Anna Belle has yet to enter the picture. This letter is from a pal in aviation school. The pal has gone to Las Vegas for his next stage of flying. Ray is down in Pecos, Texas. He's made it through Preflight and

Primary and is now in BT: basic training, which is the second-to-last step. Leo Willis is sending some gal intelligence in case Ray gets back to the Los Angeles area. He addresses it to "Heifer 'Red.' "

"Have you gotten kicked out of any more USO's for being drunk?" he wants to know. On the intel: Don't forget to look up Jackie Blackwell on 10th Avenue in L.A. "She's pretty. Works every night but Saturday." He also suggests June Faia, telephone RI-4300. "I haven't seen this one in a long time. She's a lot of fun." He adds: "All the other girls I know are married, engaged or not speaking to me. Nona would like to cut my throat." He signs off, "So long, Son."

One more. It's from his mom, back on the farm, and it, too, draws its own time-pictures. Mabel Rudkin's son is now at Luke Field in Arizona, soon to earn his wings, if he can complete the final hurdles. His mother's a little perturbed. Three times in the five-page letter she finds a way to say: *Why haven't we heard from you more?* (He's too busy flying—and chasing women.) She gives all the latest news. "Richard [Ray's kid brother] is getting the pink eye, I guess." And "Dad is up to Pauls" (a relative; there's supposed to be an apostrophe in there). And, "It was like spring to-day. No snow and the sun was shining, so guess the ground hog saw his shadow all right. We cleaned the chicken house and let the chickens out, they sure enjoyed being out. If it is nice tomorrow I will let them out again." In the third of her momly nags: "Everyone keeps asking how you are coming on and all I can say is I guess all right, I don't hear anything from him."

On and on, these time-capsule letters. Curiously, though: no letters from Anna Belle, or none that I can see.

There are also several items in the trunk relating to years after the war. The lieutenant got home to his wife and new daughter in California and didn't know what he wanted to do.

Ray: "I was picking almonds on a farm in Chico and somebody said to me, 'Hey, Ray, you should take advantage of the G.I. Bill.' Well, Anna Belle was pushing me, too. We had three mouths to feed, and old sourpuss face is picking almonds." Ray got on the G.I. Bill and earned an undergraduate degree and then later a master's, both from California state schools. A thirty-year career in school education in California followed, even though, as was said earlier, he stayed in the service for a good while, both on active duty and then in the reserves, making lieutenant colonel. One reason he got out of the active service, he says, is because doctors were advising him and Anna Belle to put Connie in a home for the deaf. "No way," Ray says. "No way on that. The government wanted to transfer me again, and I said, 'No way. Connie's with us.'"

Tacked on: "I'm not sure how everything all worked out. It just did."

Derek and his wife have said goodbye and headed back to their own home. I could stay here all day and come back tomorrow. I could go through this box item by item, but I know it's time to go.

"How are you able to remember so much about the war, Ray?" (I've asked this probably half a dozen times.)

"I don't know. I'm not sure. It's just there."

"Do you think about Iwo Jima much?" (Absurd question.)

"I guess. It comes up pretty often on the television—you know the raising of the flag on Suribachi and all that. It brings it back. In the morning, in bed, I'll lie there and think about it."

I'm lingering by the door. I know in my bones I'll never see him again.

"Hey, Ray, were you ever able to sleep in the Ready Room between hops?"

"Of course. I mean, why the heck not? If it's your time, it's your time."

On the plane home, I kept hearing in my inner ear that deflecting thing my father had said more than once: *Really, I didn't do all that much in the war, Paul. But you were there, Dad. Yes, I suppose that's so.*

Shamefully, I didn't call Ray for another several months. We had another good talk, and several briefer ones after that. In one conversation, he seemed especially focused on his father. "Remember how I told you my dad made 103? He was in a nursing home. He had a button or something he could push to call his family. He never used the thing to call me. I'd call him instead. But one day he did. I think he called all of us kids that day. The next day he died."

Pause on the line. "He knew."

I told him he was going to make 103. "Well, I'm not so sure now. Maybe before, I thought that. This damn COVID thing, you lost a little. I don't know now."

I called maybe twice more in the next couple months. I could sense him slipping.

On March 2, 2022, I dialed his cell. Maybe I knew. Derek Rudkin's wife, Jan, picked up. "He died yesterday," she said slowly. "We were going to call you today." She said it happened early in the morning. He was coming out of his room. A massive stroke. He apparently didn't suffer. Derek found him lying in the hall. Derek had arrived earlier than usual that day because he was going to take his ninety-seven-and-a-half-year-old pop to get his license renewed. The family had a small private service—everyone else he'd known was gone. The family had him cremated, and the last airman of the 549th lies now next to sweet Anna Belle, the modesty of his stone matching hers.

THE LIFELONG FATALIST mixed in with (or maybe all jumbled up with) a recessive daredevil gene, which must have had something to do with growing up in back-of-the-moon Kentucky. There was always a wild hair there somewhere inside him, even though he could be a man of a sometimes suffocating moral propriety. Rectitude.

My dad once told me that, when he was in high school, he and a buddy from town bought a third-hand Indian motorcycle, which was the hot bike manufacturer of the day. (I'm having a hard time imagining where he could have found the money for his half of the purchase.) They souped it up and went tearing around Union County back roads on Friday nights. A need for speed. After wiping out, he gave up on motorcycles. But a thirst for a certain amount of risk didn't desert. He harnessed that part of himself to his will and hunger to fly and tore off for parts unknown, spraying gravel. (In reality, as you know, the story is more prosaic: He rode, not on his Indian, but on that early-morning Greyhound out of Morganfield to Chanute Field up in Rantoul, Illinois, the week before Thanksgiving in November 1937. Metaphorically, he sprayed.)

The recessive daredevil gene must have come into play when he decided to rebuild, in the early sixties, in our garage, in the western suburbs of Chicago, from first bolt to last rivet, a stick-and-rudder, tail-dragging, rag-wing monoplane called a Luscombe—and then, when he had her finished, strapping on a parachute and flying her out of a nearby cornfield that hadn't yet given way to the latest development of split-levels.

I was in the seminary and so wasn't there to witness this Great Santini trick. I certainly heard about it. He was a captain on his airline then, in his mid-forties. The rebuilding, which I think took more than a year, or possibly even longer, gave him something to do when he was home between trips and not tending to chores around the house. My mother wasn't thrilled with the project, since she knew what its end result was. She also knew she couldn't stop it.

A Luscombe was about as rudimentary a plane as a Piper Cub—it was part of her atavistic allure. The fourteen-gallon fuel tank was located behind the two seats, which were side by side. My dad's model—I think it was the Luscombe 8A, built around 1946—had a 65-horsepower, 4-cylinder Continental engine that could allow her pilot to cruise at about 89 miles an hour. My dad was flying multimillion-dollar jets out of O'Hare International, going from Chicago to Puerto Rico and back in the same day, and he was rebuilding from scratch something in our garage that must have been taking him, if only subconsciously, back to the first open-air biplane crop dusters he'd ever spied when he was threshing barley under the hammering Morganfield sun.

I think he had found the Luscombe, which amounted, at least meta-phorically, to one big basket of wrecked parts, in a famous yellow avia-tion newspaper full of classified ads called Trade-A-Plane. *It was the bible of its day for buying and selling general aircraft.*

My kid brother Mark told me that, when he was in first grade, he used to play in the fuselage of the Luscombe when it was no more than a dented silver metal box making its way back to something recognizable as the core of an airplane. He watched my dad cut and stretch and then glue the fabric across the wings. The ribs of aircraft wings have been covered in cloth since the Wright brothers went up. My dad was using a synthetic cloth material for his wing surfaces, but it was the same prin-ciple that Orville and Wilbur had come up with in the back of the Wright Cycle Company in Dayton.

He hung the engine, the power plant, which he'd completely overhauled.

He bolted on the wings.

He painted her up and gave her a nifty pinstripe and christened her with a name: Blue Boy. *(I'm now thinking she should have been named Blue Girl.) I'm not sure if he broke a bottle of champagne over her prop. Actually, we weren't a champagne family. Maybe a Miller High Life. He got a friend to help him push her down the driveway, to the edge of County Farm Road, which fronted our house. He got a couple of cops from the Winfield Police Department (we lived between a town called Wheaton and a village called Winfield) to stop traffic. The two men pushed her up the middle of the road and into the cornfield while people gawked. As a concession to my mom, he agreed to wear the parachute, but I suspect that, had something gone wrong, the chute would have been useless anyway: He wouldn't have been up high enough to climb out and get it open in time.*

I have a picture of him in the stubbled, wintry-looking field before takeoff. He's in an old corduroy hat and beat-up jacket and the parachute is dangling rather ridiculously on his back. Mark—his favorite son, who might have been six then—is standing in front of him, clutching my dad's legs with both hands. Father and son are grinning. You could read the picture both ways: Daddy, please don't go. *Or, alternatively:* Daddy, please take me with you. *Is it any wonder Mark became an aviator?*

"How did he know it was going to get in the air?" I asked my brother the other day. "I mean, even if you get it all back together, isn't it still kind of theoretical that it's actually going to go up?" (As I write this, suddenly I am thinking of the P-61 being rebuilt, on the same kind of wing and prayer, in Reading, Pennsylvania.)

"I know what you're saying," Mark said. "On the other hand, Dad didn't have to wonder who tightened the screws to the right torque. He tightened them to the right torque. If something was going to go up, this was a good bet."

Blue Boy got into the air beautifully. Traffic resumed on County Farm Road. The local hero, whom I can almost see throwing back his head in laughter as he escaped the earth one more time, sticked and ruddered and daredeviled her around Winfield for twenty minutes or so. Then he flew her over to a nearby county airport where he had leased hangar space for his new diversion. That summer, when I got home from the seminary, neighbors were still talking about the feat. We all got some refracted glory out of it. We all got our eventual rides around the pea patch.

June–July 1945

*Gene Autry, with showgirl, on a USO tour of the Pacific, early July 1945.
I'm pretty sure this is onstage at THE FORTY-NINER'S, also affectionately
known as "The Stink Holler Radio City Music Hall." The date may be July 5.
If so, then my dad's likely not in the audience. They've got him up twice on the
5th—three hours and fifty minutes for the first hop, three hours and five minutes
for the second. That's a pity, because he truly loves "The Singing Cowboy," whose
real name is Orvon Grover Autry. He loves Hoppy and Buck Jones and Tom Mix,
too. Used to go see them all for a dime at the picture show just off the square in
Morganfield.*

IT WAS A GHOST SHIP, with maybe half a dozen dead airmen inside, and my father, who might have been asleep that midday in his bunk or maybe playing poker or writing a letter home, got a call to get to the flight line as quickly as possible and to bring with him one of the other pilots from his flight team. It's a crippled B-29 Superfortress, they told him, on the way back from a bombing run on Tokyo, and your orders are to shoot her down, that is, once the ones who are still alive inside have bailed out. And why did the gruesome thing have to be done? Because the shot-up ship, floating out there above the sea on her own devices and whims, could possibly make a sudden lazy loop and come crashing onto the island and perhaps take out a whole line of operating aircraft—or, far worse, a whole compound of off-duty men. No, she had to be destroyed.

"So we're up there and I think, 'I'm going to shoot my own airplane down.'" This is my father speaking, but not to me. He says it with something quizzical and seesawing in a voice grown slightly elevated. And slightly soft, too. I remember this precise tonal quality, the more so because it didn't happen that often. His voice could seem to raise itself by half an octave even as it was getting gentle—I almost want to say feminine. Something was disturbing him in a way his orderly mind couldn't put to rest. The softness and the raise in timbre were related, I think, to that other character trait of which I've spoken: the loquacious Kentuckian, with his sometimes faulty grammar and gift for metaphor, turning laconic and almost miserly with words in the face of something tragic and irreversible. *Wind shear got him, Paul.* (Fellow captain at Eastern, crashing a big jetliner in New York.) *Japs got him flying over the Hump.* (His best man, Barney Slamkowski, dying at the controls of his minimally armed transport.)

My father said these words into a tape recorder eleven months and two weeks before he died. It was late April 2002. He was staying at the family cabin in northern Wisconsin. Earlier, I referenced this oral history, and how none of us knew about it, and how my kid brother Mark discovered its existence only a few years ago. (*I* am the family researcher, but it had never even occurred to me to look on the internet for a possible interview my dad might have given in his late years to someone regarding his time in the war.) I don't know the circumstances of how the session came to be. Did he initiate it? (I'm half thinking he did.) Did someone find out that a World War II vet, who'd flown on Iwo, in the Black Widow, was living locally? The interview is now a part of the archives of the Wisconsin Historical Society, a major research repository in America. I can picture my dad grinning at the fact that it took us so long to find it. He was no shrinking violet about telling you, when he cared to, about all he'd accomplished in his life. And yet in other things he could be curiously modest, reticent, deferential. I'm thinking mortality came into play in this instance. Death had been dropping broad hints for a good while. Maybe, after the interview was done, with so much of Iwo having welled back up, my dad felt a melancholy come over him. In his last years, he spent a lot of time alone up there at the cabin, framed by the white birch trees on the small blue lake. He was a man uncomfortable with even saying a word like "melancholy." I remember him once saying, "Paul, I don't even have good feelings about myself anymore." He'd just had another fight with my mom, over money. It was only a couple months after he'd given the oral history that they sold off the Wisconsin property—in a rush. In almost a literal sense, he had nowhere to go.

I wish I knew the date it happened—the order for the shootdown. I've searched the declassified documents, but to no avail.[*] I remember my dad speaking of the incident once, just once, and only in the barest terms. Again, I didn't follow up. But I do recall from that quick conversation that he said it had happened a week or two after he'd been made a captain. He got promoted to captain on May 22, 1945. Which is why I'm guessing it occurred in possibly the first or second week of June.

---

[*] As for the absence of any documentary record, or at least any that I can find: One thing I have learned is that, for one reason or another, a lot of things were kept out of the documents; or, alternatively, got lost; or, alternatively again, got reshuffled to make them hard to find. You've already read one speculative account of this issue regarding the searchlight-trapping, and for more on the foggy point, and for at least one more curious example related to my dad, I refer you to the Essay on Sources.

This story is being taken almost entirely from the oral history. He gets the call to double-time it to the flight line. He scrambles Lieutenant Maxwell Julian to come with him so that there'll be two Widows in the air to shoot the plane down. (No one calls him Maxwell. He's known among his fellow officers as "Pinky" Julian. On the tape, my dad can't summon his name—"I'll think of his name in a minute"—but he does remember that he's from South Carolina, which is how I know. At the 1982 reunion in Orlando, I met Pinky Julian from Camden, South Carolina. We talked for a good while. This incident didn't come up.)

"'Emergency. Jump in the jeep and go to the line,'" he's telling the interviewer. A storytelling quality has arisen in the natural storyteller.

"So jump in the Widow, got it in the air, and I'm there talking, and they said that a crippled '29 coming in with two engines out one side and there's a lot of dead on board. Not gonna be able to land the airplane. And he's gonna come over and put it on pilot and those that's alive are gonna jump out."

The captain gets her on autopilot and parachutes out, as do the four or five others of the crew who can get free.

"So when all the men was cleared, why, they said, 'Okay, it's yours. Shoot that '29 down.'"

And: "So I made a couple passes and, and"—his voice is turning almost jokey, and the high-pitched quality, with something incredulous in it, is there—"and I find that this B-29, uh, it keeps *going!*"

He keeps making passes. Pinky the same. The ghost ship just keeps flying.

But the jokiness, if that's what it is, goes away fast.

"We finally did get the airplane shot down and it went into the ocean," he says.

Did they fire their cannons as well as the .50-caliber machine guns? He doesn't say.

"But the thing that sticks to me, my mind is, those dead men on board."

And: "Seem like to me, it could have been, uh, a different way to do it."

And: "That was the orders that I had, and I've never forgotten that." The "never" and the "forgotten" have the quizzical and soft quality.

His mind pivots to a different story. He sounds more relaxed now. It's about another crippled B-29 coming in on a different day. This ship also had two engines out on one side. He wasn't involved. Nor was it a shoot-down. The incident had a beautiful outcome.

But he's being pulled back, as if in spite of himself, to the other thing, the first thing. It had seemed over. Funny, how the mind can move back.

"I know that we shot that ship down with dead people on board. And it's . . . bothered me ever since." *Bothered* is the loudest word in the sentence. The *down* in the prior sentence also has a particular inflection. A big flaming Superfortress is spiraling into the ocean. He and Pinky are up above, bracing for the explosion, for the tremendous flashes of light. Is this the picture in his mind?

Interviewer: "They were never able to recover any of, uh, the boys?"

Interviewee, quickly: "They could have. See, I don't know. Surely, they made attempts."

Interviewer (with a seeming small discomfort of his own): "I can understand why that, uh, situation has stayed with you all these years."

They go on to something else. The tape runs for another thirty minutes or so. There are other powerful moments.

I'll pose a theoretical question: What if somebody in that shot-up ship *wasn't* dead? Did anyone in ground control consider that? Could there have been an airman (or even two) in the rear or middle of the massive eleven-crew machine who was still alive, gravely or even mortally wounded, unable to move, much less speak into a radio, and yet breathing all the same, with the faintest pulse? Or is that a too-easy moral calculation for someone like me to frame, never having been in a war, never having served my country in a uniform, never having had to jump to and obey a superior's issued orders? Who would have time for equivocal calculations in the chaotic instant it was happening? If my dad were here, he might say with mild contempt: "Those questions are for writers, Paul.

I was following my orders." I've now listened to the interview a dozen times. I somehow can't help thinking that my father, sooner or later, did come to such a thought. And, if so, how awful it must have been to bear.

I know that we shot that ship down with dead people on board. And it's . . . bothered me ever since.

I'll keep looking for documents on the matter. Not that they could ever reveal inner truths.

Documents.

In June 1945, the 549th NFS flew 576 missions and logged 827 hours and 55 minutes in the air. From the monthly squadron report: "Three thousand and eighty (3,080) rounds of twenty (20) millimeter ammunition and three thousand three hundred and fifty-five (3,355) rounds of caliber .50 ammunition were fired." A lot of ammo, a lot of time aloft. If the war was finding its torturous close, if the enemy was deep on the run, knowing it couldn't win, you wouldn't necessarily think so from these numbers.

Nor from the squadron's after-action reports, beginning with the first day of June.

A lieutenant named Jim Monaghan flew a daylight combat sortie and encountered three unidentified aircraft. From the report: "Chased for 3 minutes, closed to 2 miles. . . . Bogie went into steep dive using slight turns. . . . Lost contact. . . . Orbited for ten minutes but could not pick up Bogie."

Same day, same time, a name you'll recognize: Lieutenant Ray Rudkin. He, too, spots an enemy craft—or his R/O, Jim Spellacy, does. Chase ensues. "Bogie dived and turned port pulling away. . . . Last contact at Angels 12, on 360 degree heading. . . . Ended chase 12 miles south of Haha Jima."

Four days later, June 5, my father. This combat sortie is also by daylight. The takeoff is at 9:26 a.m. and his orders are to escort five P-51 Mustangs on a search for enemy vessels up near Muko Jima. (It's in the Bonin chain, about forty miles above Chichi Jima.) The Black Widow is sleek and fast and highly maneuverable, but she isn't a Mustang. Mustangs are one-man bands: smaller, lighter, faster. The five P-51s attack from 8,000 feet. There is intense anti-aircraft fire. The sky lights up. At least one enemy vessel is struck. *The Rita B* hangs in the background, circling—these are my dad's orders. From what I can tell, he is never directly in the line of fire. But he is there, ready to come strafing in on demand with his twenties and fifties. (The mission report doesn't say whether he's carrying the 500-pounders under his wings.) Five hours later, all the planes get back to base safe. The pilots go into the Ready and report to the intelligence guys what has happened. Five hours in the greenhouse, hardly able to move your muscles. I wonder how many times my dad used the pee tube.

Ready Room. There is a new expression for it that's creeping into the official squadron reports in the last month or so: the "alert shack." (Lowercase.)

A tropical cyclone comes through. (This is on June 21.) Each week, a boot-and-shoe inspection. The enlisted guys still take turns standing nightly guard in the compound and on the flight line, but the number on each shift has come down to ten and four, respectively. Sick call still held twice a day. From the June report: "Six (6) men were hospitalized for the following conditions: One (1) case of gastritis, two (2) cases for medical observation, one (1) for injury of second and third finger, left hand (injury occurred while placing 20mm gun in a P-61), one (1) case of nasal phyrangitis, and one (1) case of reactive depression."

My dad has a new gunner, at least for the time being. Leo E has won a furlough to the mainland. I'm not entirely sure, but I don't think they'll ever see each other again.

One more important change: All the flying officers have now moved out of their squad tents and are sleeping in Quonset huts, with real flooring.

The nightly (and sporadic daytime) missions go along. (Poet Richard Hugo: "Always the phlegm before the engines warmed.") I'll cite two such missions. "During the early morning hours of 22 June, an air attack was made against the island." This is a sentence from the monthly squadron report. It's a red alert. My dad has been scrambled along with one other Widow. From the squadron write-up: "The enemy aircraft was kept from attacking the island

and the Black Widows caused the enemy bombers to jettison their bombs in the water."

The next day, June 23, a mission for the record books: The squadron gets its first official kill. (It will turn out to be the 549th's *only* official kill of the war.) Flight Officer Donald W. Gendreau is the pilot; Flight Officer Elia A. Chiappinelli the R/O; Staff Sergeant William F. Dare the gunner. At 2:30 a.m., they're on patrol at 11,500 feet northwest of Iwo. Ground control vectors them toward an incoming object. It's a Mitsubishi G4M, which is a land-based, twin-engine, medium-range bomber known to the Yanks as a "Betty." The bomber, having now turned around, is taking violent evasive action but is beginning to lose altitude as the Widow closes. Gendreau gets to within 1,500 feet, then 800 feet, then 500 before he lets loose his cannons. The Betty's left wing is afire. She turns to port, diving and burning. From the monthly squadron report, describing the tremendous explosion when she went under the waves: "Fire on the water." It almost sounds like poetry.

In Florida, in 1982, I heard a lot about that lone confirmed kill, and some of the descriptions rose to their own poetry. Both the pilot and his R/O were there. Elia Chiappinelli traveled from Armonk, New York. The R/O looked like someone spending a lot of his retirement around golf courses: penny loafers, alligator polo shirts, shades. His old commander, Gendreau, whom everybody addressed as "Geronimo," came to the reunion from Florence, Oregon. He brought his wife. He was short and gnarled and was the life of the party. His wife kept issuing him commands: "Put that cigarette out. . . . Hush up. . . . Put that drink down." Geronimo told me that the doctors had cut out half of his stomach. He tucked at my elbow. "Shit, they want me to drink plain water. But water's got bacteria in it." He said that somewhere at home he had an 8 × 10 signed photograph of the old Hollywood star Jane Russell. She had hopped over from the States to wiggle her gams and shake her raven hair and considerable bust for the guys. He said he stole into her dressing room backstage at THE FORTY-NINER'S, and she signed the glossy. "You don't even know who Jane Russell is," the old pilot said in mock disgust. He got hold of my elbow again and nodded toward my dad: "I knew him when he was young." He pulled at my sleeve again: "We were over there at the end of the war. All these people were making these decisions over our heads. We just tried to fly our missions."

In July, the 549th flies even more missions, spends even more hours in the air, expends even more ammo. The squadron has grown to its greatest number thus far—62 officers, 250 enlisted men. The flight line for the 549th has been moved to the other side of South Field—where the taxiway is blacktopped. You don't have to get in and out of your airplane in choking dust.

Softball games have been going on. The enlisted guys thus far lead the officers' team.

There are some close calls in the air—and two sorrowful ones. I've already told what happened on July 17, 1945, when rookie Lieutenant Joe Lamont, coming in for a landing at South Field, yanked up too hard on the stick of *The Merry Widow.* On the last night of July, another 549th crew dies, and it's a shocking event, because the pilot, who is regarded as the single best flyer in the squadron, with hundreds of hours of flying time under his belt, was at the controls. But I will save the story of Larry Garland, and that of his crew, until the next chapter, because its great unsolved mysteries coincide with the end of the war itself.

The enemy is still nightly coming out of caves, desperate, starved. Quoting from an island newspaper called *Fighter Post,* mimeographed and distributed by the VII Fighter Command:

> Many of the Japs . . . had been caught on forays after water. Driven by their caves by thirst the Nips raided our water supply tanks, many of them carrying GI 5-gallon tanks and canteens. . . . The last sign of Japs still alive on Iwo came in July. On the 17th, a Jap was discovered in a hole near an anti-aircraft outfit's messhall. He was fired upon, wounded twice and taken prisoner. In the hole with him were 30 enemy dead. On July 22nd, six Japs were found in a cave on the eastern side of Iwo. Three committed suicide and the three who yield themselves were all in excellent shape and armed with hand

grenades. The books were closed on July 24th when three emaciated Japs were taken out of a cave near the Central Airfield. After three months underground, they had to be carried out on stretchers.

On the point of things happening far above your head, and you just trying to get home, to your loved ones in Xenia (or in Camden, South Carolina, or Florence, Oregon):

On June 18, 1945, the Joint Chiefs of Staff and top civilian planners had met in Washington. It was agreed that the firebombing of Japanese cities would continue, but provisions were also drawn for a seaborne invasion of the home islands. It was planned for November. Briefers with their pointers and maps projected that 25,000 troops would die in the first wave. There was no mention at the meeting of an atom bomb. Almost no one at that extreme high D.C. table had ever heard of something called the Manhattan Project, which had been formally initiated three years before. But an atom bomb was rising up out of secret ground in a high mountain and nearly walled-off desert place called Los Alamos, New Mexico.

Not quite a month after this meeting, on July 16 (my dad was in the air on the 15th, but he and his crew were resting on the 16th), the world's first nuclear test was carried out in the southern New Mexico desert. The detonation at Alamogordo, code-named Trinity, at 5:30 a.m., was equivalent to 25,000 tons of TNT. It produced temperatures hotter than the core of the sun. The following day, in Germany (my father was on a combat air patrol that night, up for two hours and forty minutes), the Potsdam Conference opened: Truman, Churchill, Stalin. Nine days into the contentious sixteen-day summit (during which Britain's national war hero and prime minister, Winston Churchill, was stunningly defeated in the general elections by Clement Attlee and his Labour Party) came the Potsdam Declaration, calling for Japan's unconditional surrender. This was on July 26, 1945. The declaration didn't make specific mention of the existence of an atomic bomb, just apocalyptic warnings of something almost beyond imagination. At the end of the declaration: "The alternative for Japan is prompt and utter destruction." In Tokyo, the Supreme War Council, a cabinet within a cabinet, was divided over whether to try to search for a negotiated settlement that might save spiritual face—or to keep fighting to the doomed end. Japan's answer to the declaration, three days later, was more or less a nonanswer: *mokusatsu,* one translation of which is "treat with silent contempt," and another meaning of which is "take no notice of." Meanwhile, Emperor Hirohito backed both factions of the Supreme Council—to attempt a negotiation which would be something less than an unconditional surrender while making plans for Operation Ketsu-Go: mobilization of the entire citizenry for suicidal protection of the empire. Some 1,470 miles away, on the island of Tinian, which sits just below Saipan in the Marianas, the materials for assembling the uranium-based "Little Boy" and the plutonium-based "Fat Man" had secretly arrived.

CALL THIS MY OWN SMALL REQUIEM *for the chapter not written.*

Approximately seventy-five times they went up into the dark together on Iwo Jima, my dad in the front, working his knobs and switches at the control wheel, the R/O in the rear, peering into his softly beeping scopes. There was no one else in the war to whom my father felt his survival was so directly tethered—he told me so himself. They slept a few feet from each other in the same squad tent and later in the same Quonset hut. I can remember with what affection his name was spoken when I was growing up: Jack Kerr, Paul. He's your godfather. Wonder whatever happened to him. *The name grew to have almost a poetic resonance in my ear. It felt faintly dreamlike. It sounded so American:* Jack Kerr.

My mom had known him well, too, while he and my dad were still stateside, training at their various airfields in Florida and California in 1943 and 1944, before they went over. My mom told me once that, since my dad's radar guy wasn't married, and was so far from home, she felt a little protective of him, almost as if he was her kid brother. (He was two years older than my mom, almost to the day.) My folks would have him over to supper, in whatever cheap rental they were living, to make sure he got some home cooking into his belly. Maybe they sat around after, listening to game shows on the radio before he went back to the base. After my christening on that May Sunday in Fresno in 1944, three weeks after the 549th got officially activated, my mom wrote in my baby book, channeling my wordless infant voice: "At three weeks to St. Theresa's Church to be baptized with my Mother, Daddy and Flight Officer Kerr. I was really angry with the priest for pouring water on my head and screamed all during the ceremony." *She slightly misspelled the church's name, very unlike her.*

So why wouldn't it have been one of my priorities, not to say great curiosities, to try to track down my "disappeared" godfather? One of the mysteries for me is that my folks should have lost touch so soon after the war, and vice versa. I knew from his obituary, easy enough to find on the web, that he had died in July 1997, six years before my father. Surely, I'd be able to locate and talk to his kids, roughly in my own age bracket.

Well, no. At least on the talking part.

I have spoken to numerous people in his extended family, including nieces and nephews and cousins (and one former in-law). I've spoken with old neighbors. I've kept in loose contact with three of his five grandchildren, who've been generous with their time. (They're roughly a generation younger than I am, with families and successful careers, including, in the case of one grandchild, a career that has included a significant stint in the FBI, as both a field agent and Washington desk person.)

But of the four biological children in Jack Kerr's nuclear family, nothing, or at least next to nothing. (For an explanation of that, please see the Essay on Sources.) That's the hole in the center. I know where they are, or approximately so. I have tried hard to reach out in various ways. Without their willingness to participate, or so I've sadly decided, there can be no Jack Kerr story, or at least there won't be one here, save for these scant paragraphs. Why? Only his children could tell me in truly meaningful and firsthand ways about things that did or did not happen in this family. But they are choosing to keep their silence, their distance, which is their absolute right. The idealist in me is willing to believe it might not always be this way.

I know this: There has been some large sorrow and deep estrangement in the family of Jack Kerr, both in the immediate nuclear unit and among certain members in the next generation down. That part is unarguable. Do I understand the sources and reasons of it all? I do not. The pain my godfather carried home from the war had its emotional residue, its capillary oozing—it's all I can conclude from my reporting. I don't feel I have the moral or ethical right to say anything more. Perhaps you are reading this and feeling a little annoyed, feeling I am trying to tantalize, trying to have it both ways. But I'm not. Nor am I trying to seem stiff-necked in my journalistic principles.

Principles? Just days ago, as I am writing this, I showed up without warning on the doorstep of the home of a close Kerr family relative and was treated with more kindliness and respect than I might have shown *had the situation been reversed. The reason I came to this relative's door unannounced was because I thought it was my best chance to show my earnestness—in person. I was doing the rude thing reporters do, and if I felt a little smutty about it, it didn't keep me from doing it. I knew that this relative was in touch with key family members. I was hoping to gain some ground.*

We stood for ten minutes on the sidewalk in the glaring August heat. The relative, also in upper age, shifted from one foot to the next, and I was doing the same. The relative was sizing me up, having heard about me and my quest. (The relative's spouse, who was the first person I had encountered when I had arrived, had been distinctly unfriendly, but I more than understand it now.) The relative said, "Oh, all right, let's go out back by the pool where there's some shade." For almost an hour, I was told many things, some of which I already knew. We spoke of the sorrow, and the residues of those sorrows, and the separation among certain members. I was trying to get at the root of the estrangements and separations. How did it happen? When did it begin happening? The relative shrugged and said, "I wasn't there." And yet this relative spoke softly, warmly, of "Uncle Jack." Others have done the same. This relative teared up more than once. Others have done the same. We walked together to my car at the curb. We shook hands—it could almost have been a hug. I could sense how torn the relative was in wanting to help.

In lieu of saying anything specific about the inside of the story, which, to acknowledge again, I know only in fractured and secondhand ways, let me say something about its outside. The outside seems so, well, nor-mal, ordinary, banal. *That's the paradox, that's the point.*

My disappeared godfather didn't disappear at all, of course. He climbed out of The Rita B *and said goodbye to my father (I know nothing of the circumstances of their parting, but it had to have been emotional) and went right back to the suburban New Jersey ground where he was born and raised. He studied education at night on the G.I. Bill at Seton Hall University. He got married to Gladys Reick, who lived a town over from his own. His first son got born. (He'd grow up to become, among other things, a champion high school wrestler, even as his own dad, in the prewar thirties, had been a statewide amateur high school boxing champ.) The three lived in a too-cramped apartment in a small building at 132 William Street in the bay town of Perth Amboy. He taught seventh* *and eighth graders and presided over homerooms in area schools called Oak Tree and Clara Barton. In 1955 he moved into his first home (which was his last home) on a nice little cul-de-sac called Robert Circle in the solidly middle-class borough of Metuchen. It was a two-story Cape Cod, like every other house on the cul-de-sac. He became a high school vice principal, where he patrolled the halls, and gave out plenty of detentions, at least to the recalcitrant boys. (I've talked to about a dozen graduates of the class of 1960 at Edison High School, who are all in their eighties now, and the consensus is that Mr. Kerr with his short haircut and neat-as-a-pin appearance was a hardass but a fair hardass, who liked throwing around the name "Sport." As in: "Guess what, Sport: you just scored yourself another detention.") At his parish he joined the Holy Name Society and the Knights of Columbus. He enlarged the garage behind his house for his power tools. He paneled his basement and put in a knotty-pine bar. He installed an aboveground pool in the backyard (first in the neighborhood, supposedly) and on summer weekends taught nieces and nephews—there were half a dozen living in nearby Jersey towns—how to do a cannonball off the makeshift diving board. He shingled a new roof with the help of his soon-to-be son-in-law. He retired after thirty years, having worked successfully as both a teacher and administrator at about six different schools, most of them in sprawling Edison Township. He assembled scale model airplanes with grandkids. He helped his grandson Scott design and build a soapbox derby wooden go-cart. Later they rebuilt a V-8 engine side by side in the garage. He let out yet another notch on his belt. He got diagnosed with cancer, and then he died. He was seventy-six. His upper-end cherry casket cost $1,690, and the whole burial bill topped out at $10,361.25. His funeral Mass was at the diocesan cathedral, St. Francis of Assisi, and then they placed him in a plot belonging to his in-laws in a Catholic cemetery that was about a five-minute drive from where he'd been born on February 19, 1921. His wife is there, too, now. She had outlived him by twenty-one years.*

I could go on, but to what end? None of it would get to the heart of what is worth writing of, which to my mind could be stated thusly: What did a seeming good American man, much loved by my parents, who went away to war at too young an age, carry back home and unwittingly foist off onto the ones he loved most in his life? If that is the Jack Kerr story, it is also the story of ten million other World War II veterans, including my own father, my own family. I hope that's clear by now.

In The Sense of an Ending, *British author Julian Barnes's magnificent 2011 novella, there are these two sentences as the story draws to
its close: "And that's a life, isn't it? Some achievements and some disap-
pointments." The author's calm and darkly spooky tale is about a man
whose existence, if you were only peering at it through its outer skin,
would strike you as so commonplace that it would seem hardly worth
commenting on. No passage in the book moves me more than this one:*

*Does character develop over time? In novels, of course it does:
otherwise there wouldn't be much of a story. But in life? I sometimes wonder. Our attitudes and opinions change, we develop new
habits and eccentricities; but that's something different, more like
decoration. Perhaps character resembles intelligence, except that
character peaks a little later; between twenty and thirty, say. And
after that, we're just stuck with what we've got. We're on our own.
If so, that would explain a lot of lives, wouldn't it? And also—if this
isn't too grand a word—our tragedy.*

*Does the Jack Kerr story—by which I really mean the Jack Kerr fam-
ily story—amount to a significant sadness, and can some or a lot of it be
laid at the foot of Iwo Jima, which he experienced in his mid-twenties?
My answer to the first part of the question would be a hedging yes. And
my answer to the second would be that it seems far too simplistic to say
so. The "tragedy" had a lot of grit and triumph in it, too, not to say heroism. What a father passed down against his will to his children, and
then what got suffered down to some of his children's children, likely had
a hundred other fathers as well. But Black Widows in the Pacific dark
had to have played their unquantifiable part. Maybe someday I'll be able
to give the John Henry Kerr story the treatment it deserves—or at least
try. For now, I need leave it here, unfinished, with its hole in its middle,
with this pale synopsis of all I had once schemed and dreamed to produce
about the godfather I never knew.*

The All-American Life and Mysterious Death
of Larry Garland
(and the Crew of Black Widow #42-39426)

Left to right: Captain Larry Garland, Major Lit Alford, my dad

I KNOW WHAT IT IS: refracted sunlight bouncing off the metal skin of the plane's fuselage. Still, the way it's shafting down the side of my father's face and across his collarbone and brushing his forearm and touching his kneecap before emptying itself into the gravel-crushed earth four inches from his left boot makes me imagine something else. I think this is God talking. I think the Almighty is transmitting a message, an illumination, and it's coming just to my dad, whether he can hear it or not: *Son, you're going to make it out of here, you're going to get home to Xenia to that beautiful waiting wife and those two little babies.*

And he will.

I wish to tell here the story of someone who had no benevolent beam, no such shaft of protective light, who didn't make it out of there—who died, along with his crewmen, at 9:15 at night, just after dark, on July 31, 1945, about fifteen miles northwest of Iwo Jima, in weather that wasn't a factor, despite what some have claimed. There have been so many claims and attempted explanations through the years for something that remains inexplicable: an apparent nosedive, with no warning, in what seemed about five seconds of elapsed time, straight into the ocean, on the way back from an uneventful patrol mission, after having been up for about two hours and fifteen minutes. (The only thing that came to the surface was one side of the ship's left wing. No bodies, or even pieces of them.)

What can be said for certain is that the person I'm speaking of— you're gazing at his picture—was sitting at the control wheel of the ship that disappeared. Captain Larry Garland was the ablest flyer in the squadron. He had more combat hours than anyone else in the outfit. He seemed possessed of a natural flying gift, as he once had a natural gift for snaring passes on his big-time Southeastern Conference college football team and sprinting for a touchdown. Squint at the photograph anew. Try mentally to remove every wartime trapping in it—the flight jackets, the fatigue pants, the caps with their insignia, the big hulking machine itself. Try to blot out my dad and the figure in the middle. (He's Major James L. Alford, the operations officer, the second-in-charge of the 549th NFS. That's his Widow behind them. He's named her *"Sleepy Time Gal"* after his baby daughter Emily back home in Mississippi. He's got a tiny pearl cameo of her affixed to the middle of his steering column. His fellow officers know him as "Lit" Alford, and that's because his middle name is Louis. Lit is its affectionate corruption. I met him at the 1982 reunion in Orlando. I didn't dare call him Lit. He was a rich lawyer with a deep Southern drawl.)

Take away maybe seven or eight years from Larry Garland's

handsome and boyish face, so that he looks even more boyish and handsome than he does here. Fashion onto his six-foot-one frame and 175 pounds some shoulder pads and a jersey and one of those old-fashioned leather helmets. Just by the ease of his body language, the way he's posed, so naturally, as if he's done this a hundred times before (and he has), can't you see that what he's really doing is taking a knee in front of his head coach in a circle of his teammates for a last-minute instruction just before the starting gun fires and the boys rise up and roar out onto the white-striped green field while the stands erupt with their own roars?

For a lot of years, in junior high and high school and college, that was the idolized life of Laurence Joseph Garland Jr. Although don't get the wrong idea: He was hardly just a star jock. If anything, he had always had an even greater life off the field. Off the field, out of his pads (or his basketball or baseball uniform for that matter), he was the all-around classroom boy, an academic star, a social star, most especially in his high-achieving Lexington, Kentucky, public high school, where he seemed, in the spring of 1935, to have walked off at graduation with every laurel, including something called the Yale Cup. (I've held it in my hand, and I'll explain more about it later.)

Something else that can't be equivocated: The death of Larry Garland, and that of his comrades, on the last night of July 1945, occurred two weeks before the end of World War II. Consider: Six days later, on August 6, the first atomic bomb got dropped on Hiroshima. Three days later the second otherworldly blast at Nagasaki. Five days after, on the 14th, Japan surrendered. Like that, the awful four-year thing was over. The next day, in Times Square, drunk sailors were grabbing white-stockinged nurses for bent-over and full lip-locks. It was as if all of America was climbing lampposts and staggering around in lascivious joy, a collective exhale of relief. V-J Day was here.

That seems a hard enough irony: that the deaths of three young men still in their twenties should have come so close to the end. But then add to it this: Their families never got word, any kind of word, until twenty-two days after the fact, eight days after Japan had surrendered. What the families of Larry Garland and Milton Gillespie and John Maxwell Hendrix believed in the eight days after August 14 was what every other family in America who had a son or brother or husband in the war believed: Their loved one would be home soon. Safe.

They didn't find out until late on the evening of August 22, when somebody came to the door with a yellow envelope, and in the envelope one of those terrifying half sheets of off-white paper on which the all-cap Teletype words are glued on in strips.

THE SECRETARY OF WAR HAS ASKED ME TO EXPRESS HIS DEEP REGRET THAT YOUR SON WAS KILLED IN ACTION ON IWO JIMA 31 JULY 45 CONFIRMING LETTER FOLLOWS EF WITSELL ACTING THE ADJUTANT GENERAL OF THE ARMY.

Surely, it was some kind of mistake, not possible this could have happened three weeks and a day ago, 10,000 miles away, and you are being informed only now, after peace has come.

I've seen two of those Western Unions. They're pasted in old passed-down Garland and Gillespie and Hendrix family albums, some of which seem in danger of crinkling into nothingness. Their present-day keepers have allowed me to run my fingers over the raised lettering.

The time stamp is 8:55 p.m. But that must represent only the time when the wires got sent out from Washington, D.C. They were delivered to their respective addresses in Kentucky and North Carolina and Connecticut at some point later that night. It's an engraved memory, part of the myth of each family's story, and "myth" here is meant in its truest sense. The lateness of the notification itself, and the lateness of the hour of delivery, whether it was at 9:30 or five minutes to midnight, were obscene. So was the cold minimalism of the message itself. Letter to follow.

The lead paragraph of a one-column, four-paragraph story on page ten of the morning *Lexington* (Kentucky) *Herald,* August 23, 1945: "Capt. Lawrence Garland Jr., 28, son of Mr. and Mrs. Lawrence J. Garland, 111 Louisiana avenue, was killed in action on Iwo Jima on July 31, according to a War Department telegram received by his parents last night." (The paper misspelled the first name of both Larry and his father; it happened all through Larry's life.)

"Yes. Well. The story I always heard, and of course I wasn't alive yet, was that Grandaddy and Grandmother had just come back with some relatives and friends from an amusement park in Lexington called Joyland," Larry Garland's niece told me quietly on the telephone the first time we spoke. Her name is Marsha Phillips. "They came home and then they found out. And all these people, you know, neighbors and so forth, standing out in the yard, not quite knowing what to say."

I can't quite get out of my head a picture of some half sheets of paper, having just been delivered, the glued-on words having just been read, or glanced at, fluttering and seesawing like little paper airplanes to a sidewalk or top step or maybe to the linoleum entryway of a house.

Does that sound overly dramatic? Fine, let it sound like that.

Thanks to COVID and other reasons, more than two years went by, after Marsha Phillips first told me about Joyland and her grandparents and the wire and neighbors in the yard, before I could get on an airplane and travel to Lexington, Kentucky, to visit her—and then she told me some other things, too. She's a few years younger than I. She is Larry Garland's closest living descendant. He was unmarried when he died, and he had only one younger sibling, Marsha's deceased mother. Marsha is an only child, so she is the last of the immediate family. She's had a large career in marketing and buying for major department stores that took her far away from Kentucky, but she is back home now. She lives alone. I have found her to be a searching and open and extremely generous person—with both her memories and her mementos. Against all my protestations, she insisted I take home her Uncle Larry's overstuffed scrapbook from his high school and college years. (His mother had kept it devotedly, scissoring out and pasting in all the pictures and stories from the local papers about her boy.)

Marsha also insisted I take home with me a little white box containing some of her uncle's personal effects. One of them is a silver bracelet, tarnished with age, surprisingly heavy, sitting on the desk where I am writing this morning. The bracelet consists of two lengths of chain hooked to a curvilinear bar with a pair of raised wings on its front. On the back side, in tiny italic script engraved into the silver, it says: *L.J. Garland O-795383.* Captain Garland wasn't wearing his beautiful Air Corps bracelet on the night he disappeared into the ocean with his twenty-one-year-old gunner and his twenty-four-year-old radar operator. My two surviving siblings and I possess a fair number of personal treasures from our dad's time in the war. Sadly, no letters at all, as you've already heard. Some of his medals and ribbons, yes. And a formal citation from his superiors, typed out on cheap newsprint, attesting to his courage. (You can read it at the back of this book.) And not least, our several dozen shared photographs. Still, I'd give a lot to have a heavy silver bracelet with our dad's name and serial number engraved in dainty script on its back side. I'm grateful beyond what I can say to have his comrade's. Every time I lift the bracelet out of the box, I get almost a tactile feeling about the person to whom it belonged.

"And you know, Paul, he was an All-American at the University of Kentucky," my dad said, the first time I ever heard him speak of the legend of Larry Garland. No, he wasn't. But that's almost beside the point.

I've known for a while I was going to try to write about what happened to Larry Garland and his crewmates on the night of July 31, 1945, and to try to understand it in the context of my dad's life. I suppose the reasons why are obvious. I don't begin to have any definitive answers to all the mysteries, which seem to spread outward like a series of concentric circles. But what I do have are some significant ironies and emotional cruelties.

The greatest poet of World War I may be Wilfred Owen. He served in the trenches of the British Army. He was a second lieutenant, with the engraved words inside him. One of his finest poems, published posthumously in 1920, is "Dulce et Decorum Est," its title in bitter reference to Horace. The words are Latin for "It is sweet and fitting," and they are meant as moral condemnation of the Roman poet's lie of how "sweet and honorable it is to die for one's country" (*pro patria mori* is the rest of Horace's line in Ode 3.2). Owen's poem is full of awful imagery (which is to say unforgettable imagery) about British soldiers getting gassed in the trenches. The oldest surviving draft of the poem is the one he sent to his mother in October 1917 with this note: "Here is a gas poem done yesterday." In 1917, Susan Owen's son had a mental breakdown at the front. Then, the condition was known as "shell shock." The shells containing the chlorine gas have just gone off, and a comrade can't get his mask on in time. The following two lines haunt me: "Dim through the misty panes and thick green light, / As under a green sea, I saw him drowning." I know they're about the exploding chlorine and the panic to get the mask on, but they make me think about something else.

Wilfred Owen got well and went back to the front. He was killed in action on November 4, 1918, one week before the Armistice was signed. He was twenty-five.

Why not reference another master? "Back out of all this now too much for us, / Back in a time made simple by the loss / Of detail, burned, dissolved, and broken off," Robert Frost wrote at the start of a hard-to-discern poem entitled "Directive." All right. Let me back out from what I've thus far related and direct you for a moment back toward something about which you already know. I mean to put a new slant on what you know. Again, you'll need to keep the photograph above much in your mind's eye. Again, I don't have the exact date, but I think it was taken in midsummer 1945, not long before a descent into the ocean with no known cause.

Go back nearly eight years before, to the fall of 1937. There isn't yet something called World War II. You could almost think of this period, at least by comparison, as one made simple, even innocent, never mind the fact of the ongoing ravages of the Depression. A recent graduate of Morganfield High School, biding his time, working daylight to dark on his father's farm, is soon to get on his

Greyhound and take himself northward with the honking geese and all his fears and curiously deep ambitions out of Morganfield to Chanute Field at Rantoul, Illinois.

In the photograph at the start, can't you still see some Union County–*ness* in my dad? I see it instantly in the flipped-up brim of the ball cap. I think he thinks he looks cool. (To be fair, I've seen a lot of pictures of old 549ers, both officers and enlisted guys, with their brims snapped up—I don't mean to imply you had to be from Morganfield to wear your hat like this when you were off duty.) Joe Paul Hendrickson (*Joepaul* Hendrickson), no matter the amazing distances he's come, no matter some of the great tests he's since faced, is still at bottom a western Kentucky shitkicker. And God bless him for it.

Let's say—and not quite arbitrarily—that it's mid-morning, September 24, 1937. In less than two months my dad will be on a bus to his new life. I have no exact idea of what he's doing on the morning of September 24. It's a Friday, not yet the end of the farming workweek (the end of the farming workweek is about five hours on Sunday afternoon, starting after church and lasting until the evening milking), so in some form or other he must be getting the grime beneath his fingernails and around the neck of his muslin shirt.

On the other hand, I know just what lithe and gifted Larry Garland is doing on the morning of September 24. He's on the other side of the state. He's up in Lexington, home of the big state university, land of private-label bourbon and Southern belles and burly tobacco and Thoroughbred breeding farms. Lexington is a small, beautiful, mid-South city, deeply provincial and self-satisfied in its own way, 228 miles east of itty-bitty Morganfield. It might as well be sitting on the other side of the moon in terms of anything a sharecropper's boy knows about university life and rich horse farms in the bluegrass country. It might as well be Athens or Rome.

Larry Garland is wearing a sport jacket and a tie—and maybe saddle shoes, too. He's about to board a private train car with coaches and trainers and thirty-one other teammates of the University of Kentucky Wildcats, bound for Nashville and tomorrow's varsity football season opener against those smarty-pant high IQ

boys from Vanderbilt. At trackside this morning, coeds are blow-
ing kisses and throwing confetti and holding up rah-rah banners.
The "Best Band in Dixie," as the UK marching band likes to pro-
mote itself, is on hand, tooting the boys off. Some of Larry's fra-
ternity brothers from Sigma Alpha Epsilon, one of the best houses
on campus, have gotten their carcasses out of bed and over to the
depot to send up a few bawdy cheers.

Larry Garland, who was second-string on the team last year as
a sophomore, has beat out "Duke" Ellington to become a starter.

The three-decker and three-column headline in this morning's
student newspaper, *The Kentucky Kernel:* "KENTUCKY NAILS
ASPIRATIONS ON NINE VETS, TWO ROOKIES, IN GRID
BOW AGAINST VANDY." And the headline below that: "MEN-
TORS, 32 VARSITYMEN BOARD TRAIN FOR NASHVILLE.
SCENE OF DIXIE'S BEST FOOTBALL GAME." And a third
headline: "WILDCATS, WITH SPRINKLED INJURIES BUT
SCORE-THIRSTY HEARTS, EN ROUTE TO DEMOLISH
COMMODORE JINX."

(Alas, they're not going to demolish the jinx; they'll go down
12–zip in the rain tomorrow.)

Let's move the calendar up by another month or so. It's Tuesday, October 19. Three days ago, on the 16th, these same campus
heroes have slaughtered Washington and Lee University, 41–6.
Tight end Larry Garland, who has been asked to do double duty
as a placekicker and point-after-touchdown specialist, has shown
some right pigskin stuff. From this morning's story in the *Kernel,*
written by one of the paper's columnists, George Kerler, in his
column, "Bull Pen," which is celebrated on campus for the quality
of its purple prose:

Speaking of Larry Garland reminds us of the cheerable extra-
pointing he did to end happily each of Kentucky's first five
touchdowns. Larry is a place-kicking rookie but the finesse
and mechanical precision with which he lifted the oval
through the one-point gate marked him as a reliable score
increaser. . . . Garland's manipulations around his wing area
become more polished and effective as the games go by. Pos-

sessed of untapped natural ability, he seems destined to be one of 1938's greats.

Which is to say that although he's doing fine things on the team this year, who knows what he'll be able to accomplish next season as a senior?

The Washington and Lee game got a recap in the sports pages of the Sunday *New York Times.* There's Larry's name at the top of the UK roster, noting his five perfect placekicks through the "one-point gate." (Not that the *Times* put it as such.)

He's still only twenty. He has always seemed about a year ahead of himself in both life and school. He was born on May 18, 1917. In nine days, my dad will turn nineteen. But he is only recently out of high school, which is as far as he's ever going to get in his formal education, while Larry, just seventeen months older, is already halfway through college. He's a psychology major. Half of these blockheads may be majoring in phys ed, but this is a real student athlete. He intends to go to graduate school and get his master's.

Last year, even though he didn't start, he still lettered (as well as played varsity basketball). Last year, he had a near-triumphant moment against the University of Tennessee. The UK-Tennessee grudge match is played on Thanksgiving Day. The football rivalry dates to 1910. But why not let the wordsmiths of the *Kernel* take over? "Tommy Coleman was sent into the game as a passer and on his first try he floated a beautiful pitch out to Lawrence Garland who gathered it in and hoofed it seventy yards only to be forced out of bounds on the Vol five-yard stripe." Alas, again: The Wildcats lost. Still, you run seventy yards in the biggest game of the season as a soph—that thrill could almost take you through a lifetime.

Finally, let's flip the calendar of 1937 forward once more, to the third week of November, to *this* year's upcoming Thanksgiving tilt against the hated Volunteers. Down in Morganfield, this is the week when my dad gets on his bus. (It was Tuesday the 16th.) In Lexington, fevered news and feature stories (not just in the *Kernel* but in the town's two dailies as well) are running about next week's game, to take place on the 25th. It'll be Homecoming week. Festivities have already begun. Today, with the game still six days off, the *Kernel* is outdoing itself. The freshmen will be parading through town in their pajamas. "PARTIES, TEAS, OPEN HOUSES INCLUDED ON CALENDAR" is one of the headlines. "ANNUAL ALUMNI HOP SET FOR THURSDAY." Larry Garland's frat, SAE, is expecting a big return of alums.★

I couldn't read those stories of Friday, November 19, 1937, without thinking of a homesick nineteen-year-old on his cot in his barracks at Rantoul. He's been at Chanute for three days. My dad told me once that there were something like a couple hundred men, raw recruits and otherwise, assigned to his first-ever barracks. "Just the snoring, Paul," he said.

Does Larry Garland understand how charmed his life is?

As under a green sea, I saw him drowning. In the beginning I thought this was going to be a story just about Larry Garland. It was almost as if I had forgotten—or at least not thought enough about the fact—that two other Americans died on the night of July 31, 1945, in Black Widow #42-39426. I can't speak about their lives in the way I wish to, but I can make some small amends to my near-obtuseness. I can offer up some further ironies.

A question for which no one seems to have an explanation: How and why did *two* sons of Lexington, the one born with a seeming gold spoon in his mouth, the other from the wrong side of the socioeconomic tracks, end up in the same airplane, sitting a few feet from each other when she seemed to hurl herself into the ocean like something out of a slingshot?

From all I can determine, it just happened, this rather amazing coincidence.

Not only were the pilot and his young gunner raised in the same town, but at one point their two families had lived one street over from each other. Larry Garland and Milton Burnett Gillespie never

---

★ Something else caught my eye in that Friday's edition of the *Kernel*, a "lighthearted" piece on the history of Lexington: "That ornate fountain by the courthouse was not always a watering trough. For many years a whipping post was there and those citizens who disliked the unpleasant task of whipping their slaves themselves could send them down-town where a man earned his living wielding a cat o'nine tails. Nearby was the block where slaves were mounted for appraisal and sale."

knew each other growing up. They were too far apart in age and in almost every other way. Figuratively, you could say, they met climbing up the same small ladder tucked behind the nosewheel of their airplane.

Leona and Edward Gillespie, with eight kids, never quite made it into the Lexington middle class, at least while those eight were getting raised. "We were poor. We were Lexington working people," Milt Gillespie's baby sister told me on the phone, the first time we spoke. I could hear the flinty pride. Again, as with Marsha Phillips, two years would elapse before I sat in her dining room, at a table with Milton's letters, with many family photographs, and hear some of the heartaches about the big brother she never knew.

Her name is Shirley Beck. She's in her mid-eighties. She is the last Gillespie child alive. Like Marsha Phillips, she seems almost startlingly forthright and generous with her feelings. We have shared many emails and phone calls. I've come to have a huge affection for her. Like Marsha, she is so alert to everything around her—as if time is running short, and she still has so many unanswered questions. She is a deep Christian who tries to read her Bible every day. In the worst of COVID, when she couldn't attend Sunday church, she told me that she'd get up at 5 a.m. to livestream a Baptist preacher. She'd pray along with him in her living room.

Shirley Beck, who paints her nails and wears stylish clothes and speaks in the soft rhythms of her native ground, lives in northern Kentucky, up close to Cincinnati, in a town called Erlanger, about an hour and a half by car from Lexington, where she was born and raised. She was a caretaker at home for her husband, who had lost a leg, and who had other ailments, right up to the end. Her middle-aged daughter, Michelle, lives with her, and she, too, has been open and generous with her time.

Shirley is fifteen years younger than the sibling she was not meant to know. Milt was the eldest, born in 1923, so if he were alive now, he'd be a centenarian. By the time Shirley, the youngest Gillespie, got born, in 1938, her brother had already left home. At fourteen he went up to Michigan (ninth grade was the highest he ever got in school) to stay with maternal relatives. He ended up staying until he was seventeen and could join the service.

"All these things. I keep thinking about them now," Shirley told me. "How did my mom allow him to go away so young like that? It was as if he went away and never got back."

Shirley's father was a Lexington fireman. The fireman used to ride the bus to the firehouse. In the early fall of 1944, he got off a city bus on Main Street and fell over dead on the sidewalk of a heart attack. He was only in his fifties. Before the police and ambulance could arrive—to try to do anything they could for one of their own—a bystander reached down and, from the fireman's fourth finger of his right hand, twisted off a black onyx ring, stuck it in his pocket, and walked away. Shirley's mom had given the ring to her husband as a present. She'd never really spent money on something like that before. She had had his initials engraved on it: *E.A.G.* Edward Austin Gillespie. A black onyx stone is said to give its wearer vibrations of willpower and strength and protection.

"My father dying on the sidewalk like that, broad daylight, some-body taking a ring off his finger, which my mother would have saved up for, and then Milton dying about ten or eleven months later in the dark. I just cannot imagine the impact of things like this on my mother."

At her father's viewing, one of Shirley's aunts took hold of her and started pulling her toward the casket. "I don't want to go," cried the six-year-old, trying to wrench free. "If you touch a dead man's hand, you'll never have bad dreams about him," the aunt said. She pushed Shirley's hand down into the folds of the casket. The child felt her father's skin and bolted backward.

Leona Gillespie knew she'd not be able to afford living in the family's current rental, so she picked up her family and moved them over to a smaller rental at 154 East Sixth Street. It was and is one of the poorer sections of Lexington, wooden shotgun houses sitting in rows. That's where a three-line telegram from the War Department got delivered on August 22, 1945.

Dead? In his war photographs, Shirley's big brother looks like he could live forever. There's one of him in uniform sitting on a striped sofa somewhere out in Hawaii. Maybe he's in an enlisted men's club at Pearl Harbor. He's holding a cig. There are potted palms behind him. He's thumbing through a picture magazine. He's got a killer grin, with something devilish in it.

Before he got out to Hawaii, the Army Air Corps had sent the soldier to stations in Oklahoma and Newfoundland and Connecticut—which is where he met Helen Muszynski. She was three years older. The good Polish Catholic girl and the Lexington boy who'd been brought up Baptist got married in just one more of those 10,000 sped-up wartime weddings. This one was in the early fall of 1941. Two years later, Milton junior was in the picture. About six months later, Milton senior got sent overseas, to Hawaii, where he trained for aerial gunnery. It would be a while before the enlisted man found himself as part of the 549th NFS, before he found himself, as if by some stroke of providence, in the same airplane as a big grid star from his hometown, sitting in a plexi bubble right behind.

A letter from Hawaii, dated September 9, 1944. (The 549th hasn't gotten to Hawaii yet.) Six days before, Milton's dad has died at the Lexington bus stop. He's trying to lift grieving hearts. The eldest son, far from home, addresses it: "Dearest Mother and All." He says, "I had a letter from Helen today, and she says the baby is getting cuter every day, and just as full of mischief." He signs it, "Sincerely your son forever and ever. Milton."

Three days later, a base newspaper at Pearl Harbor, published by the Seventh Air Force, runs a little feature on the noncom.

> Meet S. Sgt Milton B. Gillespie, who used to call Lexington, Ky. home. He moved North to Unionville, Conn. when he married. That's where his Helen and Milton, the second— are waiting to greet him after the war. Dark-haired, blue-eyed and clean-cut looking, Gil has made a host of friends in the Army because of his sincerity and friendliness. . . . Calvert's 'n' coke is his favorite refreshment. He is nertz [nuts] about horses. He will eat banana pudding any time he can get it. Next to Helen he thinks Dinah Shore is terrific.

On August 22, 1945, Helen Gillespie, with her not quite two-year-old toddler, was about to turn in for the night in her flat at 28 Railroad Avenue in Unionville, Connecticut, when a man came to the door with a Western Union telegram that could not possibly have been correct.

A week later, on the 29th, the refusing widow wrote to her mother-in-law. "Dearest Mother," she began. A few lines in: "Mother, I don't believe it, somehow I know that Milton is alive, I know I didn't wait and pray all this time for nothing, maybe I have a lot of trust in God."

The next paragraph: "Before Milton left for overseas he promised me he'd be back, that he had Milton and me to come back to and he said it was a promise, I believe him, every time he made a promise to me he kept it and I know he'll keep this one." Next paragraph: "We're having a Mass Sat. morning and it's to pray that the telegram was a big mistake, I'm sure it was." At the close: "Somehow I know that Milton is coming back to us, I just know he is."

When the eldest Gillespie child died on Iwo, it meant almost nothing to the youngest. Shirley was seven. "I think two of my older brothers—maybe it was Clyde and Marvin, I don't remember— came and found me and told me my big brother Milton was dead. I think I probably said something like, 'Oh, who's he?' Or maybe I just nodded and went outside and played."

Of the eight children in the Gillespie family, four of them served their country. Three Gillespie sons went to the Marines. Shirley herself grew up and joined up—as a lady Marine reservist. One of her brothers, Clyde, is buried at Quantico in Virginia—a Marine lifer.

Every now and then, after she was grown, Shirley used to walk by Lexington's Cathedral of Christ the King church. Larry Garland's parents, who lived two blocks away, of whom she knew nothing, had never seen or met, had arranged to have a small statue and plaque of their son placed in his memory on the cathedral grounds. Shirley had a sister who lived nearby. She'd visit with her and then go over to the church and look at the statue. This was Catholic ground, and she was Baptist, so she'd just stand on the sidewalk and look over. It made her feel very sad. It was almost as if her brother had died a Lexington unknown, at least compared to Larry Garland.

We were sitting in her dining room, fingering photographs, reading letters when she said this. She looked up. There was a sad look on her face. Funny, she said, "Milt was the brother I never knew." She paused. And now, she said, toward the end of her life, "It's almost as if I can't get my brother out of my mind."

About half a dozen times, I've heard Shirley Beck, who has been nothing but kindly to me, say that, before she goes, she wants to know what happened that night. The quiet with which she has said it belies the burn of its intensity.

I have heard some dark theories about what *did* happen that night, in Widow #42-39426, for which I can find no corroboration, so I will keep those theories to myself. (I've looked long and hard.) Was it mechanical failure? It's been ruled out. "Was it a heart attack, Paul?" I heard my dad say once. (It was in Orlando when Larry's name came into the talk around the table. My dad's voice had raised itself half an octave into that register of quizzical softness.) How does a specimen of a twenty-eight-year-old athlete have a heart attack on the way home from a routine mission? Was it a bolt of lightning, which didn't really hurt the ship but disoriented the pilot? That explanation, too, has been discarded. There is a phenomenon known as flying into a "black hole," when you can lose sudden perspective with the ground, the sea, the stars, any kind of reckoning. It's a kind of vertigo, attacking your inner ear. But night fighter pilots were aces at reckoning, at keeping themselves oriented, at managing not to get vertigo.

I have combed the accident reports. Nothing explains it with any satisfaction. There are some letters.

This one, from the CO, Major Joe Payne, dated August 8, 1945, but which didn't reach the family until sometime after the Western Union and an official War Department letter written the next day. I have come to believe (from other evidence) that Payne's letter, almost certainly against his wishes, got held on to for maybe two or three weeks before it left Iwo. It didn't get sent out until after a full investigation had been completed.

It's so heartfelt. "He was returning from a mission and called the island control and informed them he was approaching the island.

Just a few minutes later they were seen to crash into the sea. . . . There was no way of determining the cause. . . . His death came as a great shock to me and every member of this squadron. . . . Larry, as he was known to us, was held in high regard by everyone. . . . Larry was my closest friend and can never be replaced."

A second letter, from Lit Alford. It is four times as long as the CO's, and if anything, even more heartbroken, searching. It is dated September 3, 1945. It must not have reached the family until deep into that month, which would have been almost two months after the plane went down.

As a fellow officer and friend of Larry's I can truthfully say that nothing has been as hard for this Squadron to try to bear up under. . . . Larry and I alternated nights being in charge of the briefing and of the flying. . . . That was Larry's night on duty and he had been off the night before. The boys in his flight said that Larry went to bed after the show on the night of the 30th and got up about 8 A.M. the following morning. He had a short nap after lunch on the 31st. He was in perfect physical condition and was in a very happy frame of mind as the crews said that he was very cheerful at the briefing. After the briefing he had joked with the Flight Surgeon for 15 or 20 minutes before he went out to his plane to take off. The Flight Surgeon said that he knows that Larry felt fine. . . . I conducted a formal investigation of the accident and my finding for the cause of the accident was "Unknown." Larry's plane was one of the best in the Squadron and his crew chief, T/Sgt. Youra is without doubt the best and most qualified mechanic on the island. Larry was by far the best pilot in the Squadron and was not about to let himself get into trouble. He had been flying in some clouds about an hour before . . . but at the time of the crash was in clear skies. . . . Whatever happened, it happened so quickly that Larry was unable to do anything about it. Also, knowing Larry as I do, I know that if he had even a few seconds warning he would have ordered the other two members of the crew to bail out even if he had known it was impossible to save himself.

A third letter, from his crew chief, Danny Youra, dated September 10, 1945: "I was the last person to talk to Larry and he was in the best of spirits. He left on his normal mission with the parting words, 'Take it easy Danny.' His whole crew were in a very good mood. . . . I prayed all that night hoping that they would be found."

One more. It's from Captain Bill Charlesworth, a high-up pilot from Grand Forks, North Dakota. From what I've been able to determine, if Larry was regarded as #1 in the squadron in pure flying skill, then Charlesworth was probably #2, and my dad #3. His letter to the family is dated January 14, 1946, so a full six months afterward. His letter relates something I had heard about but never quite pinned down: that a select group of 549th flyers was slated to go on bombing missions to Tokyo right at the close of the war. The orders had come from high up in either the VII Fighter Command or the Seventh Air Force. The Black Widow wasn't designed for such long-range missions—she was a pursuit ship, a fighter-bomber who could do her work superlatively in tight spaces of ocean. Assigning her to do something like this seemed crazy. From the letter: "He led the Squadron in Combat flying time and was determined to bag the first Jap aircraft. . . . Larry experimented with a fully loaded P-61 in preparation for us to make night strikes on Japan. Our greatest problem was to carry enough gasoline to remain airborne for a maximum of nine hours. Then he requested that he be allowed to make the first flight to Japan. If this proposed mission had been carried out Larry would have been the first Nite Fiter pilot over Tokyo. But weather conditions and the abrupt ending of the war cancelled the missions."

I feel certain my dad would have been picked to go. And would he have made those fully loaded nine hours of round-trip and gotten *The Rita B* back down at South Field? It's something I was never able to discuss with him, because once again I never knew a thing about it.

For all the looking I've done, I've not been able to document that Larry's Widow even had a name. The ship had the squadron's insignia painted on it—I know this from photographs. People have said that very late—not out in Hawaii, not on Saipan, but on Iwo itself—he decided to get the name *Blind Date* painted on the nose of #42-39426. But I have never seen such a photograph, and indeed in some of his letters home he mentions that he can't quite decide what he wants to call his Widow. That's a little puzzling to me, but on the other hand only a small puzzle. And yet the more I've circled the mystery of Larry Garland, the more I've wondered if the name didn't fit.

To read his *own* letters is to get all a son's devotion, decency, modesty, patriotism, generosity, intelligence, hard work, bravery, otherliness. Constantly, he is writing home, most especially to his mom, whom he addresses as "Darling" or "Sweetheart" or "Honey." He is obviously close to his father, and writes to him often, too, but not in the way he wishes to tend to his mother, from so far away. Sometimes he writes to her twice a day. (He frets about her dental work; apparently, Sallie Garland tends to let this part of herself go.)

A small sampling of the scores of letters preserved in old family albums:*

From Fresno, to his mom, on Hammer Field stationery, on June 24, 1944 (the 549th was formed less than two months before):

---

* I knew I'd find mentions of my dad. What surprised me a bit was that, apparently, Larry had known my mom, too, from Fresno days. Perhaps my folks had had him, along with Jack Kerr, over to their rental on North Broadway and fixed them both supper before they went back to the BOQ—Bachelor Officer Quarters. Here's Larry on Iwo on June 3, 1945, writing to his father about a big surprise the two have lately cooked up for Larry's fellow officers: He has spent his own money to get stationery printed with each flyer's name engraved in silver on the sheets and envelopes. The boxes were produced at a Lexington printer. He and his father had worked on the secret project for several months. He handed out the gifts to his comrades, who must have been in small shock. For the married pilots, he'd gone an extra step: He'd managed to get hold of a photograph of each spouse. He had the pictures printed as cameos on the sheets, right below the flyer's name. Only thing, Larry had somehow goofed with my father's box. There was an "x" in Hendrickson, so that the spelling had come out "Hendrixson." Larry felt terrible about the mistake and quickly arranged for a new set of sheets to be printed up and shipped to Iwo—but not before my dad had mailed off a love letter to Xenia. Larry is telling his father about this in his June 3 letter. "Would you correct this with the Company, Dad—and let me know the additional cost?" He adds, "Joe's Wife, Rita, was so thrilled over the stationery that she hardly mentioned the misspelled name." I'd give anything to have one of those *Hendrixson* pieces of stationery, never mind the fixed-up one.

I'm ready to go and am perfectly willing to hurry and get where a guy like me belongs—my only regret is that I could not have gotten home to see you & Dad & Sis.

Mom—you have always worried too much about me and I've loved you for it; but by now surely you have confidence in me to know that I'll come out O.K. All I need is for you to keep praying for me and writing to me—and taking good care of yourself. . . .

Just think of this as another letter and that I'm just changing stations—I'm not saying goodbye—goodness no— just going somewhere else to do my work. . . .

Good-night, for now—my sweet and may God bless you and keep you well.

Your loving boy.

January 8, 1945, when the 549th is still in Hawaii: "I met my new crew member today—my gunner. Believe it or not he is from home. . . . His name is Gillespie. He is a nice-looking chap—and used to work for E.R. Bradley's Idle Hour furn. . . . So now there are three Lex. Ky. boys in the squadron and 5 Kentucky boys in all."

From April 16, 1945—the flyers have been on Iwo for one month, minus four days:

"Darling Mother—I'm writing in comfort now; I have built me a fine desk and my corner in the tent is fixed up somewhat like a little room. I have drawers & shelves and everything is comfy. This was made possible with empty boxes. You have to beg and steal boxes." A few lines later:

"You should call Gil's Mother often."

From his second-to-last letter home, July 16, 1945:

Good morning My Sweet! I just came in from work— and breakfast isn't ready yet. I wish I were waiting for one of your breakfasts—eggs—toast—bacon—coffee & doughtnuts. Hmm!

After breakfast I'll try to sleep—it's awfully hot here in the daytime now—but after an all night session—the weather will have a hard time keeping me awake. I wonder if I'll get back to normal living. . . .

The work here is getting a lot of our fellows down—they have lost weight and are sick; me, I'm as healthy as ever and am still going strong—I lead the outfit in missions and flying time.

That same day, to his father:

Dear Dad—When I return—wherever you and Mother are—that will be home. . . . We have been working rather hard and some of the less healthy fellows are showing the strain—they need better food and better climate to keep them healthy.

As for myself—I feel great—am healthy and know that it will never get me down. I, fortunately, have taught myself how to relax—even while flying—that makes the difference.

From his last known letter home. It's on onionskin four pages, in his strikingly fine penmanship. The date is July 23, 1945. It's eight nights from his death, not quite to the hour.

Darling Mother—

Its about 8 o'clock in the evening here—and soon I will report for work—however, before going down to the line I want to talk to you. . . .

Ever since I've been out here—you have been doing fine—your letters are encouraging & cheerful—keep it up darling! Those are the kind of letters that mean so much to me. Don't start worrying yourself and getting yourself in such a state that you find it hard to go to sleep. . . .

Honey—that is reckless worrying—away ahead of time. . . .

I may decide on taking one of the new planes we got in— mine is in perfect shape but she is just getting old—losing some of her poop—not as fast as she used to be. . . .

Gillespie has the second highest number of points in our

outfit and should get home in a couple or three months. I expect to be here eight months to a year longer—assuming the war is still in progress, which I think it will be. . . .

Guess what! I had a date last night! We have a few nurses here now. Several [of] us went to a movie—I enjoyed myself a lot—quite a change talking to a young lady. . . .

Well Honey—I've got to go now—the old Moon is out—and it will be a pretty night for working.

He closes: "With all my love—Your Son" And then a P.S. "What happened to your bowling?" (He's trying to get her to join a ladies' league.)

Five days earlier, on the 18th, fifty-year-old Sallie Garland, in her very poor handwriting, had also written a four-page letter to her boy, beginning the first paragraph with: "I have been so worried about you." In the last paragraph: "I just couldn't sleep, darling."

Her son never saw it. It came home with his personal effects, including a silver bracelet.

My father told me once that at some point after Larry's death, perhaps in the middle fall of 1945, when the crops were in, Grandma and Grandpa Hendrickson got into their Sunday clothes and backed the Chevy out of the shed and drove up to Lexington to pay their respects to Larry Garland's folks. They didn't know them, they just felt they had to do it. It would have taken the better part of a day to get there from Morganfield. I'm guessing they'd never been near Lexington before. I can see my grandparents—in the way I can see tearful neighbors standing in the moonlit Garland yard on August 22—ringing the doorbell at 111 Louisiana Avenue and asking if they might come in: Grandpa, fidgeting on the step with his deeply sunburned neck and ill-fitting tie, yellow straw fedora in his hand, Grandma wearing her best Sears, Roebuck dress and stockings and maybe even a pair of black shoes with low heels.

Grandma and Grandpa had had five sons in the war, all of them surviving. What was there to say to Laurence and Sallie Garland?

"They were inconsolable, Paul," I remember my dad saying. "Especially Mrs. Garland." Even now, I can hear my father saying "inconsolable." Such a large word on his lips.

Marsha Phillips told me that her grandparents built a kind of museum to Larry in their basement. For years they kept his old bedroom upstairs perfectly intact. Sallie Garland was Baptist, but her husband was a Catholic who attended Mass and took Communion not just on Sundays but sometimes during the week, too. Into his son's bedroom, next to the bed, the father carried a prayer kneeler. He brought in some votive lights. A statue. A rosary. A holy card. He set up a little table, and he placed the prie-dieu before it. Every night before he went to bed, he'd go into Larry's room and kneel and pray to his son in heaven.

John Maxwell Hendrix Jr.? He would have been somebody else's whole world, too, or mostly so. The third crewman of Black Widow #42-39426 was a fifth-generation son of Greensboro, North Carolina. Larry Garland's R/O was descended from shoe merchants and fox hunters and tobacco growers. (His great-grandfather had founded the J. M. Hendrix Shoe & Dry Good Store and also the Greensboro Merchants Association.) Like his pilot, Max Hendrix was a lanky drink of good-looking water. Like his skipper, he seemed possessed of a natural physical gift. He'd played on the state championship high school football team. After, he'd enrolled at Davidson College and became a starting running back on the freshman football team. (Surely, he and Larry had engaged in some fine trash-talking in their off-duty moments—and probably from the front of the plane to the back.) But Max, four years younger than his pilot, could stay only six months in college: The war had broken out. In the summer of 1942, he enlisted in the Army Air Corps, intent on winning his wings. But the natural athlete had trouble with depth perception, which is how he got pivoted by the higher-ups to become a radar guy and eventually ended up in the 549th and on Iwo Jima and in Larry Garland's airplane. He'd washed out of flight school.

I have sat in Greensboro with Max's nephew, Eric Hendrix, who's about a decade younger than I am, the keeper of the albums, of the family's collective memory. I've seen the old scissored-out and pasted-in newspaper photographs of his Uncle Max stiff-arming enemy tacklers on the championship high school football team, and I've read handfuls of his letters to his parents, and I've studied the telegram of August 22nd, and I've also looked at a typed note of condolence with this printed at the top of its thick cardlike stationery: "General Headquarters / United States Army Forces, Pacific / Office of the Commander-in-Chief." The note is signed, and to my eye looks like an *actual* signature, "Faithfully, Douglas MacArthur."

"When I was young, my grandmother was too upset to talk about any of it," Eric Hendrix told me.

There would, of course, be much more to tell of the life of Max Hendrix of Greensboro but there's still too much yet to be said about the life of Larry Garland. I've had to make my choices.

On the idea of a seeming almost effortlessly charmed existence: Yes, but no. A significant no.

Firstly, he wasn't born with a gold spoon in his mouth. I had that part all wrong. If the Gillespie family was "townie" in the usual (and elitist) way of town-and-gown divides in almost any university community, then the Garlands had far less "gownie" in their Lexington bloodstream than I understood at the start.

The real story is that his parents, not unlike the Gillespies, were Lexington renters, who'd managed, unlike the Gillespies, after long striving, and well into their middle age, to work their way into a comfortable middle-class life. But Larry was practically on his own by this time. Growing up, he'd hung with the rich kids, or at least the kids whose families didn't have to worry about paying the rent. He'd run with them at Henry Clay High School, which has always been one of the best high schools in Kentucky.[*] But he wasn't *of* them. He beat them out at almost everything he tried, but nothing was ever handed to him, which must have something to do with why he'd beat them out at practically everything. Some of this, of course, resonates with my own father's story, who came out of his Morganfield nowhere, and made his leap.

Far from ever being a bluegrasser or other kind of Lexington

[*] Elizabeth Hardwick, the great New York midcentury literary critic and essayist, grew up in Lexington and went to Henry Clay; she was in the class ahead of Larry.

gentry, Mr. Garland was a bookkeeper (as opposed to an accountant with a degree) who worked for many years for a local moving and storage company before setting up his own modest bookkeeping service at home. Laurence Garland Sr. may have had something like a year or year and a half at UK. Larry's mom, Sallie, never got beyond fifth grade. All through his growing up, the family had moved from one Lexington address to another—better places than the Gillespies ever lived in, but never their own place. It wasn't until 1939, when Larry was in his last year at UK—it was great luck, financially and otherwise, that the most prominent university in the state was almost literally down the street—that Mr. and Mrs. Garland were able to move the family into their first-ever home. The family consisted of the two parents and Larry and his kid sister, Marjorie. Mr. and Mrs. Garland were able to build their home for $12,000, which was a significant sum in 1939 and for which they must have saved up for a long time. Number 111 Louisiana Avenue was in a new residential development, at what was then the outer edge of a section called Chevy Chase. It's a handsome red-brick house with white columns out front. Chevy Chase is an upscale and partly commercial district today, but it's not Ashland Park, which sits directly above Chevy Chase. Ashland Park, with its spreading lawns and fine old trees and early-twentieth-century homes, is one of the prettier Southern residential districts I've ever come across—and I've encountered plenty. Wealthy Ashland Parkers had long sent their sons and daughters to the hometown university, and, likely as not, those sons and daughters got rushed for the best fraternities and sororities. At a place like UK, the Greek system is everything.

Larry Garland, the all-around best boy from Henry Clay High School on Main Street in Lexington, got rushed for Sigma Alpha Epsilon at the big-time backyard university, but I now wonder if he wasn't always a little hard pressed just to pay his monthly frat dues. His niece told me that she is almost certain the boy on a partial athletic scholarship lived at home, not at SAE, during some of college, just as he always had some part-time job or other, in both high school and college.

Marsha Phillips and I talked a good deal about all this when

I sat for several hours in her living room. We talked of the pressures of expectation, of the anxieties of trying to live up to yourself when you're such a star, of wearing masks of one kind or another. She said that she couldn't imagine her uncle putting on airs—he was too decent and true for that—but on the other hand, "I think Uncle Larry, and no question my mother, would have had to learn how to get good at attaching yourself to people who came easily of their money." She said it was almost an unconscious way of surviving in such a socially layered town as Lexington.

Marsha Phillips and I talked about something else, too: that her uncle was gay.

Somehow, by the time she said it, I found myself nodding. It was a little startling to me, only it wasn't. Here is what Marsha specifically said, in a very soft tone: "From everything I know, and have been able to figure out, I am pretty sure Uncle Larry was gay." She added, and I was already nodding, "And how hard that must have been." I asked how she knew. She said her father had told her when he was near his death. Marsha's father, Randall Phillips, who ended up having an unhappy life mainly due to terrible money woes and the need to try to keep up appearances, was Larry Garland's closest friend in college. He had come to Lexington from Montgomery, Alabama. They met on the freshman football team and bonded and moved up to the varsity together. They both played the end position. They were roomies together on the road. One day, the team's left end brought home and introduced to his little sister the team's right end. Things clicked. The two best friends became brothers-in-law, although this wasn't until after college. In the war, Randall went to the Army, where he made captain. Just as my dad did, Larry made captain flying Black Widows in the Pacific dark.

I asked Randall Phillips's daughter if she had any doubt about whether her father could have somehow made up the fact that her uncle was closeted gay. "No," she said quickly. "Daddy wouldn't do something like that. I think he was trying to tell me things he wanted me to know about our family before he died."

Possessed with untapped natural ability, he seems destined to be one of 1938's greats, they had written of Larry in the sports pages at the start of his junior year. Well, yes—except no, once again. Life always turns out to have its own plans. Neither the starting left end nor the starting right end in 1937 were able to play in the '38 season. Quoting again the scribes from the *Kernel:* "Both ends, Randall Phillips and Larry Garland, who were slated for the flank slots, have been weeded from the team by the injury jinx." That was published on page one on September 16, 1938, in a preview of the season opener. In horse racing, which Lexington knows all about, they talk of a Thoroughbred with so much promise suddenly pulling up lame, of getting scratched, and maybe not just for that day's race, but for the rest of a career. *Weeded from the team:* It sounds so quick and cruel. The world moves on. No question that Larry Garland had many accomplishments at UK in his last year—president of this club; president of that university society— but starring in football was not among them. Really, he had peaked the year before.

Marsha told me something else that had almost clicked in before she said it: that for almost her own entire life, her mother resented her, and that a lot of it was displaced anger. Marjorie Phillips— who was Marjorie Garland then—had grown up in the shadow of the best all-around boy. She could never get enough of her parents' attention, especially Sallie's attention, and it seems to have marked her for life. In one part of her, Marjorie adored her big brother Larry—and in another part of her glands she must have detested him. Later, when Marsha herself was in the picture, Marjorie Phillips seems to have had no way of escaping the mixed-up family feelings inside her except to take it out—although not with a belt—on the back of her only child. She took it out emotionally. "It took me so long to figure out so much of this," Marsha said. There seemed very little bitterness in it.

If Uncle Larry was Mr. Everything to his parents while he was alive, in death he became the sanctified martyr. Against this, the younger sister had no chance, and by extension, the younger sister's daughter also paid her price. "I mean, I think *I* must have heard about Uncle Larry almost every day when I was growing up," she said. But again, I heard no recrimination.

————

The more I tried to peer in, the grayer and more layered things began to seem. Earlier, I mentioned the Yale Cup at Henry Clay High School, which was the school's highest award, given annually by the Kentucky Alumni Association of Yale University. It was a loving cup, and the one given out in 1935 is now in Marsha's possession. (She insisted I take home a lot of her uncle's mementos, but not her uncle's Yale Cup.) On page ninety-eight of the *Auratum,* Henry Clay's 1935 yearbook, there is a picture of that year's winner, with thirteen lines of type below, citing his achievements: sports editor, student-teacher council, captain of the football team, alternate captain of the basketball team, class president—and so forth. But to me, what's striking is not the achievements, but the photograph of the winner. He looks so grave. He looks serious beyond his years. He looks like he's carrying something.

On page nineteen of the *Auratum,* which is devoted to class officers, it says this:

> Our efficient class president is Lawrence [*sic*] Garland, whose record is evidence of the high esteem in which he is held. His sunny disposition has won him many friends; and he will, no doubt, conquer many of the hard problems of life by beguiling them with his sunny smile.

I'm not saying the words are a lie. I'm not saying there aren't other pictures of him in the Henry Clay yearbook of 1935 when he is, in fact, smiling, when he does, in fact, seem sunny. What I *am* saying is that once you've discovered what was apparently a core truth of Larry Garland's charmed and yet not-so-charmed identity, the sunny pictures get crowded out, so that all you can see, or all I can see, is the extraordinary young man seeming to be possessed of a strange heaviness. Was his last year or so of high school the period when the best all-around boy and winner of the Yale Cup discovered who he really was, and had no choice but to keep it to himself? I have no idea—on either the first part of that sentence, or the second.

I am always amazed at how a photograph can arrow you to the truth of something in the way of almost no other document—and at other times can lie right to your teeth. In the image which I placed at the start of this chapter, do I get anything of a secret burden being borne by the best flyer of the 549th? Not in the least. I get a still boyish twenty-eight-year-old on Iwo Jima in a ball cap and a leather flight jacket, exuding his natural-born grace.

There is another set of his letters, that were written during the war to a man named Odell S. McConnell. He was twenty years older than Larry. He was a Los Angeles attorney educated at Yale and Harvard. He was a lifelong bachelor. When they met, McConnell was already a distinguished West Coast attorney, who, after Larry's death, would become far more prominent and wealthier— and philanthropic, too. (In the 1970s, he founded and funded the establishment of Pepperdine University's Odell McConnell Law Center. He seems to have been much devoted to the arts and civic causes.) He died in 1992 at age ninety-five.

I'm guessing they met at some military social function, while Larry was in training, in the months before the 549th NFS left Bakersfield and got on its troop train for Seattle in the early fall of 1944 and then onward to Hawaii and then onward to the war. McConnell was a World War I Navy veteran and had reenlisted as a reserve lieutenant commander in World War II.

What survives are not Larry's actual letters to McConnell, but McConnell's transcriptions. Ten months after the disappearance of Black Widow #42-39426, the attorney sent typed copies to Lexington, with a beautifully written cover letter to the grieving Laurence and Sallie Garland, in which he said: "It was my privilege to know your fine son all too short a while but during that period, as these letters will demonstrate, there grew between us, mutual respect and admiration and a deep and lasting friendship." He wrote of Larry's "frankness" and his "manliness."

Are the transcriptions complete transcriptions? Short of being able to read the actual letters, there's no way of knowing, but in his letter to Larry's folks, McConnell does note: "I have transcribed all of Larry's letters to me and I am enclosing them herewith." It's also important to note that what survives—or at least what came into the Garland family's possession in May 1946—is only Larry's side of the correspondence.

Marsha Phillips and I have talked about this cache of several dozen letters, and what the cache might seem to be conveying, unwittingly, between the lines.

October 26, 1944: "Hello-Fellow—Believe me, it was so good hearing from you—already I've started looking forward to mail call hours before time."

A week later, November 1: "I find myself looking forward to a letter from you. . . . Now listen, Guy, I want you to sorta take it easy. I'll allow you six out of the seven nights each week to party; but you have to save yourself for that 'Grand day a-coming' when we take over the town on our return."

November 21, 1944: "Hello Fellow: You have given me a new meaning to the cry of 'mail call'—perhaps there will be a letter from home and Odell! Your last letter . . . hit the spot—where it hurt the best. Yes, our friendship has been rather unusual, I think it is best explained not of the tempo of these days, but because there wasn't anything hidden."

December 7, 1944: "You have certainly been a Prince about writing—and, believe me I look forward to your letters so damn much."

Three days later, the 10th: "You'll never know how keenly I felt when I received the St. Christopher medal. The fact that you have worn it for Ten years proves how much it meant to you—and for you to give it up to me—well, 'Buddy' it gave me that old odd feeling way down deep inside."

In several of their exchanges, McConnell has apparently suggested that he'd like to introduce Larry to several young West Coast women; perhaps Larry will be able to get a correspondence going with them. Apparently, he's asked whether Larry's ever been truly in love.

Responding to this question, more or less: December 20, 1944, from Kipapa Airfield on Oahu: "In only five days it will be Christmas; I wish like Hell I could say 'Merry Christmas' to you over touching glasses and clasped hands. More and more I have grown to lean on you and our friendship. . . . You asked me about the girl I left behind. I wasn't holding out on you, Buddy. I really don't have the proverbial girl back home. I haven't been deeply interested in anyone for several years—I am truly a bachelor. And what I have seen of the 'situation' here, and what I know of the situation from here on down there isn't the slightest chance of changing status."

This same letter also answered for me, or seemed to, why Larry wasn't wearing his silver Army Air Corps bracelet on the night he died. I think he might have been wearing a bracelet sent to him from Los Angeles. "I have a grand gift from you on my wrist," he says.

At the close of this letter: "One thing in your letter hit me right in the heart—I only hope that I'll always be worthy of the respect & affectionate regard you hold for me."

In Larry's letters to his parents, he promises that he will get home safe to Lexington and that the three will be able to start their lives there anew. But I don't think this would have happened. It seems clear that he hoped to come back from the war and relocate to Los Angeles and study law under the guidance of McConnell. If the good son had gone ahead with this plan, I can't begin to picture him doing so without first explaining his painful decision in person to his father but most especially to his mom.

When we sat and talked of Larry's letters to McConnell, Marsha Phillips and I agreed on how things can sometimes seem much more than they are, when, in reality, they might be a lot less. My strongest gut feeling about the letters is that they reveal a longing that perhaps not even Larry was fully aware of. For the record, I believe that nothing sexual—or maybe even overtly romantic— had ever happened between the two men. Marsha said that she felt a great compassion for her uncle after reading them. I said I felt exactly the same, and also not a small sadness. I think that had her uncle survived and gone to California, he might have been able to find, to grow into, a freer and happier and thus more fully integrated self. He might have been able to shed the pressures of a lifetime of expectations. But that is just speculating from the outside. Who knows anything from the outside? Reading the letters made me think of what Norman Mailer once speculated from the outside so insightfully about Ernest Hemingway: that when it was said and done, it's reasonable to believe that Hemingway "carried a weight of anxiety within him from day to day which would have suffocated any man smaller than himself."

The National Memorial Cemetery of the Pacific is located at Punchbowl Crater in Honolulu. There are many thousands of American servicemen memorialized there. There is something called the Courts of the Missing: eight limestone panels inscribed with the names of 18,094 missing-in-action servicemen from World War II. The names of Max Hendrix, Milt Gillespie, and Larry Garland are carved on those panels. I've studied them on the web. I'd like someday to stand before them in person, but I doubt I ever will.

Really, though, I've been able to do something better, at least insofar as Milt and Larry are concerned. I've gone to Lexington Cemetery and stood in front of their gravestones. How is it that the ceremonial resting place of two lost sons of Lexington, so different in every way, should sit less than 150 feet from each other? Lexington Cemetery is 170 acres of arboretum and graves. More than 64,000 people are interred there. And, somehow, with no one ever intending it (well maybe God did), the Gillespie family plot, in section thirty-eight, under a maple, is located diagonally right across the drive, in section twenty-nine, in the shadow of a beech, from the stone of Larry and Sallie Garland. (Larry's father lies in a nearby Catholic cemetery.) Only one more mystery to contemplate, not to be answered.

Their bodies aren't beneath the markers. Those molecules are somewhere off Iwo Jima.

On July 31, 2020—which was the seventy-fifth anniversary of when Widow #42-39426 went beneath the waves—a remembrance ceremony took place at the cemetery. A Lexington motorcycle club, formally known as Rolling Thunder Kentucky Chapter 5, planned and hosted the event. The members go all over eastern and central and northern Kentucky to participate in such POW-MIA events. I have talked by phone to several RTK5 riders, and I have spent time in person with Paul Ray Key, who lives outside of Lexington and drives a big-rig truck during the week and sits on a sleek, glossy, 110-cubic-inch bike called an Indian Chief Dark Horse on weekends. He rides it wearing his leather and his head-scarf. He is Shirley Beck's nephew. (His deceased mom and Shirley are sisters.) Maybe half of his weekends during the year are given over to either planning or taking part in a POW-MIA ceremony. All of it is volunteer.

I couldn't get to Lexington for the seventy-fifth remembrance, but I have watched a video of it numerous times on Facebook. It's deeply moving to see the several dozen attendees going up, one by one, to place long-stemmed roses at each grave. It's deeply moving to see bearded, large-framed, Rolling Thunder guys, whose Harleys and Indians are parked just outside the camera's range, going up to stand solemnly before the stones. Shirley and her daughter attended and placed a rose. Marsha Phillips was there and reached down to put a rose at the base of the stone commemorating her grandmother and uncle. Both Shirley and Marsha have since told me that they would have liked to have talked afterward. But there was an awkwardness that seemed to prevent it. So many things to say—and how to say them? Someone introduced them. They greeted each other and moved on.

On a beautiful autumn Lexington day, about six weeks ago as this is being written, I visited the stones. UK was scheduled to play Northern Illinois University in football at home that evening, but all the town's bawdy celebration of that was taking place several miles away. No one was around, at least in the spot where I was. I walked back and forth between the two markers, thinking not just of Max and Larry and Milt, but of my dad, and of how he had survived when these three didn't. The opening lines of A. E. Housman's "To an Athlete Dying Young" came into my head. *The time you won your town the race / We chaired you through the market-place / Man and boy stood cheering by / And home we brought you shoulder-high.*

I kept reflecting on the gone Lexington sons (and on Max Hendrix, too) but gradually my father took over my thoughts. I thought specifically of Larry and my dad. How did he have the luck to live, to make it out of there, and the best all-around boy did not? I took out some notes and a journal that I carry with me on reporting trips. I sat on a tree stump. I looked at some lines I had typed on old newsprint having to do with August 12, 1976, when my father and I visited the Smithsonian's National Air and Space Museum on the National Mall for the first time. It was the Bicentennial year, and the three-block-long museum had opened its doors the month before. I had insisted he and my mom come over to Washington as soon as they could so that we could take a tour. He couldn't believe its size. "Shooee, Paul," he kept saying, looking upward. He couldn't believe how many aircraft were inside the building, including a silvery Eastern Air Lines DC-3, suspended from the ceiling. Through the forties, my dad had copiloted this airplane— this exact DC-3—out of Midway in Chicago. He had copiloted her to places like Charley West (Charleston, West Virginia) and Akron and Chattanooga. He had heard that Eastern had donated the old workhorse to the museum, and so, before coming over to see us, he'd looked up her serial number in his old logbooks. Sure enough, twenty-three times, this one. I was gulping my pride.

There wasn't a Black Widow on display, but that was quite okay. I think we were standing beneath a B-25. He turned and said, "I mean, when I think back on this whole part of my life, Paul, going to the war, getting back home, when all those others didn't, it's almost like it never happened to me. So far away, so gone now. I almost can't believe I was there. Just doesn't seem possible. Like a movie or something. How did I ever do that?"

What I like to think was my father's last look at the speck of Pacific earth called Iwo Jima

Epilogue

"SING ME BACK HOME BEFORE I DIE"

*My father, at our Takoma Park, Maryland, home,
a few years before he died*

*Make my old memories come alive
Take me away and turn back the years
Sing me back home before I die*

—MERLE HAGGARD

IT WAS TWENTY YEARS after that first visit to the Air and Space Museum, and four days before Thanksgiving in 1996. An old aviator, who would never pilot a plane alone again, came out of a bedroom in a Tampa condominium wearing white socks and a blue nightgown. My mom was behind him, helping to steady him. Around his shoulders like a shawl was a green flannel robe. Some sort of battery-operated pump, which was attached to a sling across his shoulder, was dripping penicillin into a vein in his heavily taped and very skinny left arm. We stood there in the doorway, a father and son, so close and pathetically far. I looked at his night-gown and thought of lines from a favorite poem by a favorite poet, James Wright:

> In a blue rag the old man limps to my bed,
> Leading a blind horse
> Of gentleness.
> In 1932, grimy with machinery, he sang me
> A lullaby of a goosegirl.
> Outside the house, the slag heaps waited.

It was impossible to hug. So we shook. But our handshake lasted a little longer than usual.

"I've got homemade vegetable soup for you," my mother said. It was 10:45 p.m., and I had just arrived, and I wasn't hungry, but once again my mom was trying to bridge all our unbridgeables with the simple pleasures of taking food. I was awkwardly facing the seventy-eight-year-old man to whom I had never really learned how to talk—and vice versa.

"You look pretty good, Dad," I lied.

"I have to think I'm on the mend—whether I am or not, son," he said.

He made his way over to a La-Z-Boy rocker and elevated his legs. They were shiny and swollen, especially his right leg. He saw me looking at it.

"I've been retaining a lot of fluids."

On Halloween, they'd cracked him open again, had filleted him down the middle again, had gone once more into the diseased chambers of his heart. Two years earlier, in August 1994, some surgeons had performed, in one marathon session, a quadruple bypass and a valve replacement. This time it was a bacterial infection in his chest cavity.

This time, by the time he had driven himself from upper Wisconsin to the Gulf Coast of Florida, and then allowed my mother to call the paramedics to take him to the hospital, and then allowed the doctors to put their high-tech cameras down his esophagus, the germs had eaten away most of the valve that had been sewn into him. And the bacteria had apparently crawled to other parts of his body, too. The doctors had told him it was his only chance, to cut again. And so on Halloween they did. After, they told him he had made it to surgery in the nick of time. I doubt he was greatly impressed. All this had taken place twenty-six days ago. I was now witnessing the aviator in his newest diminished state.

He sat across the room with his right leg looking waxy in the lamplight. Surrounding him were vials of medicine, medical literature, pillows, a blanket. In a way, it was like a cockpit.

I kept thinking how he had never wanted it to turn out this way. "I want to crash and burn, crash and burn," I had heard him say so many times. "It's the only way to go. I don't want to have this lingering death."

He reached down and ran his good arm down his bad leg. In the lamplight his hands looked almost knobby. They were always knobby. Unable to think of anything to say, I looked down at my own hands. With each passing year, they seemed to be turning into my father's.

"Sure wish I could be here Thursday," I said. It wasn't possible. I had to get back home to the Washington suburbs, to my own family, my wife and our two young sons. All I could afford was this not-even-twenty-four-hour visit—late on a Sunday and into barely half of Monday.

"All that eating of your mother's you're going to miss," he said.

How would he have the appetite for any of it?

"Will you have the scalloped oysters, Mom?" I asked.

"Already bought them," she said from the kitchen. I had gone out to the counter a moment earlier where I had seen a loose-leaf notebook, in which my mother had written instructions to herself in her somewhat shaky but still Palmer-perfect hand: "Pick up oysters at Albertson's . . . Turkey at Kash n' Karry. . . . Fruit stand—watermelon and cantaloupes."

"Remember Aunt Judith's Salad?" my dad said. Aunt Judith's Salad is a name we'd long had in our family for a whipped-cream confection of sliced oranges, apples, pears, bananas, maraschino cherries.

"It's the whipped cream that makes it," he said.

We talked of the home-health-care nurses who'd been coming twice a day. "The one in the morning helps me with my bathing. Helps me get in and out of the shower. Washes my back. I do my privates."

Through the night I heard him cough many times. I heard him get up and wander into other rooms, where he turned on the lights. I slept in fits and starts, full of strange dreams. All night it was as if an old man in a blue rag was limping to my bed, leading a blind horse of gentleness, or at least of memory.

In the morning, in Florida fall sunshine, he sat at my mom's kitchen table. He was peeling a banana. I had slept late. He had the coffee waiting for me.

"Sleepyhead."

Flat out, he started talking about his dying—what he intended for his funeral. He'd made up his mind to be cremated. And almost in the same breath he talked about next spring and going north again to Wisconsin, where his heart had always been. "'Course I don't know if that's in the plan. Nobody ever got out of this world alive, Paul."

When I left for the airport at noon, I tried so hard to make myself hug him. It didn't come close to working. We shook again. I didn't even say, "I love you, Dad." I came just short of saying it and veered off. The "I love you" got swallowed in a "Please take care of yourself."

Who would have bet my father would live on, for almost another seven years, from that overnight visit on a Sunday night and Monday morning in November 1996? He'd live on until the spring of 2003, defying the odds, all the gods, as he'd done so long ago in the war. For much of it, he would have his life, despite the various rushes to emergency rooms for urinary tract infections or alarmingly rapid heartbeats or other such onsets. Somehow, he always got better, at least temporarily. Somehow, he kept getting himself back down, at least until about the final six months or so when he even stopped riding his bicycle.

The Pacific Ocean occupies one-third of the earth's surface. Historians have said that World War II in Asia and the Pacific spread itself out over something like twenty million square miles—that was the length and breadth of what Japan had controlled in the beginning. The watery distances of the Pacific war were five times larger than what Germany had controlled at the height of its hubris and conquests. In his war room, Douglas MacArthur is said to have superimposed for his generals a sketch of a map of the United States over a chart of just the *lower Pacific* to demonstrate the effort required in transporting troops and matériel from, say, Guadalcanal in the Solomon Islands to, say, Luzon in the Philippines. It was like traveling an army from the bottom of Florida to the tip of the Pacific Northwest.

All those iconic place-names of the Pacific and Asian war, starting with Pearl Harbor itself. Corregidor. The Battle of the Coral Sea. Okinawa. Kwajalein. Not to say the speck of earth on which my dad had lived, and flew from, approximately seventy-five times, seventy-five missions, 175 logged hours, for the last five and a half months of the war. The speck of earth where so many had died in the several weeks before he landed at South Field. The speck of earth which, to my mind, is the most iconic Pacific place-name of them all.

There were something like 109,000 U.S. military deaths in the Pacific Theater, and there were many more thousands who got wounded. My dad made it through without any physical wounds. His wounds, so I believe, were the kind you couldn't see, he couldn't see. As I have said, I think it took him something like a decade to exorcise them, if never quite fully. In that decade, mid-forties to the mid-fifties, my dad was a copilot for one of America's largest airlines. He did his work, and from everything I know, he did it extremely well. He earned his way up the ladder until, in the middle of the fifties, he became an Eastern captain. But he must have had to compartmentalize so much, which would have extracted its psychic price. He paid it, and so did we. And by "we" I certainly include my mom. About whom a whole other book could be written in place of the one you've been reading.

He left Iwo on September 23, 1945—it's in his service file. So far as I know, the departure was on a military transport plane with a load of fellow officers from the 549th and perhaps some other squadrons as well. (I like to imagine him and my godfather seated side by side.) Maybe it was the same kind of transport, a C-46, that my dad's best man, Barney Slamkowski, had gone down in over the Hump in the Himalayas not quite two years before. I like to think that, from his seat in the banking plane, passing over that "glob of cold lava squatting in a surly ocean" (as William Manchester called Iwo in *Goodbye, Darkness*), my father pulled out a box Brownie and from the window made the snapshot that I have placed at the front of this epilogue—but that's just fancifulness. I have seen this same photograph in the family collections of Ray Rudkin and Leo Vough and Milt Gillespie and Max Hendrix and Larry Garland, and a few others besides. Probably it was made by someone in the historical unit of the 549th, and copies handed out.

What I do know is that *The Rita B* got left behind. What I do know, because I found it on a little card cataloguing the plane's history, is that some months later she got transported for storage to Clark Field in the Philippines. Other Widows got bulldozed into craters, dumped into the sea from aircraft carriers, shoved off cliffs. The government couldn't afford to bring them home from the Pacific. (It was true in Europe, too.) They were expendable metal. For two years, *The Rita B* lingered in her life, or half-life, or maybe no flying life at all. On September 22, 1947 (which was two years, minus one day, from when he lifted off from Iwo for the final time), she was officially—to use the official military word— "stricken." I gratefully referenced earlier the name Jeff Kolln, author of many military aviation books but none better, for my money, than *Northrop's Night Hunter*. I asked him about "stricken." I said that to my ear the word seems so freighted. Wouldn't any Black Widow pilot have been *stricken* with the beauty and power of his airplane? Wouldn't my father have been *stricken* with admixtures of emotion—dread, fear, exhilaration, godlike authority—every time he belted in? "Your dad's plane right now may be sitting under the runway at Clark Air Base, ground up into 10,000 pieces that were used for fill when they built new runways," Kolln said. That would be stricken, I suppose.

I don't know anything about the route home, but I suspect it was an island-hopping path much in the way that he'd flown *The Rita B* to Iwo in a sixteen-plane convoy. He got to Hawaii. There was the standard hurry-up-and-wait. Then it was by sea to the U.S. mainland. He told me once, and I quoted him in print: "I can tell you about that troop ship coming out of the Pacific to Seattle. I don't know how long we were on that dog, week at least. Damn, we wanted to hit the good old U.S.A. We got to the West Coast and came across the country to Chicago on a train, then changed for Indianapolis. That's where they discharged me, you know, out of Camp Atterbury, right there south of the city. Your mother came over from Xenia to meet me. That was some reunion. I'll never forget how she looked when I had that first glimpse of her. After we'd gotten reacquainted, we drove on over to Ohio, which is where we had Thanksgiving a few weeks later, right there on Edison, with Pop and Nonna and you and Marty."

The date of his official separation was October 26, 1945, a full month after leaving Iwo, two days from his twenty-seventh birthday. He was making it back, along with millions of other returning servicemen, in time to sit down, five Thursdays hence, with those he loved, to "the greatest Thanksgiving meal of the twentieth century." Earlier I used that phrase, relating how I once wrote a freelance piece for *Life* on the theme. My dad's words above are taken from that *Life* story. And this, too: "Yeah. You were just a little guy—what were you, not even two? By the way, you know that story, don't you, about how you took one look at me and ran like hell when I got out on the sidewalk and held open my arms for you?"

That story is one of our family myths.

The fresh civilian wasn't so eager to go to work. He lay around for a while on his saved-up officer's pay. At one point his father-in-law came over and said, "Uh, Joe, you know, in this life, we all have to work." The ex-captain took a job as a mechanic at a local car garage. Couldn't stand it. He worked for about another month on an assembly line at a Frigidaire factory in Dayton—he hated that even worse. Meantime he applied to all the major airlines in the country. In late 1945 and into early 1946, there was this great washing-out of pilots from the war, thousands of whom hoped to sign on at American or United or Pan Am or TWA or Braniff or Eastern. The bulk of what were known as the country's "trunk airlines" were interested in pilots who had many more flying hours in their logbooks than my dad had in his—those B-17 Flying Fortress and B-29 Superfortress guys who'd been up for nine or ten hours at a stretch. But I like to think that Eastern Air Lines recognized pure flying ability when it was standing there in the doorway with an application.

But what surprised me was to find out how much my dad wanted to go back into the service—to receive a full-time commission as a captain in the Regular Army (as it was known) as opposed to his three wartime officer commissions (second lieutenant, first lieutenant, captain). Three times in the first six months of his return to civilian life, even as he was trying to get on with the airlines, he applied for active duty. He'd been back for two months and two days the first time—and got turned down. He applied again and got a U.S. senator from Ohio to write on his behalf. Then a third time. I have studied this back-and-forth paperwork. It seems as if he got very close. It was startling to see "REJECTED" ink-stamped on the final turndown, dated October 29, 1946. He had hired on with Eastern by then and had been copiloting for three months. Our family had moved to Miami by then. One of his rejecting letters informed him that the "number of applications received by the War Department greatly exceeded the number of appointments authorized. . . . Your standing among the large number of qualified applicants on the eligible lists was not high enough." It must have been such an ego blow.

Was it because he didn't have a college degree? I have some of his fitness ratings and efficiency reports. His superior officers had always rated him in either the "excellent" or "superior" categories, which were the two highest you could earn. What then? I asked my brother Mark about why he might have wanted back in so badly in the first place. "Maybe one way to think about it, Paul, is that he'd been a captain over there. He'd been the main guy. Now he was in the second seat again. It's hard to be a copilot after you've been number one."

So, he didn't end up making the service his career for the next thirty years, and my siblings and I weren't raised as military brats. At length I think my father came to realize that not getting back in was one of the best professional things that had ever happened to him. His long and high-paying Eastern career, in the three decades when the airline industry was in its golden age, and as he moved from propellers to propjets to pure jets, could make its own book.

My father retired from Eastern in 1978—or, better said, Eastern retired him. The Hendrickson genes, known for prematurely weakening hearts, had caught up with him. He couldn't pass his flight physicals. He was almost sixty. He was no longer an airline captain, but the flyer was still a flyer—to his toenails. I'm looking at some notes dated August 1983. I was married and a *Washington Post* reporter. The flyer came over to visit us in Washington. My wife, Ceil, was pregnant with our first child. This was not quite a year after he and I had gone to the night fighter reunion in Orlando together—after my dad had done me the substantial favor of attending that reunion.

He flew his Beechcraft Debonair into a weedy little private airfield in Bowie, Maryland, which was about twenty miles from our home on Capitol Hill. I drove out to pick him up. By the time I got there, he had already landed and had parked the Deb and was tying her down, putting the foam rubber in the nose cowl. I walked out to the tarmac, spiked with grass coming up through cracks in the asphalt. Bean patches bordered the runway. An old tractor was sitting in a hangar, which was really a converted barn. This could almost have been Morganfield in the thirties. The Kentucky fly-boy, sixty-four and hale-seeming (even if the hated Feds wouldn't give him a first-class license), had on a blue-mesh ball cap with "Big Bend, Texas" on the crown. He was wearing a silver and aqua cowboy belt, white socks, ortho shoes.

A kid—he looked about seventeen—pulled up his plane alongside my dad's. It was a canary-yellow Cessna. He hopped out, drenched with sweat, grinning. An older man walked up and began pumping his hand. My dad stopped what he was doing and leaned on the wing of the Deb. "Hey, lookee there, Paul," he whispered to me. "He just soloed. That's his instructor."

He stayed with us for two or three days, and there weren't any fights. On the second day, we decided to go flying.

"So how do you like my new car, Dad?" I asked as we drove out to the airport. It was a Honda Accord, first grown-up car I'd ever owned. I had been dying for him to say something about it.

Long pause. "Yes. Very nice. But I wouldn't buy one."

I didn't even have to say *Why,* but I said it anyway.

"'Cause it's made by Japs. I buy America. If I were running General Motors, I'd tell them Japs they either take 100,000 units of ours, too, or they can go jump in Tokyo Bay. That's just what I'd tell 'em. I mean, why do you think our national deficit is so high? We trade with them, they got to trade with us. Oh, I know there are certain things you can only get over there—like the China bristle shaving brush. Hell, you're in the paper business, what are people saying at the newspaper?"

He told me of an accident with a knife he'd had in the kitchen a few days earlier. "I tried to cut off my thumb. Figured I didn't need it." I pestered him for more. He shrugged. "I was cutting something with a knife and clean missed it, can you believe it?"

I used the word "emasculate." I can no longer remember the context. We had gone on to the next subject, whatever it was.

"What was that word, Paul?"

"Emasculate, Dad."

"And it means you lose your masculinity?"

"Yes. Think of masculine, only with an 'e' in front of it."

"I didn't know the 'e' would do it."

I nearly drove off the road laughing.

At the field, we untied the Deb. He shoved the nose cowl foam at me. I didn't know where he wanted me to store it. He made three turns around the plane, moving faster, talking louder. "Well, son, I don't see anything a-hangin' or a-bangin', so we better go while we got our nerve up." I had heard him say that so many times.

We ran down the checklist and took off and flew down toward Annapolis, which he kept calling "Anna-nappolis," and then out over the Chesapeake Bay and the big silver spans of the Chesapeake Bay Bridge. It was a gorgeous day for flying. We turned inland and flew over Maryland farmland. He said he wanted to stay clear of air traffic in close to the city. He said he wanted to keep out of the path of airliners coming into and taking off from National Airport. "Us little guys have no business being around these big jets, Paul," he said. *Little guy?* He'd once commanded some of the biggest airliners in the sky. Hundreds of times in his Eastern career he'd flown into National Airport, shooting the river approach, which is to say arcing southward down the Potomac and curving her in just this side of the Washington Monument. I remember once riding family pass on an Eastern flight when my dad was up in the cockpit, arcing and curving and captaining and smoothing her onto those tight runways at National like somebody working with a hand trowel. I must have been about fifteen or sixteen and was home from the seminary for the summer. I felt so proud. My father had just done that.

After about an hour up, we headed back. I think we were at about 4,000 feet. He seemed a little unsure where the airport was. "Funny as hell, Paul, the other morning when I came in, I was having trouble finding it. I had plotted it out on the maps. I called air traffic control. I said, 'Where is the thing? I should be right on top of it.' Guy said, 'Keep a-pushin'.'"

I spotted the field before he did—it was up ahead of us two or three miles. "Say, you're getting pretty good up here, aren't you?" he said, looking over at me, his voice grown soft.

On the day he left, he was up with the chickens. "I like to get it done early," he said, peeling his banana, impatient for me to finish my oatmeal. "I like to have it done before some of these afternoon storms start and it gets to clanging and banging up there." At the field, I watched him work through his preflight. When he was ready to go, I walked to the edge of the runway. He taxied the Deb to the far end. He turned her around. The plane seemed to throb and blur in the humidity and heat already rising. A minute or more went by. I knew he was in there, reading off the checklist aloud. I knew he was in there, stoking his nerve. He rolled past me, not looking over, the plane picking up speed. She was standing up so smartly on her three wheels. Then she was off the ground, the gear retracting. He circled the field once and dipped his wings at me and turned west before disappearing into the horizon.

In January, our son Matt was born. My thrilled parents came over from Chicago. "That's new life, Paul," my dad said, holding his first grandson, that quizzical tone in his voice. Later that spring we held the christening. My parents came separately. My dad and my brother Mark flew over in the Deb. It was a tense weekend between my parents, despite the joy of the occasion. At the last minute there was a time conflict with the Jesuit priest—a friend of ours—who had agreed to do the baptizing in our living room. No problem, we'd switch the ceremony from Saturday afternoon to Sunday afternoon. My dad said the switch wouldn't work for him. He and Mark were set to fly back to the Midwest early on Sunday. "But couldn't you stay over to Monday, Dad?" I asked. No, he already had his flight plan worked out, and besides there were some things he had to do at home at the top of the week. He was sorry, but we were the ones who had changed the plans on him. I was seething. *You and your lousy stinking airplane, which always comes first,* I wanted to say. I said nothing of the kind. The next morning, in our kitchen, my dad whispered to Ceil, "Paul's really angry at me, isn't he?" Ceil told me this later.

In silence, I drove the two pilots to their plane—they had flown the Deb into a closer-in field in College Park, Maryland. Mark was caught. He was his father's closest son. He knew this was all wrong. But it wasn't his airplane. My little brother has always been such a sensitive soul who holds so much inside. It was still so difficult for any of us to stand up to this incredibly powerful man. The captain was still the captain.

At the field, they got set to go. I stood around in the wet grass, watching.

"Okeedoke, Mark, you're in the left seat this time," my father said. "I'm copilot."

"No," Mark said, looking down.

My dad did a half turn. "I had the first seat coming over. It's your turn. Only fair."

"No," Mark said softly again, still studying the ground.

My father took the pilot's seat. And off they went. He never apologized.

That was mid-1984. Over the next three years I worked myself into a deep financial and emotional hole. I had taken a leave from my newspaper job to write a major book. With each successive month, the fear got worse. I had taken a large chunk of signing money from my publisher to help support us. After almost three years, I had next to nothing to show. At times I felt almost suicidal, with my wife and baby son waiting upstairs. Ceil, who was working as well as mothering, felt helpless to help me. Over the New Year in 1987, knowing next to nothing of this, or so I believe, my parents came to visit. They were back together—for the time being. They'd sold our suburban Chicago home, which had been our family's principal residence since 1955, and just bought a small place in the Rio Grande Valley of Texas. They were trying to start over. My dad was full of beans. I couldn't bring up how badly I was failing every day on the ground floor of our rented townhouse. It was my pride. After they left, I wrote in longhand a seven-page letter, in which I off-loaded onto them my depression and anxiety and paranoia. Somehow, my inability to write the book was all their fault. I brought up old grievances. Even though I was addressing them both, I was really directing my rage at my father. When I look at this letter now (I had made a copy), I cringe. I was attacking him for his supposed cluelessness and blindness and narcissism. Except not once during their stay had I managed to speak directly about the book failure, which was my failure. Were they supposed to have divined it? I hid behind a letter.

I have already said that, as the years went on, my father wasn't one for writing lengthy letters, certainly not to me, and almost never letters revealing much emotion. His letter of reply, full of emotion, went a whole page. In his quirky spelling and capitalization and abbreviations, he said: "Didn't I offer fin. Assistance? [Yes, he had offered money, and I had conveniently omitted this fact in my letter.] More than once? What are some of the things I've done that you don't Under stand? What cues did I miss Xmas (New Years')? The others missed too, Why me only?"

Those last three words sound so out of character for a man whom I had been afraid of for my whole life. They sound almost like a small cry. Which I couldn't hear, not then.

Neither of us could stand the silence. We patched things up. I went back to the newspaper and began helping to restore my family's broken finances. Some stability returned. About a year later my dad called up and asked if I would accompany him on a fly-in fishing trip to Canada. A bunch of old Eastern pilots would be going, and a few were bringing their sons. He'd pay for everything. "Paul, there's water up in Canada man has never fished in. They've got muskie and walleye and northern pike and largemouth bass waiting up there for us." It was the wide-eyed Kentucky boy, dreaming of the north woods again.

We met in northern Wisconsin, at the cabin. (He had arrived ahead of me in the Deb and had her tied down and waiting at a local airport.) It was Memorial Day weekend. It was sleeting when we got into the air. He got her up to 5,000 feet and decided to come down to 4,000. Big chunks of ice were thwacking off the wings. He said, "Snow? Who the hell needs it? On Memorial Day? Let's get the hell out of here and go to Texas."

But the weather cleared by the time we got to International Falls, Minnesota. We crossed the border and got ready to let down for refueling and to go through customs at the municipal airport at Fort Frances, Ontario. "This is N1742-Golf," he barked on his radio to the air traffic controller. "You're clear," came the voice on the Canadian side. "Nice landing, Dad," I said, almost laughing at how a man, who'd now crossed his own border to seventy, could still stick a landing as if he were twenty-five. "Son, if you can't do it when it's like this, when you got heavy and smooth air, this time of day, these conditions, you should just hang it up."

The resort where we were headed—at a place called Eagle Lake—was less than ninety miles north and had its own 2,800-foot grass landing strip. It was clear flying all the way. Down below was a terrain of fir trees and blue water and the occasional clot of life. He was in such high spirits. He was going toward the tundra line, at least in his imagination. He started explaining his costly LORAN system, which he'd just put in. (LORAN is shorthand for "long range navigation.") He was talking about his altimeter and transponder and altitude encoder, and I understood next to none of it.

Again, he came in right on the dime—and handed the landing strip some change. Throughout the afternoon, old Eastern cronies arrived in their Cessna Skyhawk 172s and their Beech Queen Airs. He introduced me to guys nicknamed "Curly" and "Crash" and "Knobby." "Well, I better call the War Department and tell her I got here okay, she'll probably be pissed I made it," somebody said, and got a big laugh. For the next four days, there was much boozing and jesting and fishing. Except that the fishing was lousy. The Native American guides, who took us out every morning in large boats while the seabirds wheeled and cawed around us, seemed at a loss to explain. Maybe it was the weather, which had suddenly turned into summer. "I've spit on my bait, I got my favorite rod, I've said a prayer, I got a bottle of beer in my hand, hell, why can't I catch a fish?" my dad said. But neither he nor his buddies really seemed to mind. In the late afternoon, back at the lodge, they'd drift out to their planes, which were lined up beside each other on the grass in a long row. They'd lean on the wings and talk shop. I hung nearby and took notes. My dad knew what I was doing: saving string. He seemed prouder of me than I could almost ever remember. In the smallest way it almost felt as if our roles were reversing. Late one night, in our separate beds, staring at the ceiling, the lights out, he said, "Oh, I haven't accomplished very much in this life, Paul. You know, I would have liked to go to college, like you did. That's a real accomplishment."

He also said something else: "You know, before you came to the cabin, I was doing some work in the crawl space under the foundation. I got claustrophobic. I waited my whole life to feel claustrophobia in a tight space." I was thinking of a thousand cockpits.

Flying home, we went into Minneapolis–St. Paul International Airport, so I could catch a commercial flight back to Washington. He was visibly tense. The air controllers brought him in on an outer runway. He had both hands on the wheel. He was leaning forward. I had maps and approach plates in my lap—he had thrust them over at me about an hour after we had lifted off from the grass at Eagle Lake.

"Little hectic, isn't it?" I said, after we got back down and he had crossed the main runway to let me off at a satellite terminal.

"You're damn tootin'. Anytime you go into a major."

There were huge airliners all around us. We were a little puddle-jumper. Only, this was my old man at the stick of the puddle-jumper. Who'd been at Iwo Jima. Who, for thirty years, in any kind of weather, had flown in and out of those intense rookeries named Midway and O'Hare.

We said goodbye on the edge of the taxi strip. I hopped out to go into the commuter terminal. Before I could get inside, he was gone.

That was in the late eighties. Over the next few years, as his health slowly declined, our relationship grew better, more open. It was as if we both realized: Time is short. The nine-lived flyer kept flying. But his quadruple bypass and valve replacement in 1994 effectively put an end to his solo flying days. He refused to sell the Deb, though. *No, never,* I could hear him saying from hundreds of miles distant. He and Mark would fly the Deb. He'd take the second seat.

After that overnight pre-Thanksgiving visit in 1996, following his emergency heart surgery of a few weeks before, I made a vow to try to call him every other week. I tended to break it.

In 2001, he and I went on our last trip together. He was almost eighty-three. He had long wanted to see Kitty Hawk in North Carolina, to walk the sand where those two mechanical geniuses, Orville and Wilbur, proprietors of a bicycle business in Dayton, had made the world's first sustained flight in a heavier-than-air machine. He flew on an airliner over to our home in suburban Washington. I drove him down. We made a four-day trip out of it. It was the thick of summer and the Wright Brothers National Memorial at Kill Devil Hills was full of tourists. We walked the 120 feet of Orville's first flight, made at 10:35 a.m. on December 17, 1903. I could see him sagging in the heat. He unbuttoned his short-sleeved shirt to his navel. His stomach was as white as milk. It was a pretty tight stomach. We rested and then paced off Wilbur's second flight—it was the fourth attempt of December 17—in which the younger brother spanned an impossible 852 feet of Kill Devil sand—no, of Kill Devil air—in the papery Wright Flyer, staying aloft for fifty-nine seconds.

On the last night we went out to eat at a nice restaurant on the beach. He couldn't believe the prices. "Twenty-two dollars for a piece of fish, Paul?" he said, turning the menu facedown. "Shooee. Can't we go somewhere else?"

After, in the car, he said, "I just can't help it, son. It's the Depression in me. You never get over that. I don't know, lately I seem almost to be going back home to Morganfield in double time."

I've pondered that remark, the more so because of the time context in which he said it: the sell-off of the Wisconsin property. It happened only months after we'd been to Kitty Hawk. As I have already said, it was as if afterward he had no place left to go. My mother had her townhouse in the Tampa Bay area, and he had been staying there on and off for part of every year, as they tried to make things work one more time, and then one more time again. How hard it must have been for her, I understand now, to have had your husband turn up, when he wasn't living in northern Wisconsin. And then to head for Wisconsin as soon as winter up there was on its way out. Except now there was no more Wisconsin. He never liked Florida, its flatness and traffic, its year-around seeming sameness of weather. At my mom's, he would sleep in a small bedroom at the back. He'd ride his bike in a local park, where there are immense old trees and Indian mounds and beautiful views of the bay. He'd kill part of the day with some old vets down at the waterfront. He'd tinker in the garage. They'd find their ways to get along, go out to inexpensive eating joints. It was a life.

But by January 2003, I knew, we all knew: He was losing his spirit to live. He had turned eighty-four in October. In March, I was on a promotion tour for a book I had written. I called him from Atlanta. "Paul, it's time for me to leave the earth," he said, no pity in it, just stating a fact. Still, I didn't go down. In mid-April, my mom called to say he was in the hospital and that they'd found a tumor in his stomach and that I'd better come. Marty was living nearby, over near Clearwater. Mark flew in from Illinois, my little sister, Jeannie, from Ohio. I flew from Philadelphia, where we had moved not quite a year before. Of the five of us, only my younger brother Ric couldn't come. He was in his nursing home outside Chicago, too emotionally ill to travel.

I was standing behind my dad's hospital bed when his chief doctor walked in. The bed was tilted at a forty-five-degree angle. My dad was in one of those awful hospital gowns which get looped at your bare backside and have never fit anyone right in the history of medicine. Marty, Mark, Jeannie, and I were in the room. The doctor, who knew my dad pretty well, and admired him, not least for the career he'd had, said: "Joe, I know you like things straight, so here is the straight: I've studied the X-rays. We've gotten the latest labs. One problem cancels out the other. We can't operate on the tumor in your stomach because your heart would never take it."

I couldn't see my dad's face. From behind, I saw him nod. He was nodding almost before the doctor was done. He said, and not weakly: "Right. Okay. I understand." It was as if he'd just been briefed in the Ready for an intruder 150 miles north of Iwo. He had received his orders. I thought to myself: This terribly stern and often uncommunicative and occasionally violent man—which is to say the figure I had known through my childhood until I could escape home at fourteen for the seminary—is now showing me, by example more than word, how to die. He had been all those things through my childhood, true, but he had also been the other things, teaching me, by example more than word, about self-discipline, about completing a task, about self-respect, about the nature of sacrifice for a larger purpose, about honoring one's obligations. He was about to complete a task now, about to honor an obligation.

The hospital needed his room. He was expendable metal, so to speak. They wished to clear him out that day if we could arrange for it. Mark and I got in a car and spent the rest of the afternoon trying to find a hospice in the area that would take him immediately. We found one, and I have already spoken of the irradicable scent of urine seeming to come up out of the baseboard of my father's room. He didn't seem to mind. I have a feeling my beloved little sister has never quite forgiven Mark and me for settling on the place—emphasis on "settle." Of my siblings and me, Jeannie, youngest in the family, the only girl, tended him at the end with the most devotion, as she long had. She is a marvel at details and arrangements. She brought all that to bear, but mostly she brought to bear her grief and love. My mom stayed mostly in the background that final week or so.

He lived for about ten days, and I wasn't there at the end. I had to go back to Philadelphia and teach the remaining week of classes at the university where I was newly employed in a full-time capacity. (Could I have gotten out of that? Of course, I could have.) Before I left, there were some hilarious moments, when he was out of his head with morphine. Once, but only once, he broke down and cried in front of us. That was a shocking event. A time or two or three in my life, I had seen my father with tears in his eyes, but I had never come close to see him crying. "Look at me, damn baby," he'd said, as he'd welled up. The water had coursed down his hospital gown.

I told him goodbye, that I had to leave. I leaned over and told him I loved him. He wasn't awake. He'd been awake for only stray moments in the previous day or two. He made no movement, but my nurse-wife has always told me that hearing is the last sense to go.

He died on May 7, 2003. He was a man who liked to get it done early. The night fighter died in the dark. When it was light, Jeannie called me in Philadelphia. That afternoon I went out to my local trout stream, at Valley Forge, where George Washington headquartered the Continental Army in that terrible winter. I had on my waders and fishing vest and boots, and my fly rod in my hand, and my net hanging from a lanyard on my back. I didn't fish. I just sat on the bank and watched the water purl over the clean stones.

We buried him five days later, at St. Brigid's in Xenia. His stone is there, with his name on it, and my mom's, and, on the other side, Marty's name, and Ric's. Jeannie arranged for a local stone-cutter to do a rendering on the marble of a Black Widow above the words "WWII Pilot Night Fighter CPT." You can see the propellers on those Double Wasp 18-cylinder radial air-cooled Pratt & Whit-ney engines. The wheels are down. Only thing, you can't quite tell whether *The Rita B* is just lifting off, with the wheels about to retract, or just about to land, with the wheels locked in place. I've decided it's the latter. My father is feathering her in, getting back down at South Field on Iwo one more time. Safe. Home.

C I T A T I O N

Captain JOSEPH P. HENDRICKSON, O-441784, Air
Corps, United States Army. For meritorious ach-
ievement while participating in aerial flight. As a
Pilot of a P-61 Night Fighter type aircraft, he ach-
ieved an outstanding record while participating in
numerous flights against the enemy. These flights
were flown at night and frequently over enemy held
islands, during hazardous flying weather and with
no alternate airfield available upon return to home
base. They were accomplished with distinction above
that normally expected. Captain HENDRICKSON's display of high professional skill and courage reflected
great credit upon himself and the Army Air Forces.

Acknowledgments

For a book simmering on the back of my eyeball for at least half a century, there are a lot of people to thank, but I will constrain myself. In the Essay on Sources, which follows, I'll name those who came crucially to my aid while working on a specific section or chapter. In this space, as in previous works, I wish to express my gratitude to a more overarching group of individuals.

First, to speak of those not present, foremost my mother and father, deceased respectively since 2015 and 2003. To them I owe my largest emotional debt. Did they know I was one day going to attempt this reported memoir? Yes. Would they have preferred I never took it up? Probably. On the other hand, I think we sometimes greatly underestimate our parents. They can stand the story, even or especially in its harder parts. More than four decades ago, I published my first book, also a reported memoir, which had much to do with my mother and father, even if it was primarily about my seven years spent studying for the Catholic missionary priesthood. A part of me was dreading their reaction, and the dread turned out to be misplaced.

Not present: I lost two siblings while working on this book: Marty and Ric. Our original unit of seven—two parents and five children—is down to three: my kid brother, Mark, my kid sister, Jeannie, and myself. So although I dedicate *Fighting the Night* to my grandsons with pride and love, in another way I dedicate it to my entire nuclear family: my parents, and secondarily to my two gone siblings, and thirdly to Mark and Jeannie. When Mark and Jeannie came into the world, in 1958 and 1959, my father was in middle age, and my mom was just behind—so my little brother's and sister's experiences of our parents were necessarily different from my own, a fact I have tried to make clear in the text. Mark and Jeannie, you have my deep gratitude for being willing to read the work in advance of its publication. If we have our sometimes separate viewpoints, we have our great commonalities, too. And love.

Love. In a special symbolic way I codedicate this book to my next younger brother, Ric Hendrickson. As I mentioned in the text, he died of COVID. He was nearly lifelong emotionally ill, and he bore it heroically, in and out of hospitals and institutions and, for the last thirty years or so of his life, a Chicago-area nursing home. He died in November 2020, alone. None of us could get there in time. If he had lived eight more days, he would have made it to seventy-one. I was able to speak to him the night before his death and say to him—on a nurse's cell phone that she had put up to his ear—that I loved him.

Not present: For seven decades, one of my most ardent moral supporters was Michael Woyahn of Greensboro, North Carolina. We started first grade together at St. Patrick's Elementary in 1950 in Kankakee, Illinois. He used to check in by phone almost weekly, and to my shame I sometimes felt I was too busy to pick up. He died in the fall of 2022 when I was in the final stretch of the writing. I also lost my best friend from my years at *The Washington Post,* Bill Gildea. I also lost Dennis Gildea (no relation to Bill), my best friend from graduate school more than five decades ago. I am fresh out of Gildeas.

I wish to single out two extraordinary people in my extended family on my father's side: my Aunt Margena Mason, my dad's youngest sibling and lone survivor of what were once nine sharecropping children, and my Morganfield in-law relative, Beth Hendrickson, the wife of my farming first cousin, Keith Hendrickson. Both Margena and Beth helped sustain this project more than they were aware, and not only in the Kentucky parts. In another life Beth could have gone to Washington, D.C., and run a huge government agency.

Aviation journalists and historians. The reader has encountered Jeff Kolln's name. I've spoken of his *Northrop's Night Hunter,* the best Black Widow book I know. (Please see the Essay on Sources for the full citation as well as a list of other P-61 books and monographs which were important to the research.) But I must remark again on Jeff's generosity. Early in the project, I called him up cold. He helped throughout the entire project, with documents, photographs, and technical questions. We've yet to meet in person, but I feel I've made a lasting friend. Stephen Joiner's name also appears in the text. Again, the generosity from someone I've never met. And to make it a trifecta: Mark Stevens, president of the VII Fighter Command Association World War II, as well as the historian of the 20th Air Force Association World War II. All three of these experts are West Coast–based, and I hope to make a round-robin thank-you tour.

Reference librarians at major institutions as well as local historians and genealogists. To repeat what I've said in other acknowledgments in other books: Where would I be without their help? There are too many to name, but three must be cited: Mike Watson, genealogy and history researcher at the Adair County Public Library in Columbia, Kentucky, with whom I've had sweet country lunches and rides through Cane Valley, where the Hendricksons of my line got this whole show on the road, at least in Kentucky; Bill Bauer, retired schoolteacher in Morganfield, Kentucky, who is a walking encyclopedia of the county where my dad was born and raised; and the reference librarian at the Air Force Historical Research Agency at Maxwell Air Force Base in Montgomery, Alabama, who asked to remain anonymous but who, I will say again, seemed to take it upon himself/herself to aid me in enormous ways, not to say to provide by electronic transfer thousands of pages of declassified government documents, many of them relating specifically to the 549th Night Fighter Squadron.

In no particular order: university colleagues, comrades from journalism, longtime friends, former students, fellow authors, several physicians, a lawyer, a family accountant, along with various others in and out of publishing whose steady presence in one way or another I could sense: Wil Haygood, Neenah Ellis and Noah Adams, Lysa Bennett and Greg Djanikian, JoAnn and Bill Lanouette, Robert Fry, Tim Samuelson, Keiran Murphy, Mark Hertzberg, John Baskin, Kim and Tom Hayes, Jim Godsil, Linda and David Maraniss, Sandy Tedeschi, Linda Patterson Miller, Tom Rankin, Henry Hart, Ed Murphy, Jim Sullivan, Joe Appollo, Eric Carroll, Bob Rink, Pete Krebs, Bob Burns, Kathy Milton, Diana and Howard Kohn, Mary Bennett, Paul Burch, Al Filreis, Julia Bloch, Jessica Lowenthal, Allie Katz, Zach Carduner, Jamie-Lee Josselyn, Shelby Coffey, Mary Hadar, John McDonnell, Elizabeth Taylor, David Von Drehle, David Shipley, Hope Rogers, Michael Gerstein, Alison and Kyle Brown, Chris McConnell, Jessica Yu, Elaine Wong, Michael Morse, Naomi Shavin, Sabrina Qiao, Sebastian Stockman, Eric Moskowitz, Gabe Oppenheim, Dan Kaplan, Jessica Goldstein, Julie Steinberg, Shrestha Singh, Susie Cook, Amanda Van Scoyoc, Margo Crawford, Paul Saint-Amour, Jim English, Herman Beavers, Rita Barnard, David Wallace, Dagmawi Woubshet, Jean-Christophe Cloutier, Buzz Bissinger, Carlin Romano, Cher Bryant, Loretta Witham Turner, Stephanie Palmer, Mike Drake, Hope Rogers and Mary Rogers, Burma Mathews, Cherrie Curran, Lynn McClellan, Sunita Nasta, Richard Toof, Stephen Solotoff, Ed Woehling, and Bonnie Youra Krug.

Gratitude to the Sachs Program for Arts Innovation at the University of Pennsylvania, which funded parts of my research.

Gratitude to the Camera Shop in Bryn Mawr, Pennsylvania, for some amazing photographic restoration work.

With particular gratitude: to my longtime literary agent, Kathy Robbins, and her associate, David Halpern, at The Robbins Office, such wise counselors and decent human beings. David is an old-school gent. Kathy is a mensch, a mom who goes to the mat for her authors. My thanks also to their efficient and always courteous staff.

This book couldn't have gotten done without the computer help of my best friend at the University of Pennsylvania: Brian Kirk. It embarrasses him when I call him a tech genius, but that's what he is. And my office at Penn is right next door to his. The gods worked it out.

At Alfred A. Knopf, finest publisher in America, my respect and gratitude to, and in memory of, the late Sonny Mehta. My sincere thanks to Reagan Arthur, Jordan Pavlin, John Freeman, Dan Novack, Chip Kidd, Nicholas Latimer, Emily Reardon, Sarah Perrin, Maggie Hinders, Nicole Pedersen, and Isabel Ribeiro: all dedicated professionals and lovers of books. But most of all, my gratitude to my editor, Jonathan Segal. I remember the winter afternoon so long ago when I came back from lunch and was walking across the several-acre newsroom at *The Washington Post*. One of the ladies who sat on a raised dais and took telephone messages for the entire staff called out to me, waving a sheet of notepaper. She was just about to put the pink sheet in the "H" slot in the oversized, wooden, pigeon-holed mailbox sitting below the dais. "Mr. Paul," Joyce said. "This man from New York just called for you. He's a book editor. His name is Mr. Segal. Here's his number." A relationship with one of the great nonfiction book editors of our time was about to begin. This was forty-four years ago. The relationship has long since transcended books. It hasn't always been smooth going. Who would want it to be? First and last, we meet at the words. Jon is a master at making them better, making the ideas better. In the revolving door of book publishing, I am the luckiest author I know to have had such an experience.

Largest gratitude of all to my immediate family: Ceil, believer of believers, friend of friends, strength of strengths, who so long ago presented me with a T-shirt printed on the front with the words "Caution: Book in Progress." More than anyone, my wife of forty-five years knows the family costs of all this—and yet keeps nudging me forward. Then our son Matt, father of our two astonishing grandsons. Matt, you are twice the father I have been, and you are such a huge professional success. Then our son John, fellow Knopf author, and a world-class journalist to boot. And not least our amazing daughters-in-law, Jennie and Liz. You two have rounded us out, bridged us, enhanced us, beyond anything Ceil or I could have hoped for.

Finally: To all the servicemen of the 549th Night Fighter Squadron who went to Iwo Jima: heroes each one. May you stay forever young.

Essay on Sources

William Maxwell, who for forty years was a fiction editor at *The New Yorker*, once wrote an essay for *The New York Times Magazine* entitled "Nearing Ninety," in which he said: "I have liked remembering almost as much as I have liked living." This is a book about remembering, no matter its reporting and research. It is a hybrid work, like most of my books. If it is a memoir, I also was privileged to go out into the world as a shoe-leather reporter to try to discover what was in my own heart. On the most basic level, I went searching for the documents—and, not least, for people. I come proudly from the journalistic tradition. It's the only way I know how to proceed.

Significant parts of this book rely on note-taking I did decades ago in skinny spiral-ringed reporter's notebooks and in leatherbound journals. I also was thrilled to call on material typed out in a pre-digital age on a trusty Smith Corona portable. The paper that got rolled into the carriage of that fondly remembered machine were usually those off-white, rustle-free, penny-cheap sheets of newsprint that used to fill every newsroom in America. I cadged wads of them from my employer. Through the years, as I worked on other book projects, I squirreled away my notes and notebooks and journals on what I thought of as "The Father Book," dreaming of being able to go back someday and discover inside them the form of a story, the bones of a narrative, about fathers and sons—about *my* father and *his* son.

I don't have to glance over at the mounds of *new* paper I've accumulated. If I've been writing this book in the back of my head for fifty years, it's also true I've acquired what seems like a small dump truck of documents in just the past several years. (Much of it remains on digitized microfilm; more on that in a minute.)

The "outside" material for *Fighting the Night* has been gathered in three ways: First, from my own reporting and interviewing. Second, from documentary material—letters, manuscripts, photographs, films, newsreels, audio recordings, declassified government records. Third, from secondary sources, by which I principally mean books and articles and monographs and textbooks and, in a few instances, unpublished academic dissertations or theses.

There turned out to be a lot. This only speaks to the Black Widow's myth. The myth has always been much greater than the record. As the reader knows, the P-61's arrival in World War II came too late. Even though she served in the

European Theater, the Pacific Theater, the China-Burma-India Theater, and the Mediterranean Theater, the Black Widow's record against the enemy cannot compete with, say, what the P-51 Mustang fighter, the B-25 Mitchell bomber, the B-29 Superfortress, the B-24 Liberator, the P-38 Lightning, the P-47 Thunderbolt, or the P-40 Warhawk accomplished. (Only 706 Widows came off the assembly lines as opposed to 13,738 Warhawks.) And yet there she is, settled in her place in aviation history, in her fame in the war, amid all these other iconic craft. As the reader also knows, what has helped stoke the legend of my father's ghostly black night ship is that she has all but vanished. (A legend-making fact which I didn't note in the text: On the overnight of August 14–15, 1945, a P-61 was credited with the last Allied kill of World War II. Her name was *Lady in the Dark*. She belonged to the squadron just below my dad's: the 548th NFS. She is one of the most photographed Black Widows of all.)

I know of two dozen books on the Black Widow, and probably there are a good deal more. Some are esoteric and difficult to lay hands on. I don't pretend to have collected them all.

The following works, full-length and small-sized, were of help: Larry Davis and David Menard, *P-61 Black Widow in Action* (Carrollton, TX: Squadron Signal Publications, 1990); Jesse Gardner, *Beachheads and Black Widows: A South Pacific Diary* (Pittsburgh: Hermann Printing, 1995); Frederick A. Johnsen, *Darkly Dangerous: The Northrop P-61 Black Widow Night Fighter* (Tacoma, WA: Bomber Books, 1981); David McLaren, *Black Widow: The Story of the Northrop P-61* (Colorado Springs, CO: VIP Publishers, 1993); Garry R. Pape, with John M. and Donna Campbell, *Northrop P-61 Black Widow: The Complete History and Combat Record* (Atglen, PA: Schiffer Publishing, 1997); Warren Thompson, *P-61 Black Widow Units of World War 2* (Oxford, UK: Osprey Publishing, 1998); Thompson, *Combat Chronicles of the Black Widow* (Carrollton, TX: Squadron Signal Publications, 2011); Thompson, *Northrop P-61 Black Widow* (North Branch, MN: Specialty Press, 1997).

Six other works, full-length and otherwise, not solely devoted to the P-61, were important: Fred Anderson, *Northrop: An Aeronautical History* (Los Angeles: Northrop Corp., 1976); Bill Gunston, *Night Fighters: A Development and Combat History* (Gloucestershire, UK: Sutton Publishing, 2004); John W. Lambert, *The Pineapple Air Force: Pearl Harbor to Tokyo* (Atglen, PA: Schiffer Publishing, 2006); Stephen L. McFarland, *Conquering the Night: Army Air Forces Night Fighters at War* (Washington, DC: Air Force History and Museums Program, 1998); William Odell, *Those Few Who Dared: The History of World War II Night Fighters* (Albuquerque, NM: WWII Night Fighters, 1994); Garry R. Pape and Ronald C. Harrison, *Queen of the Midnight Skies: The Story of America's Air Force Night Fighters* (Atglen, PA: Schiffer Publishing, 1997). Of these, I found Anderson's *Northrop* and Lambert's *Pineapple Air Force* and Pape and Harrison's *Queen of the Midnight Skies* the most thorough and helpful for my purposes. McFarland's *Conquering the Night* remains perhaps the most authoritative overview of the night fighter story.

But none of these books comes close to what Jeff Kolln's *Northrop's Night Hunter: P-61 Black Widow* (North Branch, MN: Specialty Press, 2008) did in helping me to understand both the mechanics and soul of my father's airplane. It is the reason I am citing it separately. I have already spoken of Jeff's generosity, a man of both mechanics and soul, or so it seems to me from our numerous talks. Every writer of deeply researched nonfiction, if the gods are smiling, finds his own Jeff Kolln somewhere along the way.

Although I dug up many articles in newspapers and magazines and journals (some will be cited below, as they relate to specific sections or chapters), the rabbit's foot I carried in my metaphorical back pocket for the last several years was "Welcome to the Night Shift," by Stephen Joiner (named in the acknowledgments), in the August 2016 *Air & Space/Smithsonian*. The piece is eight pages long but has the overview and the juice. Joiner and I have had our fruitful talks.

The work I carried almost literally the whole way in my pocket is a cheap paperback edition of William Manchester's *Goodbye, Darkness: A Memoir of the Pacific War* (New York: Dell, 1987). I have made my hosannahs to this magisterial tone poem on the horrors of war. The Iwo Jima part is small. There is barely a mention about my father's airplane. It doesn't matter. *Darkness* was the talisman for what I knew I would never achieve in my own book but would aim toward anyway. If Manchester had still been alive when I began this book in earnest, I would have tried to go to his door (in Middletown, Connecticut) to thank him.

I spoke of a small dump truck of documents, and I am referring specifically to what my anonymous guardian angel at the Air Force Historical Research Agency at Maxwell Air Force Base in Montgomery provided. Again, I have already paid tribute, but I will add here that it seems inconceivable to me now that *Night* could have gotten done at all without his/her help. This help supersedes even Jeff Kolln's. I refer to the literally thousands of pages of declassified documents which got sent my way electronically in a period when I couldn't travel because of the coronavirus. I can't pretend to have read all the pages, not even close. Maybe less than 5 percent of the documents (I am only guessing) relate specifically to my father's squadron. Most of the pages in my possession remain on digitized microfilm reels—such as Reel A7535, which is 1,430 pages and titled, "History of the Seventh Air Force, 1 April 1945–14 July 1945." There are nuggets in this document pertaining to my father's island and squadron. I have mined them as I could. But just knowing these reels were there, stored safely in my Dropbox folder, provided psychological comfort in keeping the writing going.

What gave a psychological comfort *and* crucial documentary help for the writing were the declassified monthly squadron reports of the 549th NFS. They were the ingots of gold because they are solely about my dad's squadron. My Montgomery guardian angel supplied them all, from the first month's report when the unit was activated back in Fresno (two days after I was born) until way past the point when my father flew off Iwo for the final time in a transport, bound for home. I printed out the entirety of them and pored over each page multiple times. In fact, it was the "monthlies" (I have also heard them called the unit histories) that arrived first from Montgomery. They tend to be styled this way: "549th Night Fighter Squadron, VII Fighter Command, Army Air Forces, Pacific Ocean Areas, APO 86, 1 March 1945–31 March 1945." That one runs to some twenty pages of main text, with twelve pages of supporting documents, including hand-drawn maps of the squadron's bivouac on Iwo and the flight line at South Field. The documents are full of banalities and terrors. (I am speaking, although not exclusively, of the attached mission reports.) In some of the monthlies, there are photographs at the back. It was the texture of these reports that took me across. To see my dad's name cropping up seemed like magical realism: proof, once more, as if I really needed any, that he was actually there. I combined the squadron reports with my father's service file at the National Personnel Records Center in St. Louis, along with another document also housed there and known as the Individual Flight Record. The IFR tries to catalogue every hour that a particular flyer was in the air. (Not possible; I found conflicts with my dad's record in the monthlies.)

I need add that Jeff Kolln also gave me—to keep—a declassified 8-millimeter microfilm reel of the squadron history. Much of it duplicates what my angel from Montgomery provided.

Magical realism: I got the critical documents from Montgomery without setting foot there. A couple years earlier, I went to St. Louis and spent two days standing at the copier machine in the reading room, madly duplicating the military record of an Army Air Corpsman from Morganfield, Kentucky, whose file just as easily could no longer have existed. I said in the text, but will repeat it here: Somehow, the 1973 fire that destroyed something like 70 to 80 percent of the records ended up not even singeing the edges of my dad's file. How could this be? I asked that question several times to the reference assistants. None had a satisfying answer. But it was as if God was telling me I had no choice but to try to write this book.

I traveled to other archives across the country (I am not speaking of what is held in local libraries), and at least one is worth mentioning: The Night Fighters of World War II Collection in the Department of Special Collections and Archives at Wright State University in Dayton, Ohio. It is a significant collection, although a teacup compared to what is held at Montgomery. Nonetheless, I found helpful the papers of William C. Odell and also the papers and photographs and notebooks of Earl Tigner. My father served with both. Tigner was a fellow flyer in the 549th. Odell was one of my dad's superior officers when he was still stateside.

Not least in importance was my dad's oral history, which informs this entire book but comes downstage for my chapter "June–July 1945." The oral history is part of "Listening to War: Wisconsin's Oral Histories," and was conducted by James Ogilvie on April 25, 2002, at our former family cabin in Iron River, Wisconsin. The tape is held at the Richard I. Bong Veterans Historical Center in Superior, Wisconsin, but, as was said in the text, it's a part of the statewide archives of the Wisconsin Historical Society, headquartered in Madison.

As with previous books, what follows isn't meant to be an all-inclusive source-noting, but rather a kind of prose-form road map of my own devising, both the left-out anecdote and the specific citation. Not every cite, no, but ones in which I feel the reader will be interested. I'll use abbreviations where it feels appropriate and not confusing. This time, as is probably already apparent, rather than presenting a formal bibliography at the end, I am folding into this essay as I go the key book-length works on which I relied. (Some are named in the text.) The same fold-in goes for newspapers and periodicals. Again, my intention is to join conventional nonfiction sourcing to some things I was unable to weld onto the main frame of the narrative. Again, as with the acknowledgments, I'll constrain myself.

PROLOGUE: AMARILLO GOODBYE

It was put together, chiefly, from talks with my parents through the years, and from my dad's service file, which has amazingly detailed dates of transfers and promotions, of start-up dates and ending dates for a particular training school or temporary duty assignment. My folks had no memory of the name of the Texas motor lodge where they stood in the sun and said goodbye. I halfheartedly tried to find out the name by calling up the Amarillo City Library and speaking to someone at the local history desk and then emailing several photographs. No luck. However, I am convinced the goodbye occurred early in the day, probably right after breakfast. As noted in the text, later that same day, back in California, my dad was practicing turns and rolls at Bakersfield—I have his Individual Flight Record for proof. My mom? She was headed tearfully east toward Xenia all that day with her sister war-wife and Marty and me. It's all I know. (Note: A version of this prologue appeared in *Literary Hub*, on September 23, 2020, entitled "Snapshots Before the War: Saying Goodbye in 1994.")

LONG AGO IN KENTUCKY

Interchapter. The quote is from p. 31 of *Seminary: A Search* (New York: Summit Books, 1983).

Chapter. The quotes from the after-action battlefield report at the Battle of Shiloh are in the Regiment History of the Thirteenth Kentucky Volunteers. Mike Watson (named in the acknowledgments) of the Adair County Public Library at Columbia, Kentucky, helped me locate that document, as he helped me locate numerous other documents. One of them was the original Book of Record documenting the February 6, 1854, marriage of my great-great Civil War grandfather, George Hendrickson, to Martha Winfrey. The marble-backed book, in fragile condition, maybe six inches by seven inches, was probably carried in the vest pocket of the circuit-riding minister who performed the ceremony. Watson keeps the document in a safe at the library. When I was researching *Night,* I was a stranger to this part of Kentucky. By the time I left Cane Valley, I almost felt I had known the place my entire life.

Which is something I can say almost literally as regards Morganfield and Union County, some 200 miles to the north and west of Adair County and Cane Valley. It was blissful to go back to the place where I spent several weeks of so many boyhood summers in the late forties and into most of the fifties. Blissful to go back almost for the barbecue alone at Peak Brothers in the hamlet of Waverly, ten minutes outside of Morganfield.

I consulted local histories, census records, newspaper files, slave schedules, tax rolls, cemetery records, the books of deed in the basement of the courthouse on the square in Morganfield. An astounding resource was *Union County, Past and Present* (Louisville: Schumann Printing Company, 1941), part of the American Guide Series, written by formerly out-of-work writers of the Kentucky Writers' Project of the New Deal's WPA (Work Projects Administration).

I've spoken of researcher Bill Bauer's great help. Nancy Voyles, in the genealogy/local history room of the Henderson County Public Library in Henderson,

Kentucky, was also generous with her time. (Henderson is the next county up from Union, but its history holdings are rich and include the far more rural Union County.) In the *Union County Advocate* Nancy found this old ad.

My grandfather's half-brother, Noel Hendrickson, is selling out. It's Christmas 1936. It almost seems as if he's pre-empting the bankers. He's going to let the auctioneer's song take it down to the bone. Just in this public notice of giving up, there seems a quiet, fatalistic poetry.

The Morganfield phone directory has many listed Hendricksons, but the Hendrickson to bet on if you're on a research mission is Beth Hendrickson. I spoke of her earlier. She knows our genealogical history better than anyone. One late spring day in 2021 we got into Beth's SUV. She was at the wheel; I had the county maps and my notebooks in my lap. The men were out planting. We sped around on back roads. We pulled up at a neck of green hilltop land. Two of her—and her husband, Keith's—sons had just taken out a monstrous loan to buy it. It was the same land, off the Crawley Road, which, almost a hundred years before, the New York Life Insurance Company had seized from our great-grandfather Kincheloe Hendrickson because he couldn't find $148.33 to pay his bundled yearly taxes. "We got it back," Beth crowed, leaning on the steering wheel, waiting for her son Bryan to come back up the rise on a monster corn-planting machine, which, like the new land, was being bought on time and dreams. (Bryan's own small son was riding in the cab with his daddy, already a pint-sized farmer.) "Your sons have redeemed Kincheloe's shame," I said.

One other note: There is some slight doubt among some of my kin whether that's my dad in the photograph at the front of the chapter. Beth and Aunt Margena have wondered whether the figure holding the bridle is really my Uncle Tommy, who went to the Navy in the war and was two rungs below my dad on the ladder of kids. But I am certain the figure is my dad for two reasons: He once said so to me. And I recognize, unforgettably, the way the figure in the picture is holding his cig, down low, ready to flick the ash. That's my dad.

THE ROAD TO SOUTH FIELD ON IWO JIMA (1)

Interchapter. My notes and reporting and memories.

Chapter. My notes and reporting and memories. The figure of 300,000 American warplanes in World War II: from the National Air and Space Museum of the Smithsonian. The figure of roughly sixteen and a half million men and women serving in the war: from both the U.S. Census Bureau and the National WWII Museum in New Orleans. My portrait of Chanute Field was drawn principally from materials in the local history and genealogy division of the Urbana (Illinois) Free Library. The library's Chanute holdings are vast and are part of the Champaign County Historical Archives. The Chanute archive has an extremely detailed finding aid. The collection includes many photographs: one more proof of how local libraries (even if this one is in a university community) are often such an unsung and underprized resource for researchers. Other: In addition to my dad's oral history, I used his service record, along with the Xenia and Morganfield newspapers, to track his moves after graduation from Chanute. Barney Slamkowski's too-brief life was drawn from newspaper reports and biographical material on Ancestry.com and, not least, from the War Department's official, two-page "Report of Aircraft Accident." Jack Benny's live radio show was April 12, 1942. Bosley Crowther's *New York Times* review of *This Gun for Hire* was May 14, 1942. A particularly good overview of the prewar buildup of the Army Air Forces, just as my dad was entering the service, is Wesley Frank Craven and James Lea Cate, eds, vol. 6, New Imprint series, "Men and Planes," in *The Army Air Forces in World War II* (Washington, DC: Office of Air Force History, 1983).

THE ROAD TO SOUTH FIELD ON IWO JIMA (2)

Interchapter. My notes and reporting and memories. Lessing's "My Father" is in the American edition of *The Doris Lessing Reader* (New York: Alfred A. Knopf,

1989). My "The Best Thanksgiving" appeared in the November 1990 issue of *Life.*

   Chapter. For the mini-portrait of the making of my father's airplane, I drew from some of the works cited above about the Black Widow. But I chiefly drew from Anderson's *Northrop* (it's a company-commissioned history, but well done and fairly objective) and Joiner's "Welcome to the Night Shift." (All the quotes, including "Jack, you've got a damn fine airplane," are from that piece.) The Los Angeles Coliseum story about the first public sighting of the plane is on p. 54 of Anderson's history. Other: Once again, my dad's service record was invaluable for tracking his moves, but I also used my old notes from talks with my folks through the years, as well as his oral history. For my dad's time at Thunderbird II in primary training, where he soloed in a PT-13 Stearman: At the Scottsdale Airport, built on the site of the old Army Air Corps training facility, is a small, albeit wonderful, museum and veterans memorial. It charts the history of Scottsdale's contribution to training pilots for the war. A beautifully restored Stearman is suspended from the museum's roof. I stood under it for some hours. The museum's guiding light is Steve Ziomek; he was generous with his time. At Yuma, where my dad got his wings: Librarian Laurie Boone, in the archives of the Heritage Library of the Yuma County Library District, directed me to a trove of old photographs and base newspapers and other ephemera. I didn't get to use it, but the trove informed the narrative. The greatest Yuma resource, informing the narrative, was my dad's yearbook. It contains a long essay by a fellow airman (and aspiring journalist) named Lindell Hendrix. The piece describes all phases and stages of the steps to earning one's wings. Other: My dad's middle-of-the-night taxiing accident in Florida: The twelve-page official War Department report is dated December 27, 1943, seven days after it happened. Re Jack Kerr: The "STUDIES RADAR" story was in the *Raritan Township* (NJ) *Fords Beacon,* July 30, 1943. For the nearly six-month Fresno stay: The Fresno County Public Library has a large Hammer Field collection. I found copies of the base newspaper, the *Night Hawk,* published in the same week that the 549th was being activated. (The base movie theater was playing *Between Two Worlds,* with John Garfield.) George F. Gruner's *Into the Night* (Clovis, CA: Clovis Veterans Memorial District in cooperation with Linden Publishing, 2012) is a comprehensive history of Hammer. For the Hawaii portion of this chapter: David Trojan sent via email maps and photographs and other documents. He is a preeminent authority about aviation in Hawaii during the war, and especially about Kipapa Field. But the monthly squadron histories were the ingots, supplying precise dates of, say, when my dad and his fellow flyers left for "the forward area," and all stops in between before touching down at South Field in the forenoon of March 20, 1945.

   Finally, a nomenclature note: The reader may have noticed by now that I have used the terms "Army Air Corps" and "Army Air Force" and "Army Air Forces" a bit indiscriminately. Which is it, which was it? In a word, often all three, even if not officially so, not correctly so. I have seen occasions and documents when the three terms seemed to be in use rather interchangeably. The facts: The U.S. Army Air Corps was the aviation arm of the U.S. Army between 1926 and 1941. In June 1941, the Air Corps officially became the United States Army Air Forces. And yet, during the war, the Air Corps, although no longer a separate administrative entity, continued as one of the combat arms of the army. In 1947, the Army Air Forces formally became the United States Air Force. It all sounds a bit confusing. I have seen pieces of government paper pertaining to my father (for instance, when he was up for a rise in rank or change in station) when the term "Air Corps" or "Army Air Force" or "Army Air Forces" appears at the bottom of a particular page atop an official signature. All were correct, sort of. My take is that everyone was too busy trying to defeat Hitler and the Emperor to care all that much about when the names and dates had changed. Maybe I've got that part wrong, but that's what it feels like from afar. As for my own usage, I admit to being somewhat chronologically loose and arbitrary. I have tended to employ what has sounded right to my ear in a particular sentence, especially when using "Army Air Force" or "Army Air Forces." So far as I know, "Army Air Force" was never a technically correct term, even if you can find it in plenty of official and semiofficial places.

CLEAR PICTURES

Interchapter. My notes and reporting and memories. Re James Salter quote preceding the interchapter: He is a literary hero of mine who was a fighter pilot in the Korean War and wrote an unforgettable flying memoir entitled *Burning the Days.* Michael Herr? I honor him even more than Salter. The quote is from p. 67 of the Avon paperback edition of *Dispatches.*

Chapter. Manchester's "The deaths on Iwo" quote is on p. 392 of the Dell edition of *Darkness.* The casualty statistics and other numbers related to the Battle of Iwo Jima come from standard government military reference works—of which I consulted many. Samuel Eliot Morison's "The operation looked" quote is on p. 35 of chapter 3, "D-day at Iwo Jima," in vol. 14, *Victory in the Pacific,* of the author's *History of United States Naval Operations in World War II* (Boston: Little, Brown, 1947–62). Portrait of General Kuribayashi in *Japan Times* ("His Emperor's Reluctant Warrior") is August 13, 2006. Letters of the general: The great majority are taken from two sources, one of which was referenced in the text: Kumiko Kakehashi's *So Sad to Fall in Battle: An Account of War Based on General Tadamichi Kuribayashi's Letters from Iwo Jima* (New York: Ballantine, 2007). The other work is Tsuyuko Yoshida, ed, *Picture Letters from the Commander in Chief* (San Francisco: VIZ Media in conjunction with Warner Bros. Entertainment, Inc., and DreamWorks LLC, 2006). There are sometimes small variations in the English translations of the same letter, appearing in both books, and I went with the translation that most struck my imagination. "The carnage was terrible" quote is on p. 125 of Lambert's *Pineapple Air Force.* Cyndy Carrington Miller (now a friend) published her tribute to her father, Ralph J. Carrington, *Iwo Jima Album,* in 2012. Lester Friedman's "God/County/Family" is in *Tough Ain't Enough: New Perspectives on the Films of Clint Eastwood* (New Brunswick, NJ: Rutgers University Press, 2018). My talks with Iris Yamashita and Tim Moore were in February 2022. The "It does not seem impossible" quote is on p. 190 of the Presidio Press paperback edition of *So Sad.*

Fighter Post, an Iwo newspaper mimeographed and distributed to units of the VII Fighter Command, was helpful to understand the texture of daily life.

As the reader knows, the Battle of Iwo Jima occurred before my dad's squadron arrived on the island. But I knew I had to steep myself in what happened there. There is so much literature. Manchester's *Darkness* was where I started. I read in and out of a handful of well-known works. I looked at military newsreels. But in truth, three unsung—and diverse—sources aided most. The first is a short video of an old man who's gone back to Iwo in March 2015, the seventieth anniversary of the battle. Jerry Yellin, P-51 Mustang pilot of the 78th Fighter Squadron, is remembering. The old airman, ramrod-straight, is in uniform. The outline of Suribachi is in the background. It's not so much what Yellin says (the clip is on the web as part of Defense Visual Information Distribution Service), but the humility and the quiet with which he says it. The second source is a nearly 500-page work by Robert D. Eldridge, *Iwo Jima and the Bonin Islands in U.S.-Japan Relations* (Quantico, VA: Marine Corps University Press, 2014). Chapter two is "The War and the Battle of Iwo Jima." I contacted Eldridge—who is based in Japan and has had a lengthy career in teaching and consulting, in and out of the military—for help in understanding Chichi Jima and Haha Jima. The third source is independent scholar and Pacific War historian Dan King, who has devoted much of his life to trying to understand the story from the Japanese side. His *A Tomb Called Iwo Jima: Firsthand Accounts from Japanese Survivors* (North Charleston, SC: CreateSpace Independent Publishing Platform, 2014) gave me an emotional feel for my father's island. From King— based in Texas, who, as with others, was generous with his telephone and email time—I learned the essential difference between a *banzai* charge and a *kirikomi* attack.

Finally, a note on the photograph at the start of this chapter. As was said in the text, I do not know whether my father saw *this* ditch. He never talked of any of it. I only know he had to have seen scenes very close to this one. As was said in the text, in Ralph Carrington's *Iwo Jima Album,* there are similar photographs. Other families of men in my dad's squadron also have small bundles of these same pictures. Bonnie Youra Krug—whose dad was the crew chief of the Widow piloted by Captain Larry Garland (the Garland story, as the reader knows, takes up the closing chapter)—has pictures in photo albums of the bodies and the ditches. She has a picture of an airman standing over a ditch with a shovel and peering in. We have shared much talk.

WHERE LEO E SAT

Interchapter. My notes and memories and reporting. My talks with Russ Strine were in spring 2022. It was inspiring to discover a man pursuing such a bold dream. A good book of the Widow under restoration is Sharon Wells Wagner and Stephen Wagner, *Forgotten Widow: The Incredible True Story of Two Men's Efforts to Recover and Restore a Rare World War II P-61 Black Widow Night Fighter Against Overwhelming Odds* (Reading, PA: Aperture Press, 2010).

Chapter. My reporting and research. Richard Hugo's "Home. Home," is from his "The Only Bar in Dixon." Kolln's "made up of molded Lucite" quote is on p. 48 of *Northrop's Night Hunter.* Michelle McGowan and her husband, Leo, opened their family albums and trunks of memories. John Litzy, who has lived in the valley most of his life, spent half a day driving me around. Rev. Thomas J. Petro, who serves the faithful at Sacred Heart of Jesus Church in the area, was generous with his time.

EIGHTY-THREE YEARS LATER, NOT QUITE TO THE DAY

Interchapter. My notes and memories—and talk with my brother Mark.

Chapter. My notes and memories and reporting. But the documents—and my Montgomery guardian angel—were the key to it all. As much as I could, I embedded into the chapter itself the relevant dates of a particular document. The quotes by Joiner are in his *Air & Space* "Night Shift" piece. Again, help came from Robert Eldridge and his work on Iwo and the Bonins (cited above). The "Dr. Teraki cut" quote is in Colin Fraser's May 16, 2016, article, "George H. Bush Narrowly Escaped Being Executed and Eaten by the Japanese in WWII," in *War History Online.* Hemingway's line about the "duration of a sensation" is from an unpublished (and undated) fragment about fishing he probably wrote in Paris in the mid-twenties. One other note: My dad, in his Wisconsin oral history, remembered that the searchlight incident happened on Haha Jima instead of Chichi. He got the island wrong but not the fright.

OF JAMES DICKEY AND MY FATHER

Interchapter. My notes and reporting.

Chapter. Bill Moyers's "A Conversation with James Dickey" was recorded in late 1975 and aired on *Bill Moyers Journal* on PBS on January 25, 1976. Bly's take-down of Dickey is in "The Collapse of James Dickey" in the journal *The Sixties,* No. 9, 1967. MacLeish's lines about Hemingway are in his 1948 poem "Years of the Dog." Chris Dickey's "The Poet's Family Album" was published as "The Family Album" in Sarah Ban Breathnach's *A Man's Journey to Simple Abundance* (New York: Scribner, 2000). Again, Robert Eldridge was very helpful on the culture and texture of Haha Jima, as was another Japan-based scholar-friend of Eldridge's, Daniel Long. (Note: A longer version of this chapter was published online, in *Literary Hub,* on December 7, 2020, entitled "On James Dickey and the Truths That Matter.")

THE SHORT UNHAPPY LIFE OF *THE MERRY WIDOW*

Interchapter. My notes and memories. "On the Sadness of a Family Photograph" is a fugue in an essay entitled "Fantasia on the Relations Between Poetry and Photography" in Mark Strand's *The Weather of Words* (New York: Alfred A. Knopf, 2001).

Chapter. My notes and reporting. Once again, the squadron monthly enabled me to get it done. Re *The Merry Widow.* A document known as the Individual Aircraft Record Card (sometimes more commonly called the aircraft record card) had the dates of the airplane's history starting from when she left the Northrop assembly lines. (I have used the record card to track all *The Rita B*'s relevant dates; ditto with other Widows in this narrative.) The March 24, 1945, footage of *The Merry Widow* is on the web, extracted from United States Naval Photographic Center, film #11083. My talks with Tim Lamont were in the fall of 2018. The Albert Speer quote is in Gilbert King's "The Candor and Lies of Nazi Officer Albert Speer," January 8, 2013, *Smithsonian.*

Re my dad's May 23 accident in *The Merry Widow:* two curious facts. First, the official report wasn't written and signed for a full two months—on July 23. Second: The operations officer of the squadron had a similar accident that same night, and I think at roughly the same hour. And yet that accident was omitted from the monthly report. Kolln, in *Northrop's Night Hunter* (p. 168): "Major Alford, with the weather closing in, had poor visibility as he approached South Field at Iwo Jima for landing. Fog had reduced visibility to such an extent that the runway could not be seen on final approach." Kolln got the accident report not from an official government source, but from an authoritative civilian website, Accident-Report.com, run by a New Jerseyite named Mike Stowe. He and I have become something of friends (though we've not met), and he has advised this project at several critical turns. Stowe has spent a lot of years prying information from government records. I asked him why my father's accident would have been noted in the 549th's monthly history (albeit with forgiving language), but nothing of Alford's. He said he didn't know. He elaborated in an email: "I have found very many accidents in the Pacific area were just not reported. I believe many were deliberately (and falsely) attributed to combat which eliminated the requirement for reporting. I once tried to compare the Pacific to the other air forces to see if I was right. Just the 8th Air Force [in Europe] created over 5000 accident reports. The 5th, 7th, 13th, and 20th Air Forces combined created about 900. I know there was a big difference in flying, but not that much!" Was Alford's accident kept out of the squadron monthly report to the higher-ups at the VII Fighter Command to shield the unit's second-ranking officer? If so, it ultimately didn't work, because the accident report does exist, although you have to search for it. I know Alford was loved by the officers serving under him. I know my dad and he were good friends and visited after the war. I met him in Orlando (I reference this in the chapter on Larry Garland). In the footnote on p. 198, of the "June–July 1945" chapter, I address the question of omissions—but I don't have answers.

THE LAST LIVING AIRMAN OF THE 549TH
Chapter. The chapter is entirely the product of my own reporting.

JUNE–JULY 1945
Interchapter. My notes and memories.

Chapter. My dad's oral history was crucial. But the monthly squadron report was even more of a core document. The "Many of the Japs" extract is from the October 13, 1945, *Fighter Post*.

THE ALL-AMERICAN LIFE AND MYSTERIOUS DEATH OF LARRY GARLAND (AND THE CREW OF BLACK WIDOW #42-39426)
Interchapter. The "Does character develop" extract from Barnes's *The Sense of an Ending* is on p. 113 of the Vintage International softcover edition (New York: Vintage, 2012). Jack Kerr. As was said in the text, I hope someday to be able to give the story of my "disappeared" godfather the treatment it deserves—even if I get to do it only for my private satisfaction. My Kerr folder may be about my most bulging research-and-reporting file. I am certain I have spoken to in excess of three dozen people for the chapter not written. I don't intend to name all of those to whom I spoke by phone or email or in person. But I will crucially name Richard Veitch, a New Jersey attorney and a former Kerr son-in-law. He and I have been talking on and off for about four years. He had nothing to gain by trusting me—but he generously did. The same goes for his two sons, Scott and Andrew, as well as his daughter, Catherine. (Scott and Andrew knew their grandfather well. Scott, who lives in Rhode Island, was the first Kerr grandchild I approached. He was guardedly open, and I wish to thank him sincerely.) One more inside-but-still-outside name on this foreshortened list: Bill Kerr. He is a nephew. But he knows much. And he was willing to share a lot of it. And I thank him in the same way. All the other names, I will let go.

To state it again for the record: The reason there can be no Jack Kerr chapter is because I was unable to talk directly to my godfather's four biological children. I tried very hard. There were a couple fleeting interactions. In the summer of 2019, I spoke once on the phone to the youngest Kerr child. The talk was cordial. I explained what I was trying to do—write a portrait of the R/O of *The Rita B,* since he seemed so vital to the story—but the youngest child said it wasn't a good time; maybe later. I could never make contact after that. Two of the youngest child's siblings live in the southwestern United States. I contacted each by letter, which I know were received. With one of the older siblings in the Southwest, I made contact through a third party. Again, the word that came back was that now wasn't a good time; maybe later. There wasn't a later. So I closed the book on the Kerr story, or at least the one I had hoped to write. It was the immediate family's perfect right not to wish to speak to me, although that silence in its own way seemed to be conveying much. One last note: Perhaps the reader is wondering how I found out the price of my godfather's casket. That was easy: Flynn & Son Funeral home still had an index card from 1997 with each itemized cost of the funeral. I stopped in one day, and they pulled it right out.

Chapter. Which, of course, isn't about my godfather at all. Life has its own way of threading ironies: The Larry Garland story turned out to be no substitute, but its own almost impossibly rich thing. The chapter is a product of my own reporting and research. I have sought to embed in the text the relevant dates for all the relevant documents—governmental and otherwise. Which leaves me free, in this space, to cite the *real* sources, namely, the people. Above all: Marsha Phillips and Shirley Beck, who each gave so much. They opened their lives, not to say all the documents in their possession. (Where would I have been in this chapter without the Garland and Gillespie and Odell McConnell letters?) I have been talking to Marsha and Shirley for four years and consider them friends for whatever time remains to each of us. In Greensboro, Eric Hendrix was generous with his time and albums. The seventy-fifth remembrance ceremony can be viewed at: https://ne-np.facebook.com/RollingThunderKY5/videos/2720422121567960/.

EPILOGUE: "SING ME BACK HOME BEFORE I DIE"

Like the prologue, it was primarily put together from my notes and memories and talks with my parents through all the years. In another sense, it was put together from our family myths, which I kept trying to substantiate with as much fact as possible. My dad's service file was of great relevance for tracking specific dates in the period of his coming home and the weeks and months afterward. Other: A different version of the opening pages of this epilogue was published in *The Washington Post* on November 28, 1996, entitled "A Day for a Son to Give Thanks." The James Wright lines are from his poem "Stages on a Journey Westward." My source for the hard-to-come-by figure of 109,000 U.S. military deaths in the Pacific is Richard B. Frank, "US Battle Deaths, Asia-Pacific Theaters," in his *Memorandum to the National WWII Museum,* May 5, 2016. The date for my father's airplane getting "stricken" is written on *The Rita B*'s aircraft record card. Maybe such a layered word is the right word and way to end a book about fathers and sons.

Index

Page numbers in *italics* refer to captions.

A NOTE ON THE PHOTOGRAPHS AND ILLUSTRATIONS

All photographs and illustrations are courtesy of the author, with the following exceptions: Photo of Black Widow, p. ii, Hulton Archive, Archive Photos, via Getty Images. Illustration of Chanute Field, Army Air Forces Technical Training Command brochure, p. 45, Army Forces Collection. Photo captioned "Airplane Engine Mechanics Course, 1938," p. 51, from Chanute Collection, Champaign County Historical Archives, the Urbana Free Library, Urbana Illinois. Photo of Japanese bodies, p. 88, National Archives and Records Administration. Illustration of Mission Report, p. 160, courtesy Air Force Historical Research Agency. Photo of Ray Rudkin and crewmates, p. 178, courtesy Ray Rudkin family. Photo of Gene Autry, p. 196, from the Collection of the National World War II Museum. Public auction notice, p. 278, courtesy Henderson County (Kentucky) Public Library.

A NOTE ABOUT THE AUTHOR

Paul Hendrickson is a three-time finalist for the National Book Critics Circle Award and a winner of it once—for his 2003 *Sons of Mississippi.* His *The Living and the Dead: Robert McNamara and Five Lives of a Lost War* was a 1996 finalist for the National Book Award. His 2011 *Hemingway's Boat* was a *New York Times* best seller. He has been the recipient of writing fellowships from the Guggenheim Foundation, the National Endowment for the Arts, the Lyndhurst Foundation, and the Alicia Patterson Foundation. Since 1998 he has been on the faculty of the creative writing program at the University of Pennsylvania, and for two decades before that he was a staff writer at *The Washington Post.* In 2009 he was a joint visiting professor of documentary practice at Duke University and of American Studies at the University of North Carolina at Chapel Hill. He lives with his wife, Cecilia, a retired nurse, outside Philadelphia and in Washington, D.C.

A NOTE ON THE TYPE

This book was set in Aldine 401, a digital version of the typeface Bembo released by Bitstream, Inc.

Created in 1495 by the punch cutter Francesco Griffo for Aldus Manutius, Bembo represented a shift from calligraphy- to engraving-inspired letterforms. It was first used for *De Aetna,* a book by the poet Pietro Bembo which descibed his journey to Mt. Etna.

Composed by North Market Street Graphics, Lancaster, Pennsylvania

Printed and bound by Berryville Graphics, Berryville, Virginia

Designed by Maggie Hinders